ANSWER BOOK

JOHN R. MARTIN

Tarrant County College, Northeast Campus

TECHNICAL CALCULUS WITH ANALYTIC GEOMETRY

FOURTH EDITION

ALLYN J. WASHINGTON

Dutchess Community College

Addison Wesley

Boston San Francisco New York
London Toronto Sydney Tokyo Singapore Madrid
Mexico City Munich Paris Cape Town Hong Kong Montreal

ISBN   0-201-74557-7

1 2 3 4 5 6 7 8 9 10 CRW 04 03 02 01

CONTENTS

CHAPTER 4 APPLICATIONS OF THE DERIVATIVE

CHAPTER 5 INTEGRATION

CHAPTER 6 APPLICATIONS OF INTEGRATION

CHAPTER 7 DIFFERENTIATION OF THE TRIGONOMETRIC AND INVERSE TRIGONOMETRIC FUNCTIONS

CHAPTER 8 DIFFERENTIATION OF THE EXPONENTIAL AND LOGARITHMIC FUNCTIONS

CHAPTER 9 INTEGRATION BY STANDARD FORMS

CHAPTER 10 METHODS OF INTEGRATION

CHAPTER 11 INTRODUCTION TO PARTIAL DERIVATIVES AND DOUBLE INTEGRALS

CHAPTER 12 POLAR AND CYLINDRICAL COORDINATES

CHAPTER 13 EXPANSION OF FUNCTIONS IN SERIES

CHAPTER 14 FIRST-ORDER DIFFERENTIAL EQUATIONS

CHAPTER 15 HIGHER-ORDER DIFFERENTIAL EQUATIONS

CHAPTER 16 OTHER METHODS OF SOLVING DIFFERENTIAL EQUATIONS

APPENDIX A SUPPLEMENTARY TOPICS

APPENDIX C

FUNCTIONS AND GRAPHS

1.1 Introduction to Functions

1. (a) $A(r) = \pi r^2$ (b) $A(d) = \pi \dfrac{d^2}{4}$

2. (a) $c = 2\pi r$ (b) $c = \pi d$

3. $V = \dfrac{1}{6}\pi d^3$ **4.** $e = \sqrt{\dfrac{A}{6}}$ **5.** $A(l) = 5l$

6. $V = \dfrac{8}{3}\pi r^2$ **7.** $A = s^2,\ s = \sqrt{A}$

8. $p = 4s,\ s = \dfrac{p}{4}$ **9.** $3, -1$ **10.** $1, -19$

11. $11, 3.8$ **12.** $0.7, 17.2$ **13.** $\dfrac{5}{2}, -\dfrac{1}{2}$

14. $6, 50.8$ **15.** $\dfrac{1}{4}a + \dfrac{1}{2}a^2,\ 0$

16. $15,\ 6\sqrt{a^2 + 1} - 3$ **18.** $3s^2 - s + 6,\ 12s^2 - 2s + 6$

18. $-10t + 7,\ 5t + 12$

19. -8 **20.** $8x + 6$

21. 3 is an integer, rational, real. $-\pi$ is irrational, real.
$-\sqrt{-6}$ is imaginary; $\sqrt{7}/3$ is irrational and real.

22. $\dfrac{5}{4}$: real, rational

$\sqrt{-4}$: imaginary

$-\dfrac{7}{3}$: real, rational

$\dfrac{\pi}{6}$: real, irrational

23. $3, \dfrac{7}{2}, \dfrac{6}{7}, \sqrt{3}, 3 - \sqrt{5}$.

24. $4, \sqrt{2}, \dfrac{\pi}{2}, \dfrac{19}{4}, \pi - 3$

25. (a) $<$ (b) $>$ (c) $>$

26. (a) $<$ (b) $>$ (c) $<$

27. (a) positive integer
     (b) negative integer.
     (c) positive rational number less than 1

28. (a) positive integer
     (b) positive rational
     (c) positive integer

29. (a) yes (b) yes   **30.** (a) yes (b) yes

31. to the right of origin

32. (a) $-1 < x < 1$ (b) $x < -2$ or $x > 2$

33. 10.4 m   **34.** 55°F

35. 75 ft, $2v + 0.2v^2$, 240 ft, 240 ft   **36.** $\dfrac{200(R+10)}{(110+R)^2}$

1.2 Algebraic Functions

1. $\sqrt{x^2 - 2x + 5}$ **2.** $x^3 - 3x^2 + 3x - 1$

3. $\dfrac{x - 1}{\sqrt{x^2 + 4}}$ **4.** $x^2 - 2\sqrt{x^2 + 4} + 5$

5. $\sqrt[6]{x^6 + 1}$ **6.** $\sqrt{x^3 - 1}$ **7.** $(4x - 5)^{7/2}$

8. $\dfrac{}{3\sqrt{x^2 + 4}}$ **9.** $\dfrac{3x + 4}{\sqrt{2x + 1}}$ **10.** $\dfrac{2 - 4x}{(3x - 1)^{2/3}}$

11. $\dfrac{1}{(x^2 + 1)^{3/2}}$ **12.** $\dfrac{2x}{(1 - 2x^2)^{5/4}}$

13. domain and range: all real numbers.

14. domain is the set of all real numbers, range is all real numbers $g(u) \le 3$

15. domain: all real numbers except 0. range: all real numbers except 0.

16. domain: all real numbers $r \ge -4$, range: all real numbers $F(r) \ge 0$

17. domain: all real numbers except zero; range: all positive real numbers.

18. domain is all real numbers, range is all real numbers $T(t) \ge -1$

19. domain: all real numbers $h \ge 0$. range: all real numbers $H(h) \ge 1$.

1

20. domain: all real numbers $x < 2$,
range all real numbers greater than 0

21. all real numbers $y > 2$

22. domain: all real numbers except 3

23. all real numbers except $2, -4, 6$.

24. domain: all real numbers $x \geq 2$, except $x = 3$

25. 2, not defined

26. $-16, \dfrac{1}{2}$ **27.** $2, \dfrac{3}{4}$ **28.** $5, 0$

29. $d(t) = 80 + 55t$ **30.** $C = 12\pi r + 6\pi r^2$

31. $w = 5500 - 2t$ **32.** $p = 100c - 300$

33. $m(h) = 0.5h - 390$ **34.** $n = 0.5x + 70$

35. $C = 5l + 250$ **36.** $M = \dfrac{8}{h}$

37. **(a)** $y(x) = \dfrac{1200 - 0.1x}{0.4}$ **(b)** 2900 L

38. $c = 2\pi\sqrt{36d - d^2}$ **39.** $A = \dfrac{p^2}{16} + \dfrac{(60 - p)^2}{4\pi}$

40. $A = \dfrac{1}{4}\pi d^2 + d^2$

41. $A = \pi(6 - x)^2$ with domain $0 \leq x \leq 6$, range: $0 \leq A \leq 36\pi$.

42. $d = \sqrt{14400 + h^2}$
domain: $h \geq 0$
range: $d \geq 120$

43. $s = 300/t$, domain: $t > 0$, range: $s > 0$ (upper limits depend on truck)

44. $l = \dfrac{8}{w}$
domain: all real numbers $0 < w < 8$
range: all real numbers $0 < l < 8$

45. domain: is all values of $C > 0$, with some upper limit depending on the circuit.

46. domain: all real numbers greater than zero and less than 550

47. $m = \begin{cases} 0.5h - 390 & \text{for} \quad h > 1000 \\ 110 & \text{for} \quad 0 \leq h \leq 1000 \end{cases}$

48. $C = \begin{cases} 5l + 250 & \text{for} \quad l > 50 \\ 500 & \text{for} \quad 0 \leq l \leq 50 \end{cases}$

1.3   Rectangular Coordinates

1. $(2, 1)$, $(-1, 2)$, $(-2, -3)$

2. $(3, -2)$, $(-3.5, 0.5)$, $(0, -4)$

3.

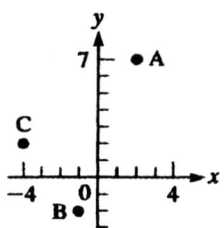

4.

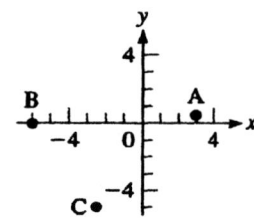

5. isosceles triangle

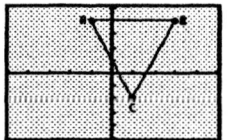

6. isosceles right triangle

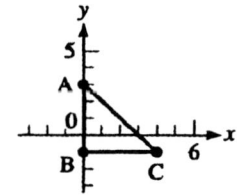

7. Rectangle

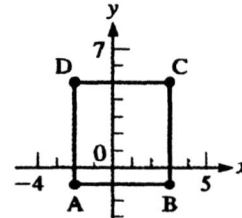

8. parallelogram

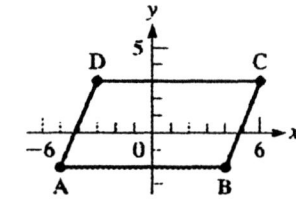

9. $(5, 4)$

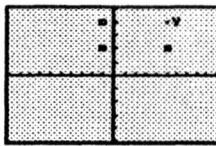

10. $\dfrac{9}{2}$ **11.** $(3, -2)$ **12.** $(4, -1)$

13. on a line parallel to the y-axis, 1 unit to the right.

14. a line parallel to the x-axis, 3 units below

15. on a line parallel to the x-axis, 3 units above

16. on a line parallel to the y-axis, 2 units to the left

17. on a line bisecting the first and third quadrants

18. on a line bisecting quadrants two and four

19. 0   **20.** zero

21. to the right of the y-axis

22. below the x-axis

23. to the left of a line that is parallel to the y-axis, one unit to the left

24. above a line parallel to the x-axis, 4 units above it

25. first, third   **26.** two, four

27. (a) 8   (b) 6

28. 10

1.4   The Graph of a Function

1.

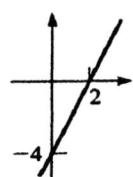

2.

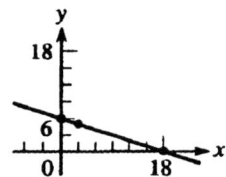

3.

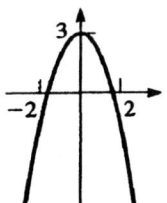

4.

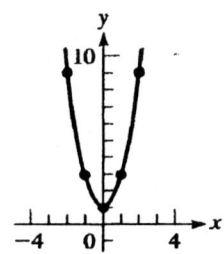

5.

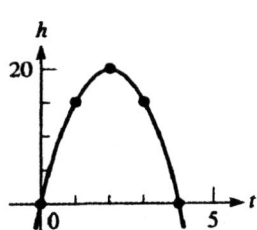

6.

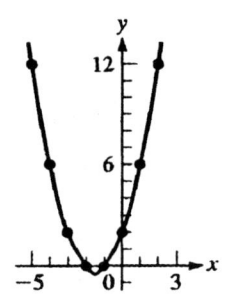

7.

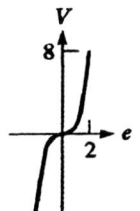

8.

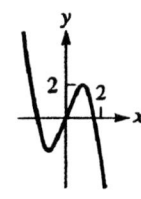

9.

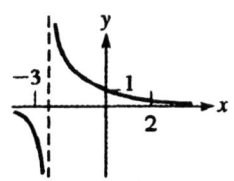

10.

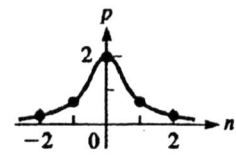

11.

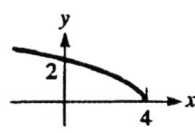

12.

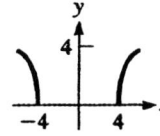

13.

14.

15.

16.

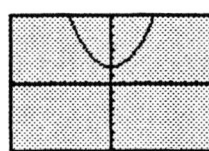

17.

18.

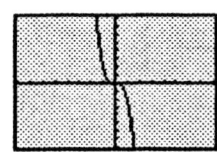

19.

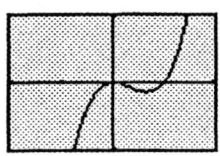

20.

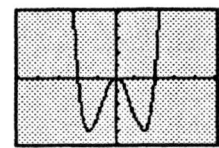

21.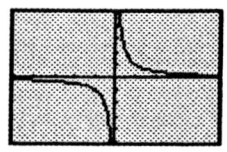

22.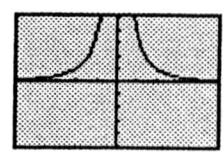

34. range: all real numbers excluding $-\frac{1}{2}$

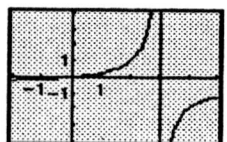

23.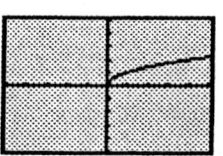

24.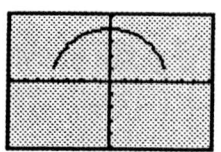

35. all real numbers

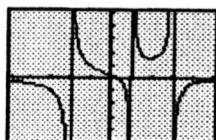

36. range: all real numbers

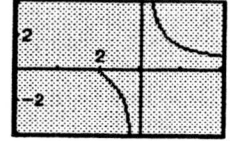

25. -6.4 and 6.4

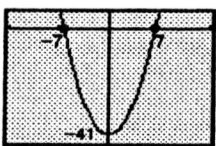

26. $-1.6, 5.6.$

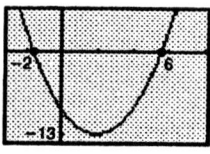

37.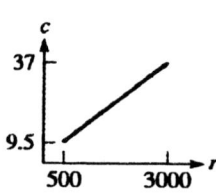

38.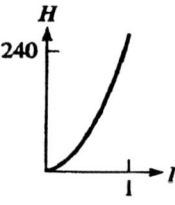

27. 1.4

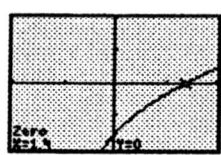

28. $-0.4, 2.4$

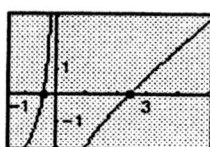

39.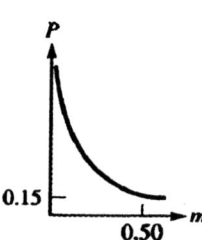

40.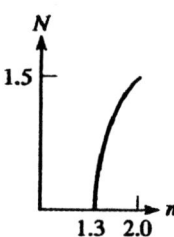

29. $y \leq -1$ or $y > 0$

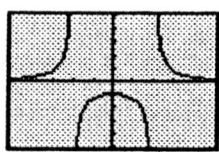

30. range: all numbers greater than -0.25

41. 24.4 cm, 29.4 cm

42. $w \approx 18$ cm, $l \approx 30$ cm

31. $y \geq 0$ or $y \leq -4$

32. range: all real numbers

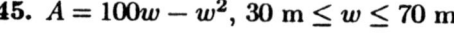

43. 18 s   **44.** 67 ft

45. $A = 100w - w^2$, 30 m $\leq w \leq 70$ m

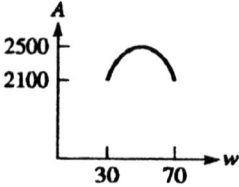

33. all real numbers $Y(y) \geq 3.464$ (approx.)

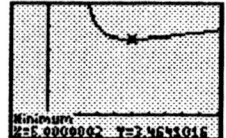

46. 1.3 in, 2.4 in   **47.** 0.25 ft/min

48. 96.8 in^3

49. $y = x$ is the same as
$y = |x|$ for $x \geq 0$.
$y = |x|$ is the same as
$y = -x$ for $x < 0$.

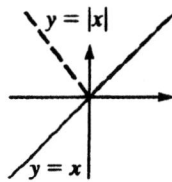

50. The graphs differ because the absolute value does not allow the graph to go below the x-axis.

51.

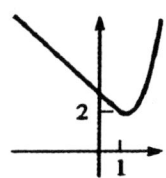

52.

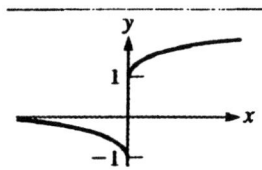

53. yes   **54.** no   **55.** no   **56.** yes

Chapter 1 Review Exercises

1. $A = 4\pi t^2$

2. $A = 3\pi\sqrt{h^2 + 9}$

3. $y = -\dfrac{10}{9}x + \dfrac{250}{9}$

4. $C = 50w + 600$

5. $16, -47$

6. $\dfrac{15}{2}, 20$

7. $3, \sqrt{1 - 4h}$

8. $8, \dfrac{3v + 1}{v + 2}$

9. $6xh + 3h^2 - 2h$

10. $h^3 + 11h^2 + 36h$

11. -3

12. $2x^4 - 2x^2$

13. $-3.67, 16.7$

14. $-1778, -630.4$

15. $0.16503, -0.21476$

16. $0.0344, 0.0982$

17. domain: all real numbers;
range: all real numbers

18. domain: all real numbers except 0,
range: $y \neq 0$

19. domain: all real numbers $t > -4$;
range: all real numbers $g(t) > 0$

20. domain: all real numbers $y \geq 0$,
range: all real numbers $F(y) \leq 1$

21.

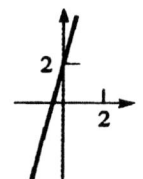

22.

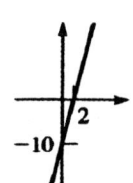

23.

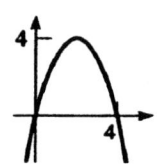

24.

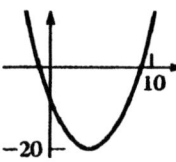

25.

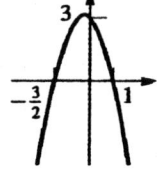

26.

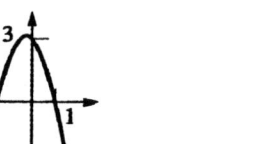

27.

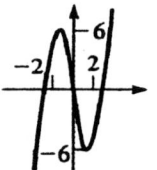

28.

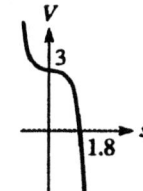

29.

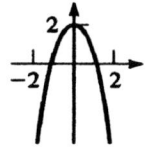

30.

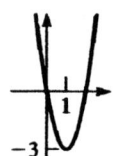

31.

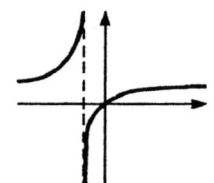

32.

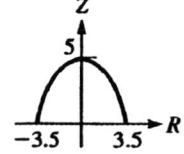

33. 0.4

34. −3.7

35. 0.2, 5.8

 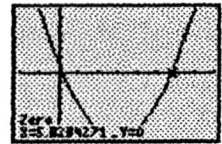

36. 1.0, 2.0

37. 1.4

38. 1.2

39. −0.7, 0.7

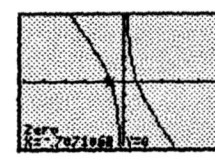 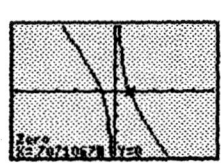

40. 1.0

all real numbers $y \geq -6.25$

41.

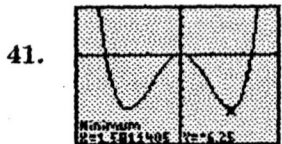

42. range: $-2 \leq y \leq 2$.

43.

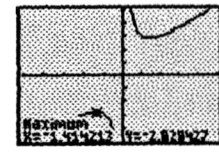 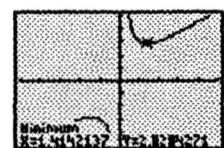

all real numbers $w \leq -2.83$ or $w \geq 2.83$

44. range: all real numbers $y \geq 4.95$

45. either a or v is positive, the other negative

46. $\sqrt{a^2 + b^2}$

47. $(1, \sqrt{3})$ or $(1, -\sqrt{3})$

48. $(6, 2)$, $(6, -3)$; $(-4, 2)$, $(-4, -3)$

49. 13.4   **50.** 20   **51.** 72.0°   **52.** 8.6 W

53.

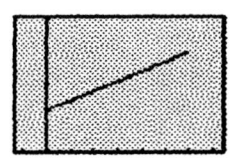

54.

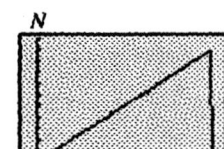

55.

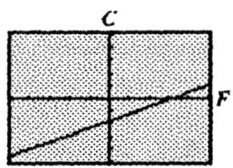

56.

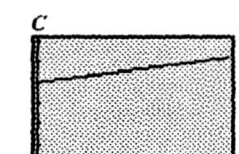

57.

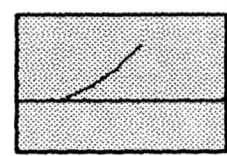

58.

59.

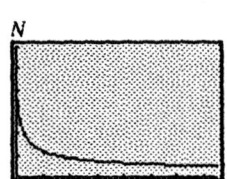

60.

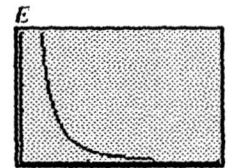

61.

62.

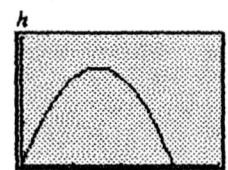

63.

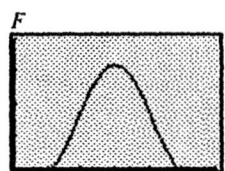

64. $V(x) = x^3 - 2.0x^2$

65. 3.5

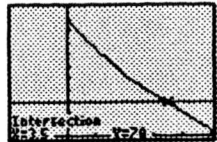

66. 140 gal   **67.** 33°C

68. $A(r)\pi r^2 + \dfrac{4000}{r}$

780 cm^2, 725 cm^2, 701 cm^2

69. 1.03 ft

70. 3.85 mm, 4.85 mm

71. 6.5 h   **72.** 11 Ω

PLANE ANALYTIC GEOMETRY

2.1 Basic Definitions

1. $2\sqrt{29}$
2. $7\sqrt{2}$
3. 3
4. $\sqrt{34}$

5. 55
6. 52
7. $2\sqrt{53}$
8. 8.15

9. 2.86
10. 16.9
11. $\dfrac{5}{2}$
12. 1

13. undefined

14. $\dfrac{3}{5}$
15. $-\dfrac{3}{4}$
16. $-\dfrac{5}{12}$
17. $\dfrac{-5}{9}$

18. 0
19. 0.747
20. -0.71

21. $\dfrac{1}{3}\sqrt{3}$
22. 1.92
23. -1.084

24. -1
25. $20.0°$
26. $39.5°$

27. $98.50°$
28. $125°$
29. parallel

30. perpendicular
31. perpendicular

32. parallel
33. $-2, 8$
34. $\pm 2\sqrt{5}$

35. -3
36. $-4 \pm 3\sqrt{3}$

37. two sides equal $2\sqrt{10}$

38. $m_1 = \dfrac{1}{2}, m_2 = -2$
39. $m_2 = \dfrac{4}{3}, m_1 = \dfrac{5}{12}$

40. $d = \sqrt{29}; m_1 = m_4 = \dfrac{2}{5}, m_2 = m_3 = -\dfrac{5}{2}$

41. 10
42. 29 square units

43. $4(\sqrt{10} + \sqrt{2}) = 18.3$
44. 36 units
45. $(1, 5)$

46. $(-7, -1)$
47. $(-2.8, 4.2)$
48. $(-0.8, 1.3)$

2.2 The Straight Line

1. $4x - y + 20 = 0$
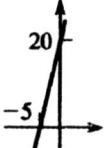

2. $2x + y + 5 = 0$
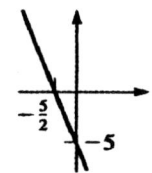

3. $7x - 2y - 24 = 0$
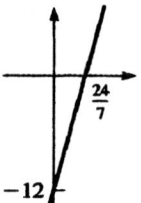

4. $2x + y + 1 = 0$
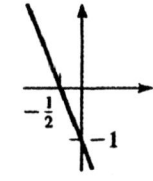

5. $x - y + 2 = 0$
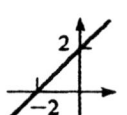

6. $\sqrt{3}x + y + 2 = 0$
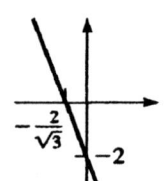

7. $y = -2.7$
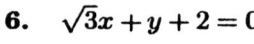

8. $x = -4$
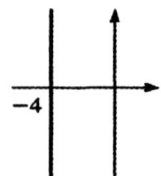

9. $x = -3$
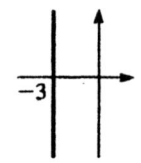

10. $y = -4.1$
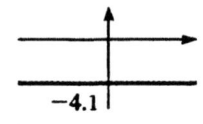

11. $3x - 2y - 12 = 0$ **12.** $2x - y + 6 = 0$

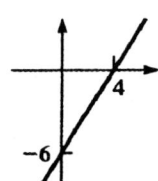   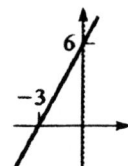

22. $y = \dfrac{2}{3}x - 2, m = \dfrac{2}{3}, b = -2$

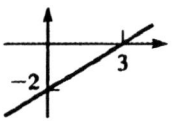

13. $x + 3y + 5 = 0$ **14.** $x - 4y + 12 = 0$

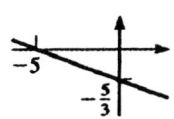   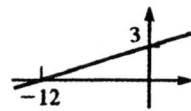

23. $y = \dfrac{-3}{5}x + 2, m = \dfrac{-3}{5}, b = 2$

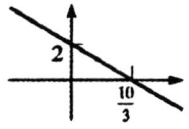

15. $x + 4y - 9 = 0$ **16.** $4x + 3y + 6 = 0$

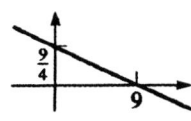   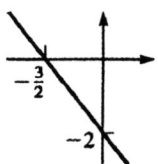

24. $y = \dfrac{3}{2}x - \dfrac{9}{4}, m = \dfrac{3}{2}, b = \dfrac{-9}{4}$

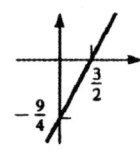

25. $y = \dfrac{3}{2}x - \dfrac{1}{2}, \dfrac{3}{2} = m; -\dfrac{1}{2} = b$

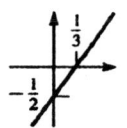

17. $0.4x + y + 1.7 = 0$ **18.** $3x - y + 7 = 0$

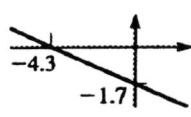   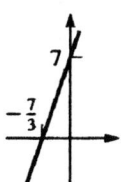

26. $y = -2x + \dfrac{5}{2}$

Slope $= -2$; y-intercept $= \dfrac{5}{2}$

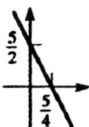

19. $3x + y - 18 = 0$ **20.** $x + y - 1 = 0$

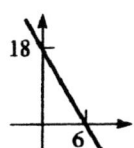   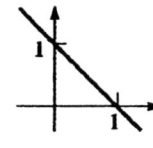

27. $y = 3.5x + 0.5$, $m = 3.5$; y-intercept $= 0.5$

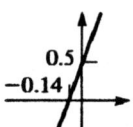

21. $y = 4x - 8, m = 4, b = -8$

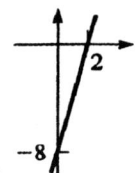

28. $y = -2.50x + 1.30$, $m = -2.50$; y-intercept $= 1.30$

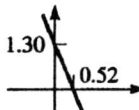

29. $k = -2$ **30.** $k = 8$ **31.** $k = 1$ **32.** $k = -9$

33. parallel   **34.** neither   **35.** perpendicular

36. parallel   **37.** neither

38. perpendicular   **39.** perpendicular

40. parallel

41. $v = 12.2 + 5.16t$

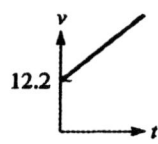

42. $V = 6.00 - 180i$

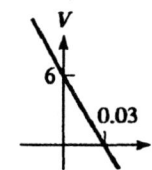

43. $v = 0.607T + 331$

44. $2x + 3y = 200$

45. $5x + 6y = 1220$

46. $T = \dfrac{4}{3}x + 3$

47. $y = 150,000 - 0.80x$

48. $p = 4w + 20$

49. $y = (-5.6x + 2.4)10^{-5}$

50. $y = 3.38x$

51. $n = \dfrac{7}{6}t + 10$

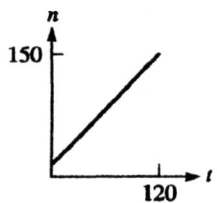

n at 6:30 $(t = 0) = 10$; at 8:30
$(t = 120) = 150$

52. $w = -2t + 30$

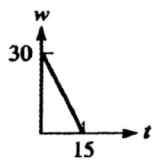

53.

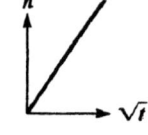

54.

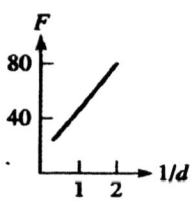

55.

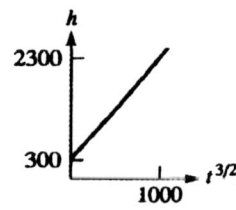

56.

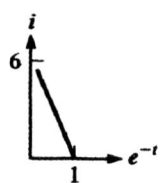

57.

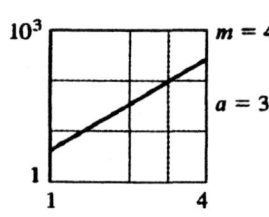

58.

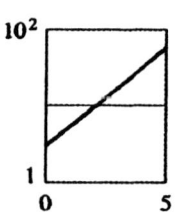

59.

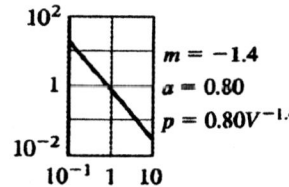

60. $v = 40(0.952)^{t}$

2.3   The Circle

1. $(2, 1)$, $r = 5$ **2.** $(3, -4)$, $r = 7$

3. $(-1, 0)$, $r = 2$ **4.** $(0, 6)$, $r = 8$

5. $x^2 + y^2 = 9$ **6.** $x^2 + y^2 = 1$

7. $x^2 + y^2 - 4x - 4y - 8 = 0$

8. $x^2 + y^2 - 4y = 0$

9. $x^2 + y^2 + 4x - 10y + 24 = 0$

10. $x^2 + y^2 + 6x + 10y + 22 = 0$

11. $x^2 + y^2 - 24x + 30y + 45 = 0$

12. $4x^2 + 4y^2 - 12x + 16y = 0$

13. $x^2 + y^2 - 4x - 2y - 3 = 0$

14. $x^2 + y^2 + 2x - 8y + 15 = 0$

15. $x^2 + y^2 + 6x - 10y + 9 = 0$

16. $x^2 + y^2 - 4x + 8y + 16 = 0$

17. $x^2 + y^2 - 4x - 4y + 4 = 0$

18. $x^2 + y^2 + 8x - 8y + 16 = 0$

19. $x^2 + y^2 + 4x + 10y + 4 = 0$

20. $x^2 + y^2 - 8y - 9 = 0$

21. $r = 2,\ C(0,3)$ **22.** $r = 7,\ C(2,-3)$

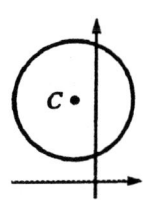   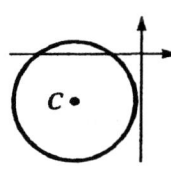

23. $r = \dfrac{9}{2},\ (-1,5)$ **24.** $C(-4,-3);\ r = \dfrac{5}{\sqrt{2}}$

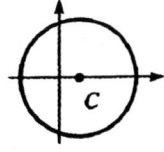   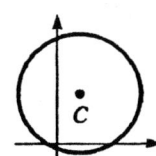

25. $r = 3, C(1,0)$ **26.** $r = 5;\ C(2,3)$

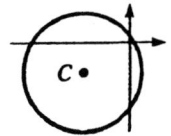   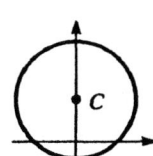

27. $(2.10, 1.30),\ r = 3.1$

28. $C(-11,-7), r = 14$ **29.** $r = \dfrac{5}{2}, (0,2)$

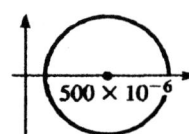

30. $C(0,-1), r = \dfrac{4}{3}$ **31.** $C(1,2), r = \dfrac{\sqrt{22}}{2}$

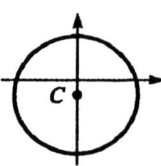   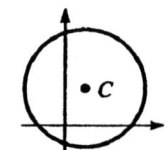

32. $C(2,0), r = \sqrt{\dfrac{8}{3}}$

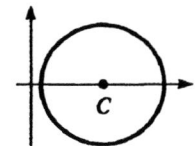

33. symmetrical to both axes and origin

34. symmetrical to x-axis

35. symmetrical with respect to y-axis

36. no symmetry

37. $(-1,0),\ (7,0)$ **38.** $(2,1),(1,0)$

39. $3x^2 + 4x + 3y^2 + 8y - 20 = 0$, circle

40. $x^2 + y^2 = 4$, circle

41.   **42.**

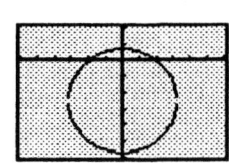   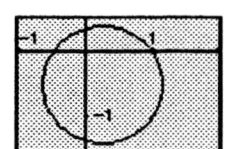

43. 2.82 in.   **44.** 3.10 in

45. $x^2 + y^2 = 0.0100$

46. $v_H^2 + v_V^2 = v^2 = 4.80 \times 10^7$

47.

$$(x - 500 \times 10^{-6})^2 + y^2 = (400 \times 10^{-6})^2$$
$$= 0.16 \times 10^{-6}$$

48. 4.57 m^2

2.4   The Parabola

1. $F(1,0)$, $x = -1$

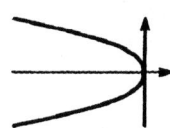

2. $F(4,0)$, $x = -4$

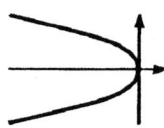

3. $F(-1,0)$, $x = 1$

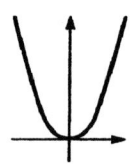

4. $F(-4,0)$, $x = 4$

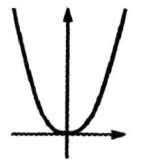

5. $F(0,2)$, $y = -2$

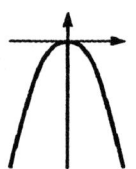

6. $F\left(0, \dfrac{5}{2}\right)$, $y = -\dfrac{5}{2}$

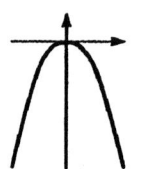

7. $F(0,-1)$, $y = 1$

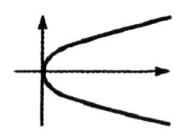

8. $F(0,-3)$, $y = 3$

9. $F(\dfrac{5}{8},0)$, $x = -\dfrac{5}{8}$

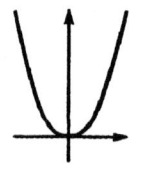

10. $F\left(0, \dfrac{2}{3}\right)$, $y = -\dfrac{2}{3}$

11. $F\left(0, \dfrac{25}{48}\right)$, $y = -\dfrac{25}{48}$

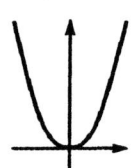

12. $F\left(\dfrac{5}{152}, 0\right)$, $y = -\dfrac{5}{152}$

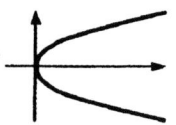

13. $y^2 = 12x$ **14.** $y^2 = -8x$ **15.** $x^2 = 16y$

16. $y^2 = -12x$ **17.** $x^2 = 0.64y$ **18.** $x^2 = -9.2y$

19. $x^2 = \dfrac{1}{8}y$ **20.** $y^2 = \dfrac{1}{2}x$

21. $y^2 - 2y - 12x + 37 = 0$

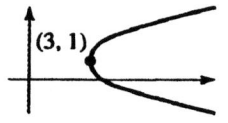

22. $x^2 - 2x + 8y - 23 = 0$

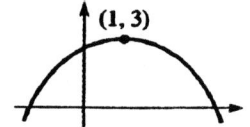

23.

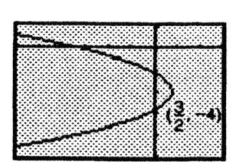

24.

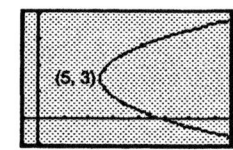

25.

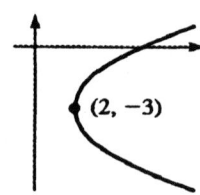

26.

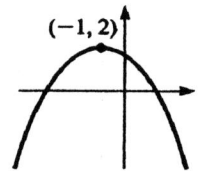

27. $4p$ **28.** $x^2 + y^2 - 2y = 0$

29. $x^2 = 14,700y$ **30.** $x^2 = -2.44y$

31.

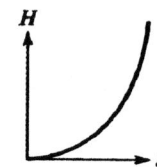

32. 2.97 ft

33. 57.6 m

34. $y = \dfrac{g}{2v_0^2}x^2$

35. $y^2 = 1.2x$

36. 31.5 ft

37.

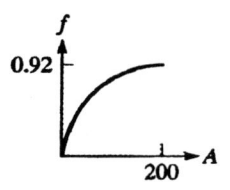

38.

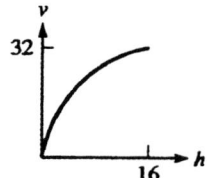

39. $x^2 = 8y, \ y^2 = 8x$

40.

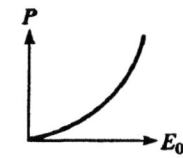

2.5   The Ellipse

1. $V(\pm2,0), F(\pm\sqrt{3},0)$

2. $V(\pm10,0), F(\pm6,0)$

3. $V(0,\pm6), \ F(0,\pm\sqrt{11})$

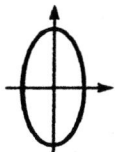

4. $V(0,\pm9), \ F(0,\pm4\sqrt{2})$

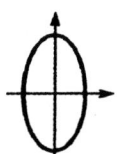

5. $V(\pm3,0), F(\pm\sqrt{5},0)$

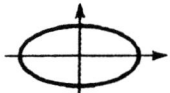

6. $V(\pm12,0), \ F(\pm2\sqrt{35},0)$

7. $V(0,\pm7), \ F(0,\pm3\sqrt{5})$

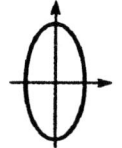

8. $V(0,\pm5), \ F(0,\pm2\sqrt{6})$

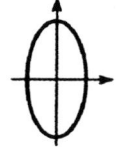

9. $V(0,\pm4), F(0,\pm\sqrt{14})$

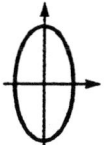

10. $V(\pm\sqrt{300},0), F(\pm10,0)$

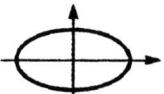

11. $V(\pm0.25,0), F(\pm0.23,0)$

12. $V\left(0,\pm\dfrac{3}{20}\right), F\left(0,\pm\dfrac{\sqrt{5}}{20}\right)$

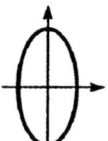

13. $144x^2 + 225y^2 = 32,400$

14. $25x^2 + 16y^2 = 400$

15. $9x^2 + 5y^2 = 45$

16. $\dfrac{x^2}{25} + \dfrac{y^2}{16} = 1$

17. $3x^2 + 20y^2 = 192$

18. $3x^2 + y^2 = 6$

19. $4x^2 + y^2 = 20$

20. $2x^2 + 3y^2 = 20$

21. $16x^2 + 25y^2 - 32x - 50y - 359 = 0$

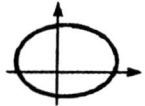

22. $3y^2 - 12y + 4x^2 - 8x - 32 = 0$

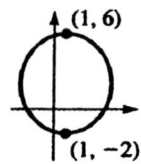

23.

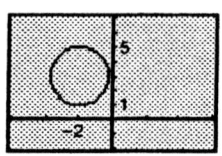

24.

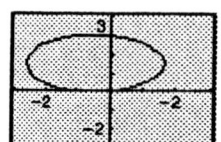

25.

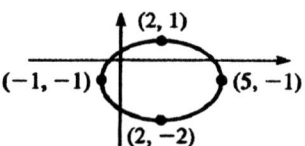

26.

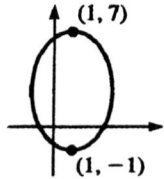

27. $0 < k < 1$

28. $k = \pm\dfrac{5}{4}$

29. $2x^2 + 3(-y)^2 - 8x - 4 = 2x^2 + 3y^2 - 8x - 4$

30. $5x^2 + y^2 - 3y - 7 = 5(-x)^2 + y^2 - 3y - 7$

31. $\dfrac{2\sqrt{2}}{3} \approx 0.943$

32. 0.24

33. $7x^2 + 16y^2 = 112$

34. $i_1^2 + 4i_2^2 = 32$

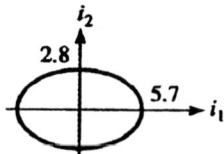

35. 27.5 m

36. $x^2 + 49y^2 = 17.6$

37. 13 ft

38. 12.1 ft

39. 843 ft^3

40. 41.1 mm^2

2.6   The Hyperbola

1. $V(\pm 5, 0), F(\pm 13, 0)$

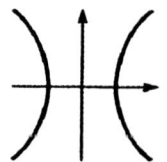

2. $V(\pm 4, 0), F(\pm 2\sqrt{5}, 0)$

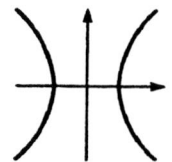

3. $V(0, \pm 3), F(0, \pm\sqrt{10})$

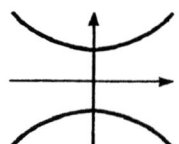

4. $V(0, \pm\sqrt{2}), F(0, \pm 2)$

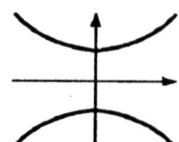

5. $V(\pm 1, 0); F(\pm\sqrt{5}, 0)$

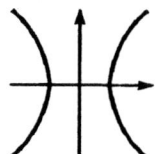

6. $V(\pm 9, 0), F(\pm 3\sqrt{10}, 0)$

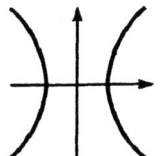

7. $V(0, \pm\sqrt{5}), F(0, \pm\sqrt{7})$

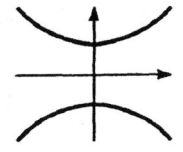

8. $V(0, \pm 10), F(0, \pm 5\sqrt{10})$

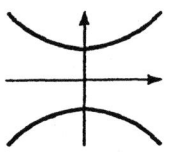

9. $V(0, \pm 2), F(0, \pm\sqrt{5})$

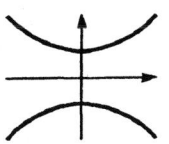

10. $V(\pm 1, 0), F(\pm\sqrt{10}, 0)$

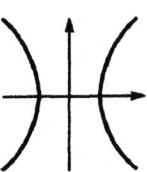

11. $V(\pm 0.4, 0), F(\pm 0.89, 0)$

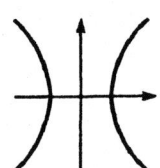

12. $V(0, \pm 0.2), F\left(0, \pm\dfrac{\sqrt{10}}{5}\right)$

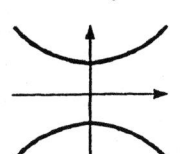

13. $16x^2 - 9y^2 = 144$ **14.** $2y^2 - x^2 = 2$

15. $9y^2 - 25x^2 = 900$ **16.** $\dfrac{x^2}{64} - \dfrac{y^2}{36} = 1$

17. $3x^2 - y^2 = 3$ **18.** $x^2 - 16y^2 = 16$

19. $4x^2 - 5y^2 = 20$ **20.** $3y^2 - 4x^2 = 8$

21.   **22.**

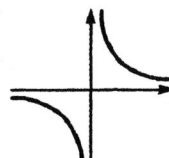   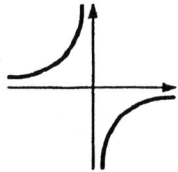

23. $9x^2 - 16y^2 - 108x + 64y + 116 = 0$

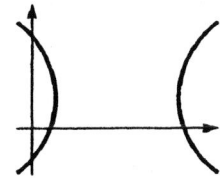

24. $4y^2 - 9x^2 - 8y - 36x - 68 = 0$

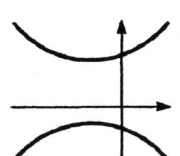

25.   **26.**

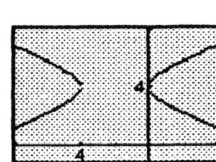   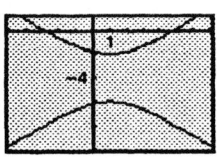

27.   **28.**

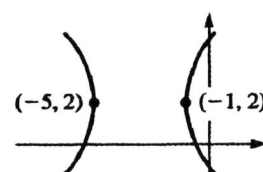   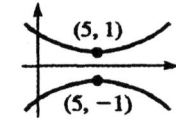

29. $x^2 - 2y^2 = 2$ **30.** 1.29

31. $l^2 - x^2 = 2000^2$

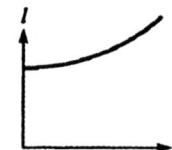

32. $\dfrac{R^2}{24/\pi} - \dfrac{r^2}{12} = 1$, hyperbola

33. $i = \dfrac{6.00}{R}$

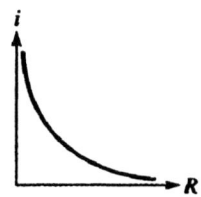

34. $\dfrac{x^2}{7.84} - \dfrac{y^2}{4.41} = 1$

35.

36. $3x^2 - y^2 = 3$

2.7   Translation of Axes

1. parabola, $(-1, 2)$

2. ellipse, $(-4, 1)$

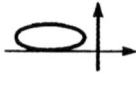

3. hyperbola, $(1, 2)$

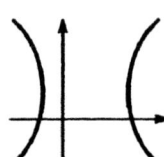

4. parabola, $(2, -5)$

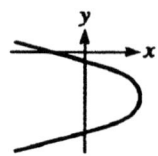

5. ellipse, $(-1, 0)$

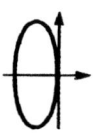

6. hyperbola, $(-2, 4)$

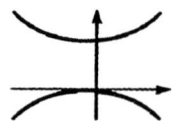

7. parabola, $(-3, 1)$

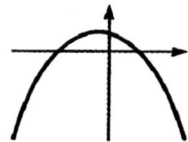

8. ellipse, $(0, -1)$

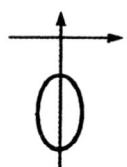

9. $y^2 - 6y - 16x - 7 = 0$

10. $x^2 - 4x + 16y + 20 = 0$

11. $y^2 = 24(x - 6)$

12. $y^2 - 8y + 8x - 16 = 0$

13. $16x^2 + 25y^2 + 64x - 100y - 236 = 0$

14. $25x^2 + 169y^2 - 1014y - 2704 = 0$

15. $4x^2 + y^2 + 16x - 2y + 1 = 0$

16. $676x^2 + 100y^2 - 1352x - 800y - 1949 = 0$

17. $x^2 - 3y^2 + 2x + 12y - 8 = 0$

18. no hyperbola.

19. $16x^2 - 9y^2 + 32x + 18y - 137 = 0$

20. $9y^2 - 16x^2 + 32x + 72y - 16 = 0$

21. parabola, $(-1, -1)$

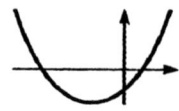

22. parabola, $(-5, 1)$

23. ellipse, $(-3, 0)$

24. ellipse, $(-2, 4)$

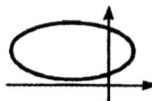

25. hyperbola, $(0,4)$

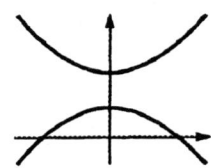

26. hyperbola, $(-2,1)$

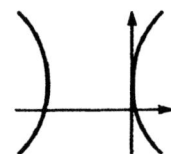

39. $y^2 + 4x - 4 = 0$

40. hyperbola

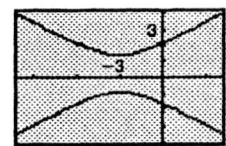

27. parabola, $(1,0)$

28. ellipse, $\left(0, \dfrac{1}{32}\right)$

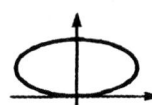

41. $(x - 95)^2 = \dfrac{95^2}{-60}(y - 60)$

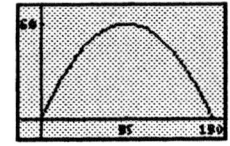

29. hyperbola, $(-4,5)$

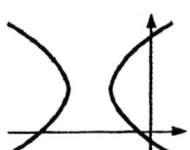

30. circle, $(6,-4)$

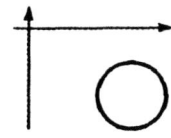

42.

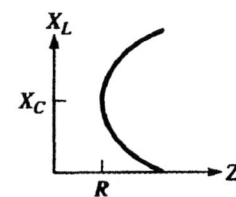

31. ellipse, $\left(\dfrac{2}{3},-2\right)$

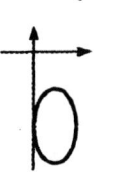

32. hyperbola, $(4,0)$

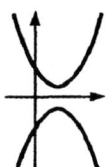

43. $\dfrac{y^2}{16} + \dfrac{x^2}{9.0} = 1$, $\dfrac{(x - 7.0)^2}{16} + \dfrac{y^2}{9.0} = 1$

44. $A = 240w - w^2$, parabola, 120 m

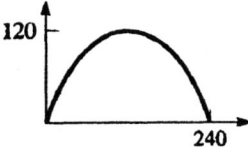

33. hyperbola, $(1,-8)$

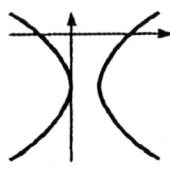

34. hyperbola, $(0,3)$

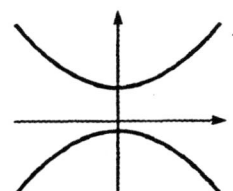

2.8 The Second-Degree Equation

1. ellipse   **2.** parabola   **3.** hyperbola

4. not second degree   **5.** circle

6. not second degree   **7.** parabola

35. circle, $\left(\dfrac{1}{3},\dfrac{4}{3}\right)$

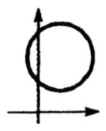

36. parabola, $\left(\dfrac{4}{3},\dfrac{3}{2}\right)$

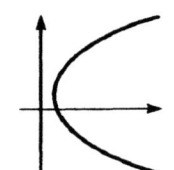

8. ellipse   **9.** hyperbola

10. ellipse   **11.** circle   **12.** parabola

13. line   **14.** circle   **15.** hyperbola

37. $x^2 - y^2 + 4x - 2y - 22 = 0$

38. $x^2 + 2y^2 + 4x - 14 = 0$

16. parabola   **17.** ellipse   **18.** hyperbola

19. ellipse   **20.** circle

21. parabola, vertex $(-4,0)$, focus $(-4,2)$

22. ellipse, $(h,k) = (3,0), V(3 \pm 2\sqrt{2}, 0)$

23. hyperbola, $C(1,-2), V(1,-2 \pm \sqrt{2})$

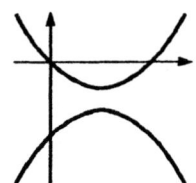

24. circle, $(h,k) = (-1,0); r = \dfrac{3}{2}$

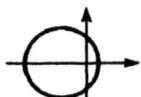

25. ellipse, $C(5,0), V(5, \pm 2\sqrt{2})$

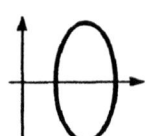

26. hyperbola, $C(-2,-2); V(0,-2); V(-4,-2)$

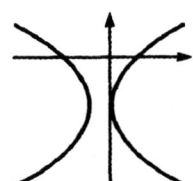

27. parabola, $V\left(-\dfrac{1}{2}, \dfrac{5}{2}\right), F\left(\dfrac{1}{2}, \dfrac{5}{2}\right)$

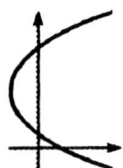

28. ellipse, $C(0,1); V(0,4), V(0,-2)$

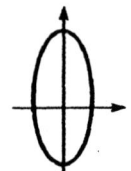

29. ellipse   **30.** hyperbola

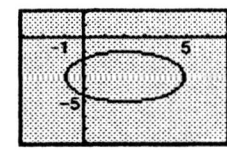   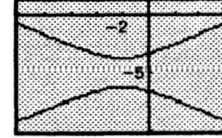

31. $y = \dfrac{-3x \pm \sqrt{60x + 139}}{9}$

32.

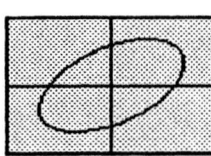

33. (a)   circle

(b)   hyperbola

(c)   ellipse

34. (a) ellipse   **(b)** hyperbola

35. a point at the origin   **36.** no real solution

37. parabola   **38.** parabola

39. (a) Beam is perpendicular to floor. We have a circle.

(b) Beam is not perpendicular to floor. We have an ellipse.

40. hyperbola

Chapter 2 Review Exercises

1. $4x - y - 11 = 0$

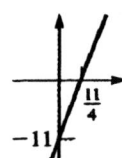

2. $8x - y + 13 = 0$

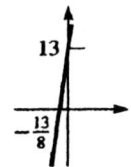

3. $2x + 3y + 3 = 0$

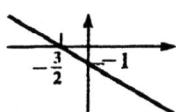

4. $2x - 5y - 4 = 0$

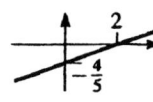

5. $x^2 + y^2 - 2x + 4y - 5 = 0$

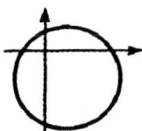

6. $x^2 + y^2 - 10x - 2y + 22 = 0$

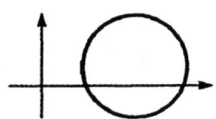

7. $y^2 = 12x$

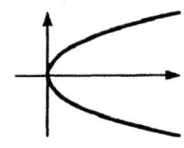

8. $x^2 = 20y$

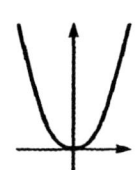

9. $9x^2 + 25y^2 = 900$

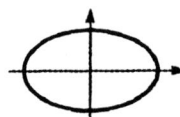

10. $2x^2 + y^2 = 9$

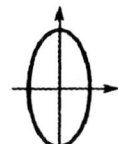

11. $144y^2 - 169x^2 = 24{,}336$

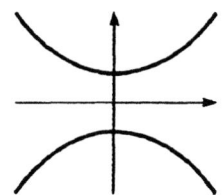

12. $9y^2 - 16x^2 = 576$

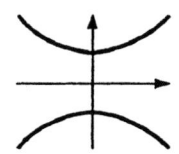

13. $(-3, 0)$, $r = 4$

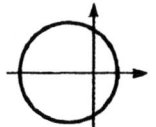

14. center $(h, k) = (2, -1)$; radius $r = 5$

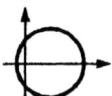

15. $(0, -5)$, $y = 5$

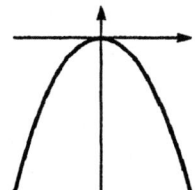

16. focus $(6, 0)$, directrix, $x = -6$

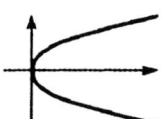

17. vertices: $(0, 4)$, $(0, -4)$
foci: $(0, \sqrt{15})$, $(0, -\sqrt{15})$

18. vertices: $(0,3), (0,-3)$.
foci: $(0, \sqrt{11}), (0, -\sqrt{11})$

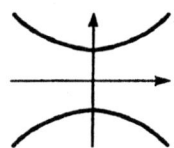

19. vertices: $\left(\dfrac{1}{2\sqrt{2}}, 0\right)$, $\left(\dfrac{-1}{2\sqrt{2}}, 0\right)$

foci: $\left(\dfrac{\sqrt{70}}{20}, 0\right)$, $\left(\dfrac{-\sqrt{70}}{20}, 0\right)$

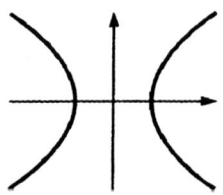

20. vertices: $(20,0), (-20,0)$
foci: $(4\sqrt{23}, 0), (-4\sqrt{23}, 0)$

21.   vertex: $(4,-8)$; focus: $(4,-7)$

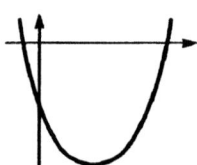

22. vertex: $(5,-2)$, directrix: $x = 4$

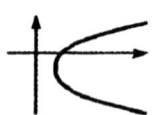

23. $(2,-1)$ **24.** center $(-2,1)$

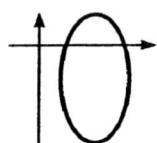   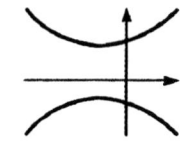

25. four real solutions

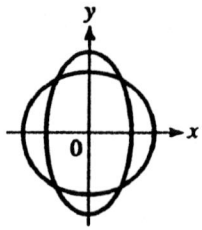

26. no real solutions

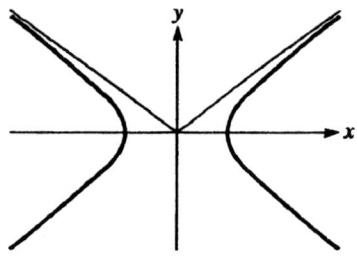

27. 2 real solutions

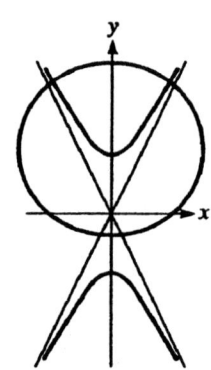

28. 2

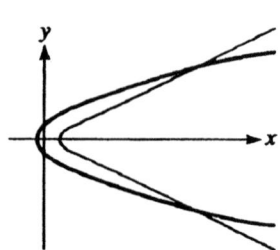

29. $y = \pm\sqrt{0.25x^2 + x - 3} + 3$

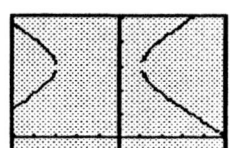

30.

31.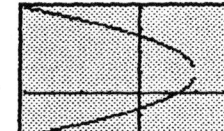

32.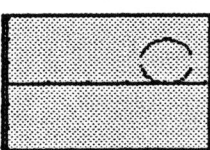

33. (a) $-\dfrac{12}{5}, \dfrac{5}{12}$

  (b) $d_1 = 169, d_2 = 169, d_3^2 = 338$

34. $\left(\dfrac{60}{7}, \dfrac{31}{21}\right)$

35. 8

36. (slope of PA)(slope of PB)

$$= \left(\frac{y-0}{x-a}\right)\left(\frac{y-0}{x+a}\right)$$

$$= \frac{y^2}{a^2 - \frac{a^2 y^2}{b^2} - a^2}$$

$$= -\frac{b^2}{a^2}$$

37. $x^2 - 6x - 8y + 1 = 0$

38. $-1 < k < 0$

39. $R_T = R + 2.5$

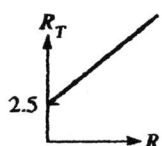

40. $v = 20t + 5$

41. $y = -\dfrac{5}{3}x + 25$

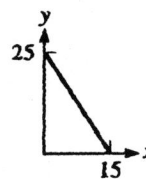

42.

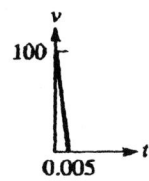

43. $y = 100.5T - 10{,}050$

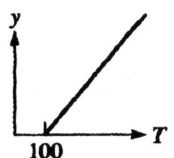

44. $T = -0.006h + 27$

45. $11{,}000 \text{ ft}^2$

46. $x^2 + y^2 - 64.8y + 126 = 0$

47. $y^2 = 32x$

48.

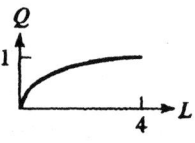

49. $A = 300w - w^2$

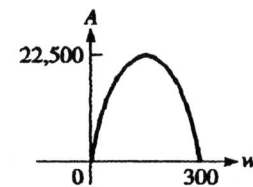

50.

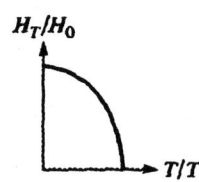

51.

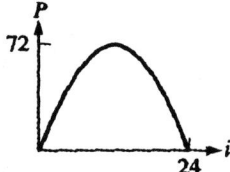

52. $2.3 \times 10^4 \text{ m}^2$ **53.** 7500 ft^2

54. $\dfrac{(d-10)^2}{100} + \dfrac{f^2}{1} = 1$

55. 18 cm, 8 cm

56. $\dfrac{x^2}{1.464 \times 10^6} + \dfrac{y^2}{1.461 \times 10^6} = 1$

57. 37.8 ft

58. $\dfrac{y^2}{8100} - \dfrac{x^2}{57{,}000} = 1$ **59.** $3y^2 - x^2 = 27$

60. $h = \sqrt{36 + x^2} - 50$

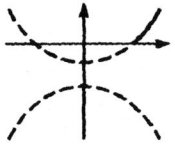

THE DERIVATIVE

3.1   Limits

1. Continuous for all real x.

2. Continuous for all x.

3. Not continuous for $x = 0$

   or for $x = 1$; division by zero.

4. Continuous for all $x > 0$ division by zero, square roots of negative numbers.

5. Continuous for $x \leq 0$ and $x > 2$. function is not defined.

6. Continuous for $-2 \leq x < 0$ and for $x > 0$. division by zero.

7. Continuous for all x.

8. Continuous for all x.

9. Not continuous at $x = 1$, small change.

10. Not continuous at $x = 2$. Function does not exist at $x = 2$.

11. Continuous for $x \leq 2$

12. Continuous for $-2 < x \leq 2$

13. Not continuous at $x = 2$, small change.

14. Continuous for all x.

15. Continuous for all x.

16. Not continuous at $x = -2$.
    $f(x)$ not defined at $x = -2$.

17.

x	2.900	2.990	2.999
$f(x)$	6.700	6.970	6.997

x	3.001	3.010	3.100
$f(x)$	7.003	7.030	7.300

$$\lim_{x \to 3} (3x - 2) = 7$$

18.

x	3.900	3.990	3.999
$f(x)$	8.210	8.920	8.992

x	4.001	4.010	4.100
$f(x)$	9.008	9.080	9.810

$$\lim_{x \to 4} (x^2 - 7) = 9$$

19.

x	0.900	0.990	0.999
$f(x)$	1.7100	1.9701	1.9970

x	1.001	1.010	1.100
$f(x)$	2.0030	2.0301	2.3100

$$\lim_{x \to 1} f(x) = 2$$

20.

x	−3.100	−3.010	−3.001
$f(x)$	13.7100	13.0701	13.0070

x	−2.999	−2.990	−2.900
$f(x)$	12.9930	12.9301	12.3100

$$\lim_{x \to -3} f(x) = 13$$

21.

x	1.900	1.990	1.999
$f(x)$	−0.2516	−0.2502	−0.25002

x	2.001	2.010	2.100
$f(x)$	−0.24998	−0.2498	−0.2485

$$\lim_{x \to 2} f(x) = -0.25$$

22.

x	3.900	3.990	3.999
$f(x)$	0.2516	0.2502	0.25002

x	4.001	4.010	4.100
$f(x)$	0.24998	0.2498	0.2485

$$\lim_{x \to 4} f(x) = 0.25$$

23.

x	10	100	1000
$f(x)$	0.4468	0.4044	0.4004

$$\lim_{x \to \infty} f(x) = 0.4$$

24.

x	10	100	1000
$f(x)$	−0.1230	−0.12498	−0.1249998

$$\lim_{x \to \infty} f(x) = -0.125$$

25. 7   **26.** 3   **27.** 1   **28.** $\dfrac{1}{9}$

29. 1   **30.** 8   **31.** $-\dfrac{2}{3}$ **32.** -4

33. 2   **34.** $\dfrac{3}{7}$ **35.** 2   **36.** 4

37. Does not exist   **38.** Does not exist

39. 0   **40.** 6   **41.** 3

42. $\dfrac{1}{7}$ **43.** 0   **44.** $\dfrac{-1}{8}$

45.

x	-0.1	-0.01	-0.001
$f(x)$	-3.10	-3.01	-3.001

x	0.001	0.01	0.1
$f(x)$	-2.999	-2.99	-2.9

$$\lim_{x \to 0} \frac{x^2 - 3x}{x} = -3$$

46. $\displaystyle\lim_{x \to 3} \frac{2x^2 - 6x}{x - 3} = 6$

x	2.9	2.99	2.999	3.001	3.01	3.1
$f(x)$	5.8	5.98	5.998	6.002	6.02	6.2

47. $\displaystyle\lim_{x \to \infty} \frac{2x^2 + x}{x^2 - 3} = 2$

x	10	100	1000
$f(x)$	2.1649	2.0106	2.0010

48.

x	10	100
$f(x) = \dfrac{x^2+5}{\sqrt{64x^4+1}}$	0.1312498975	0.1250625

x	1000
$f(x) = \dfrac{x^2+5}{\sqrt{64x^4+1}}$	0.125000625

$$\lim_{x \to \infty} \frac{x^2 + 5}{\sqrt{64x^4 + 1}} = \frac{1}{8}$$

49. 3 cm/s   **50.** 92 cm   **51.** 34.9°C, 0°C

52. 5 Ω   **53.** e **54.** $\displaystyle\lim_{x \to 0} \frac{\sin x}{x} = 1$

55. no, div. by 0; $\displaystyle\lim_{x \to 0^+} f(x) \neq \lim_{x \to 0^-} f(x)$

56. $\displaystyle\lim_{x \to 0^+} 2^{1/x} = \infty$

$\displaystyle\lim_{x \to 0^-} 2^{1/x} = 0$

3.2   The Slope of a Tangent to a Curve

1.

$m = \dfrac{y_2 - 4}{x_2 - 2}$	3.5	3.9	3.99	3.999
$m_{\text{tan}} = 4$				

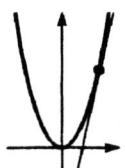

2.

$m = \dfrac{y_2 + 1}{x_2 - 2}$	-1.75	-1.95	-1.995	-1.9995
$m_{\text{tan}} = -2$				

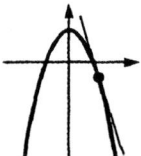

3.

$m = \dfrac{y_2 - (-2)}{x_2 - (-2)}$	-2	-2.8	-2.98	-2.998
$m_{\text{tan}} = -3$				

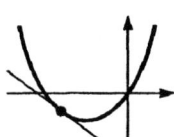

$y = x^3 + 1;\ p = (-1, 0)$

4.

$m = \dfrac{y_2}{x_2 + 1}$	1.75	2.71	2.9701	2.99700000
$m_{\text{tan}} = 3$				

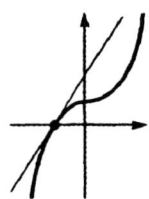

5. 4   **6.** -2 **7.** -3 **8.** 3   **15.** $m_{\tan} = 6 - 2x_1; 10, 0$

9. $m_{\tan} = 2x_1, 4, -2$

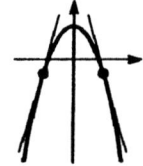

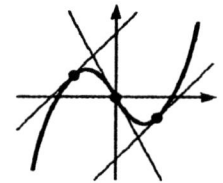

10. $m_{\tan} = -x_1, -2, 2$

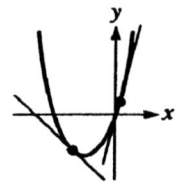

16. $m_{\tan} = 3x_1^2 - 2, 1, -2, 1$

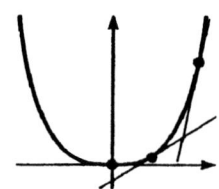

11. $m_{\tan} = 4x_1 + 5, -3, 7$

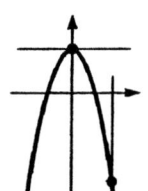

17. $m_{\tan} = 4x_1^3; 0.5, 4$

12. $m_{\tan} = -6x_1, 0, -12$

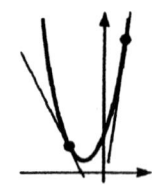

18. $m_{\tan} = -4x_1^3, 0, -4, -32$

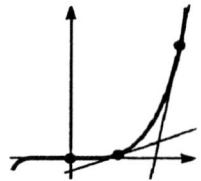

13. $m_{\tan} = 2x_1 + 4; -2, 8$

14. $m_{\tan} = 4x_1 - 4, 0, 2$

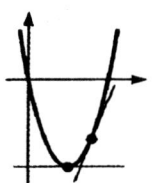

19. $m_{\tan} = 5x_1^4; 0, 0.31, 5$

20. $m_{\tan} = \dfrac{-1}{x_1^2}, -4, -1, -\dfrac{1}{4}$

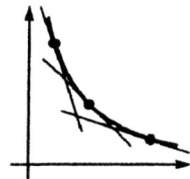

21.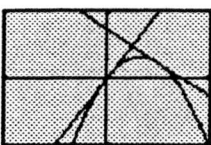

22.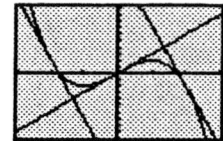

23.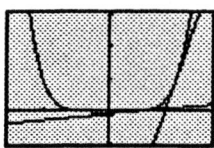

24.

25. $\dfrac{\Delta y}{\Delta x} = 4.1, \ m_{\tan} = 4$

26. $\dfrac{\Delta y}{\Delta x} = -4.2, \ m_{\tan} = -4$

27. $\dfrac{\Delta y}{\Delta x} = -12.61, \ m_{\tan} = -12$

28. $\dfrac{\Delta y}{\Delta x} = 21.91, \ m_{\tan} = 21$

3.3   The Derivative

1. 3 **2.** 6 **3.** −2 **4.** −5

5. $2x$ **6.** $-2x$ **7.** $10x$ **8.** $-12x$

9. $2x - 7$ **10.** $2x + 4$ **11.** $8 - 4x$

12. $3 - x$ **13.** $3x^2 + 4$ **14.** $2 - 12x^2$

15. $\dfrac{-1}{(x+2)^2}$ **16.** $\dfrac{-6}{(2x+1)^2}$ **17.** $1 - \dfrac{4}{3x^2}$

18. $\dfrac{-1}{(x-1)^2}$ **19.** $\dfrac{-4}{x^3}$ **20.** $\dfrac{-4x}{(x^2+4)^2}$

21. $4x^3 + 3x^2 + 2x + 1$ **22.** $x^2 + x + 1$

23. $4x^3 + \dfrac{2}{x^2}$ **24.** $\dfrac{-1}{x^2} - \dfrac{2}{x^3}$

25. $6x - 2; \ -8$

26. $9 - 3x^2; \ -3$ **27.** $\dfrac{-33}{(3x+2)^2}; \ \dfrac{-3}{11}$

28. $2x + \dfrac{2}{x^2}; \ -\dfrac{7}{2}$

29. $-\dfrac{2}{x^2}$, all real numbers except 0.

30. $\dfrac{-20}{(x-4)^2}$; all real numbers except 4.

31. $\dfrac{-6x}{(x^2-1)^2}$, all real numbers except ± 1.

32. $\dfrac{-4x}{(x^2+1)^2}$, all real numbers

33. $\dfrac{1}{2\sqrt{x+1}}$ **34.** $\dfrac{x}{\sqrt{x^2+3}}$

35. $\dfrac{1}{2\sqrt{x}}$

36. $\dfrac{1}{2\sqrt{x-2}}$, differentiable for $2 < x$.

3.4   The Derivative as an Instantaneous Rate of Change

1. $m = 4$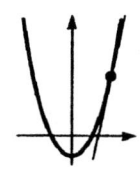

2. $m = 4$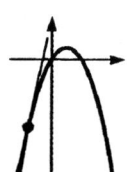

3. $m = \dfrac{-3}{4}$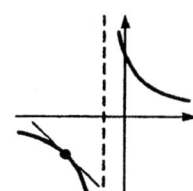

4. $m = 4$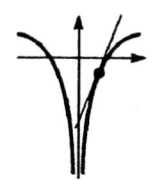

5. $4.00, 4.00, 4.00, 4.00, 4.00$

$\lim_{t \to 3} \dfrac{\Delta s}{\Delta t} = 4$ ft/s

6. $-3.0, -3.0, -3.0, -3.0, -3.0$

$\lim_{t \to 4} \dfrac{\Delta s}{\Delta t} = 3$ ft/s

7. $5.0, 6.5, 7.7, 7.97, 7.997$

$\lim_{t \to 2} = v = 8$ ft/s

8. $105.6, 104.8, 104.16, 104.016, 104.0016$

$\lim_{t \to 0.5} \dfrac{\Delta s}{\Delta t} = 104$ ft/s

9. $4; 4$ ft/s

10. $-3; -3$ ft/s   11. $6t - 4; 8$ ft/s

12. $120 - 32t; 104$ ft/s

13. $3 + \dfrac{2}{5t^2}$ 14. $\dfrac{4}{(t+2)^2}$ 15. $6t - 6t^2$

16. $v_0 - at$ 17. $12t - 4$ 18. $\dfrac{1}{\sqrt{2t+1}}$

19. $6t$ 20. $-a$ 21. -2 22. $5 - x$

23. $6w$ 24. 1510 m   25. 460 W

26. $6.8 \dfrac{\text{cm}^3}{\text{cm}}$ 27. -83.1 W/(m$^2 \cdot$ h)

28. $\dfrac{-48}{(t+3)^2}$, $-\$1300$/year   29. πd^2

30. 9.77×10^{-3} s/cell   31. $\dfrac{24.2}{\sqrt{\lambda}}$

32. -0.50 N/m

3.5   Derivatives of Polynomials

1. $5x^4$ 2. $12x^{11}$ 3. $-36x^8$ 4. $-42x^5$

5. $4x^3$ 6. $15t^4$ 7. $2x + 2$

8. $3x^2 - 4x$ 9. $15r^2 - 2$ 10. $12x - 6$

11. $8x^7 - 28x^6 - 1$ 12. $16x^3 - 2$

13. $-42x^6 + 15x^2$ 14. $52x^3 - 18x^2 - 1$

15. $x^2 + x$ 16. $-2z^7 + 2z^3$

17. 16 18. 16 19. 33 20. 49

21. -4 22. 0

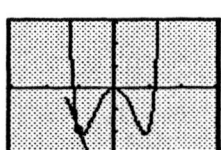   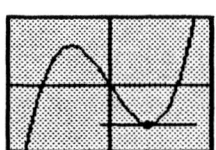

23. -29 24. -30

   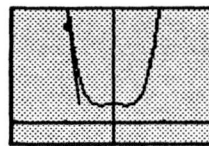

25. $30t^4 - 5$ 26. $60 - 9.8t$ 27. $-6 - 6t^2$

28. $v_0 + at$ 29. 64 30. 0 31. 45

32. 70 33. 1 34. $-\dfrac{3}{2}$ 35. $(2, 4)$

36. $\dfrac{dy}{dx} = 15x^2 + 4$; since $x^2 \geq 0$, minimum value of $\dfrac{dy}{dx} = 4$.

Therefore, $m \geq 4$.

37. $-\dfrac{1}{4}$ 38. $\dfrac{1}{2}$ 39. $3\pi r^2$ 40. $12e$

41. 84 W/A   42. $3220d^2$

43. $a(c_1 + 2c_2 E + 3c_3 E^2)$

44. $kx(5x^3 + 1350x - 7000)$

45. -80.5 m/km   46. -12 N/cm

47. 391 mm^2 48. -13.3 in^2

3.6   Derivatives of Products and Quotients of Functions

1. $x^2(3) + (3x + 2)(2x)$
$= 3x^2 + 6x^2 + 4x = 9x^2 + 4x$

2. $3x(3x^2) + (x^3 + 1)(3) = 9x^3 + 3x^3 + 3$
   $= 12x^3 + 3$

3. $6x(6x - 5) + (3x^2 - 5x)(6)$
   $= 54x^2 - 60x$

4. $2x^3(12x^3 + 1) + (3x^4 + x)(6x^2)$
   $= 42x^6 + 8x^3$

5. $(3t + 2)(2) + (2t - 5)(3)$
   $= 12t - 11$

6. $24x^2 - 16x + 12x^2 + 9$
   $= 36x^2 - 16x + 9$

7. $-6x^6 + 18x^4 - 18x^2 + 4x^3 - 8x^6 - 6x + 12x^4$
   $= -14x^6 + 30x^4 + 4x^3 - 18x^2 - 6x$

8. $(x^3 - 6x)(-12x^2) + (2 - 4x^3)(3x^2 - 6)$
   $= -24x^5 + 96x^3 + 6x^2 - 12$

9. $(2x - 7)(-2) + (5 - 2x)(2) = -8x + 24$

10. $(5s^2 + 2)(4s) + (2s^2 - 1)(10s)$
   $= 20s^3 + 8s + 20s^3 - 10s$

11. $(x^3 - 1)(4x - 1) + (2x^2 - x - 1)(3x^2)$
   $= 10x^4 - 4x^3 - 3x^2 - 4x + 1$

12. $(3x^2 - 4x + 1)(-12x) + (5 - 6x^2)(6x - 4)$
   $= -72x^3 + 72x^2 + 18x - 20$

13. $\dfrac{3}{(2x + 3)^2}$

14. $\dfrac{2x + 2 - 2x}{(x + 1)^2}$

15. $\dfrac{-2x}{(x^2 + 1)^2}$

16. $\dfrac{11}{(2i + 3)^2}$

17. $\dfrac{6 - 2x^2}{(3 - 2x)^2}$

18. $\dfrac{-12x + 10}{(3x^2 - 5x)^2}$

19. $\dfrac{-6x^2 + 6x + 4}{(3x^2 + 2)^2}$

20. $\dfrac{-4x^3 + 24x^2}{(4 - x)^2}$

21. $\dfrac{-3x^2 - 16x - 26}{(x^2 + 4x + 2)^2}$

22. $\dfrac{-48x^5 - 12}{(4x^5 - 3x - 4)^2}$

23. $\dfrac{-2x^3 + 2x^2 + 5x + 4}{x^3(x + 2)^2}$

24. $\dfrac{6x^4 - 30x^3 + 38x^2 - 4}{(2x^2 - 5x + 4)^2}$

25. -107 **26.** 2 **27.** 75 **28.** 3.875

29. 19 **30.** $\dfrac{15}{32}$ **31.** -5.64 **32.** 0.42

33. (1) $\dfrac{-12x^3 + 45x^2 - 14x}{(3x - 7)^2}$

   (2) $\dfrac{-12x^3 + 45x^2 - 14x}{(3x - 7)^2}$

34. (1) $\dfrac{8x^3 - 16x^2 + 8x + 1}{(x - 1)^2}$

   (2) $\dfrac{8x^3 - 16x^2 + 8x + 1}{(x - 1)^2}$

35. 12 **36.** -61

37. $1, -1$

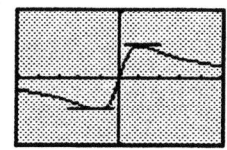

38. $x = -2, \dfrac{dy}{dx} > 0$; $x = -1, \dfrac{dy}{dx}$ undefined;

   $x = 0, \dfrac{dy}{dx} > 0$; $x = 1, \dfrac{dy}{dx}$ undefined;

   $x = 2, \dfrac{dy}{dx} > 0$

   m_{tan} is never negative.

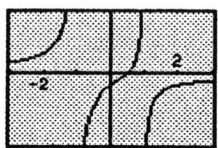

39. $8t^3 - 45t^2 - 14t - 8$

40. $\dfrac{-150,000(e + 3)}{e^2(e + 6)^2}$

41. -0.07 V/Ω **42.** 0.24 g/s

43. $1.2°$C/h   **44.** 0.925 V/s

45. $\dfrac{2R(R + 2r)}{3(R + r)^2}$ **46.** $\dfrac{pV^3 - aV + 2ab}{RV^3}$

47. $\dfrac{E^2(R - r)}{(R + r)^3}$ **48.** $\dfrac{2kf(w^2 - wf + a^2)}{(w^2 - 2wf + f^2 + a^2)^2}$

3.7　　The Derivative of a Power of a Function

1. $\dfrac{1}{2x^{1/2}}$　　　2. $\dfrac{3}{4\sqrt[4]{x}}$　　　3. $\dfrac{-6}{t^3}$

4. $\dfrac{-8}{x^5}$　　　5. $-\dfrac{1}{x^{4/3}}$　　　6. $\dfrac{-2}{5\sqrt[5]{x^7}}$

7. $\dfrac{3\sqrt{x}}{2}+\dfrac{1}{x^2}$　　　　8. $-6x^{-4}+6x^{-3}$

9. $10x(x^2+1)^4$　　　　10. $-8(1-2x)^3$

11. $-192x^2(7-4x^3)^7$　　　12. $288x(8x^2-1)^5$

13. $\dfrac{2x^2}{(2x^3-3)^{2/3}}$　　　14. $-9(1-6x)^{1/2}$

15. $\dfrac{24y}{(4-y^2)^5}$　　　16. $\dfrac{6}{(1-3x)^{3/2}}$

17. $\dfrac{24x^3}{(2x^4-5)^{1/4}}$　　　18. $\dfrac{60\theta^5}{(3\theta^6-4)^{1/3}}$

19. $\dfrac{-4x}{(1-8x^2)^{3/4}}$　　　20. $\dfrac{8x^5}{(4x^6+2)^{2/3}}$

21. $\dfrac{12x+5}{(8x+5)^{1/2}}$　　　22. $x(1-3x)^4(2-21x)$

23. $\dfrac{-1}{\sqrt{2R+1}(4R+1)^{3/2}}$　　　24. $\dfrac{-14(2x+1)}{(3x-2)^3}$

25. $\dfrac{3}{10}$　　　26. $-\dfrac{2}{9}$　　　27. $\dfrac{5}{36}$

28. 9　　29. $\dfrac{-3}{x^4}$　　30. $\dfrac{-8}{(4x+3)^2}$

31. $x=0$　　　　　32. $x=\dfrac{1}{2}$

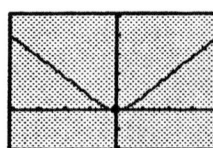　　　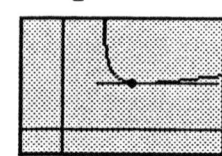

33. 1　　34. $-\dfrac{4}{3}$　　35. -1.35 cm/s

36. 0.801　　37. $\dfrac{-450{,}000}{V^{5/2}}$, -4.50 kPa/cm^3

38. -2.9×10^5/ft　　　39. $-45.2\ \text{W/(m}^2\text{·h)}$

40. $\dfrac{x}{v_1(a^2+x^2)^{1/2}}+\dfrac{x-c}{v_2[b^2+(c-x)^2]^{1/2}}$

41. $\dfrac{8a^3}{(4a^2-\lambda^2)^{3/2}}$　　　42. $\dfrac{-\omega^2 LV}{[R^2+(\omega L)^2]^{3/2}}$

43. $\dfrac{2(w+1)}{(2w^2+4w+2)^{1/2}}$　　　44. $\dfrac{x-3}{\sqrt{x^2-6x+34}}$

3.8　　Differentiation of Implicit Functions

1. $-\dfrac{3}{2}$　　　2. 2　　　3. $\dfrac{1+6x}{4}$

4. $\dfrac{5x^4+1}{5}$　　　5. $\dfrac{x}{4y}$　　　6. $\dfrac{-x}{2y}$

7. $\dfrac{2x}{5y^4}$　　　8. $\dfrac{9x^2-1}{4y^3}$　　　9. $\dfrac{2x}{2y+1}$

10. $\dfrac{4x^3}{1-6y^2}$　　11. $\dfrac{-3y}{1+3x}$　　12. $\dfrac{y}{8-x}$

13. $\dfrac{-2x-y^3}{3xy^2+3}$　　　14. $\dfrac{(x+1)^2(3+y^2)+5y}{(5-2xy-2x^2y)(x+1)}$

15. $\dfrac{3(y^2+1)(y^2-2x+1)}{(y^2+1)^2-6x^2y}$　　　16. $\dfrac{2+2x-3x^2y^2}{1+2x^3y}$

17. $\dfrac{4(2y-x)^3-2x}{8(2y-x)^3-1}$　　　18. $\dfrac{4x^3y}{6y(y^2+2)^2-x^4}$

19. $\dfrac{-3x(x^2+1)^2}{y(y^2+1)}$　　　20. $\dfrac{2(3y-1)}{2y-6x-3}$

21. 3　　22. -4　　23. $-\dfrac{108}{157}$　　24. $-\dfrac{27}{44}$

25. 1　　26. 0.363 m/s　　27. $\dfrac{-x}{y}$

28. $\dfrac{-r}{r+h}$　　　29. $\dfrac{r-R+1}{r+1}$.

30. $-\dfrac{b^3+3bh^2}{h^3+3b^2h}$　　　31. $\dfrac{2C^2r(12CSr-20Cr-3L)}{3(C^2r^2-L^2)}$

32. $0.638, 0.143$

3.9 Higher Derivatives

1. $y' = 3x^2 + 2x$; $y'' = 6x + 2$; $y''' = 6$; $y^{(n)} = 0$; $n \geq 4$

2. $f'(x) = 3 - 4x^3$; $f''(x) = -12x^2$; $f'''(x) = -24x$; $f^{(4)}(x) = -24$; $f^{(n)}(x) = 0$, $n \geq 5$

3. $f'(x) = 3x^2 - 24x^3$; $f''(x) = 6x - 72x^2$; $f'''(x) = 6 - 144x$; $f^{(4)}(x) = -144$; $f^{(n)}(x) = 0$, $n \geq 5$

4. $\dfrac{ds}{dt} = 10t^4 + 20t^3$,

   $\dfrac{d^2s}{dt^2} = 40t^3 + 60t^2$,

   $\dfrac{d^3s}{dt^3} = 120t^2 + 120t$,

   $\dfrac{d^4s}{dt^4} = 240t + 120$,

   $\dfrac{d^5s}{dt^5} = 240$,

   $\dfrac{d^n s}{dt^n} = 0$, $n \geq 6$

5. $y' = -8(1 - 2x)^3$; $y'' = 48(1 - 2x)^2$; $y''' = -192(1 - 2x)$ $y^{(4)} = 384$; $y^{(n)} = 0$, $n \geq 5$

6. $f'(x) = 9(3x + 2)^2$; $f''(x) = 54(3x + 2)$; $f'''(x) = 162$; $f^{(n)} = 0$, $n \geq 4$

7. $f'(r) = 256r^3 + 144r^2 + 24r + 1$ $f''(r) = 768r^2 + 288r + 24$ $f'''(r) = 1536r + 288$ $f^{(4)}(r) = 1536$ $f^{(n)}(r) = 0$, $n \geq 5$

8. $y' = (x - 1)^2(4x - 1)$; $y'' = 12x^2 - 18x + 6$; $y''' = 24x - 18$; $y^{(4)} = 24$; $y^{(n)} = 0$, $n \geq 5$

9. $84x^5 - 30x^4$

10. $-40x^3$

11. $\dfrac{-1}{4x^{3/2}}$

12. $6 - \dfrac{3}{8\theta^{5/2}}$

13. $\dfrac{-12}{(8x - 3)^{7/4}}$

14. $\dfrac{-8}{(6x + 5)^{5/3}}$

15. $\dfrac{12}{(1 + 2p)^{5/2}}$

16. $\dfrac{60}{(3 - 4x)^{5/2}}$

17. $600(2 - 5x)^2$

18. $480(4x + 1)^4$

19. $30(3x^2 - 1)^3(27x^2 - 1)$

20. $144x(2x^3 + 3)^2(11x^3 + 3)$

21. $\dfrac{4}{(1 - x)^3}$

22. $\dfrac{4}{(1 + R)^3}$

23. $\dfrac{2}{(x + 1)^3}$

24. $\dfrac{3x}{(1 - x^2)^{5/2}}$

25. $\dfrac{-9}{y^3}$

26. $\dfrac{8}{(x + 2y)^3}$

27. $\dfrac{-6(y^2 - xy + x^2)}{(2y - x)^3}$

28. $\dfrac{2y(x - y)}{(x - 2y)^3}$

29. $\dfrac{9}{125}$

30. 24

31. $-\dfrac{13}{384}$

32. 576

33. -50

34. $\dfrac{4}{9}$

35. 48

36. 540

37. -32.2 ft/s^2

38. 0 ft/s, -28.8 ft/s^2

39. $\dfrac{-1.60}{(2t + 1)^{3/2}}$

40. 24.8 W/(m^2·h^2)

Chapter 3 Review Exercises

1. -4

2. 8

3. $\dfrac{1}{4}$

4. 0

5. 1

6. $\dfrac{10}{3}$

7. $\dfrac{7}{3}$

8. -6

9. $\dfrac{2}{3}$

10. 7

11. -2

12. 0

13. 5

14. 6

15. $-4x$

16. $4x - 3x^2$

17. $\dfrac{-4}{x^3}$

18. $\dfrac{4}{(1 - 4x)^2}$

19. $\dfrac{1}{2\sqrt{x + 5}}$

20. $\dfrac{-1}{2x^{3/2}}$

21. $14x^6 - 6x$ **22.** $56x^6 - 1$ **23.** $\dfrac{2}{x^{1/2}} + \dfrac{3}{x^2}$

24. $\dfrac{6}{x^3} - \dfrac{2}{x^{3/4}}$ **25.** $\dfrac{3}{(1-5y)^2}$

26. $\dfrac{-2(x^2 - x - 1)}{(x^2+1)^2}$ **27.** $-12(2-3x)^3$

28. $24x(2x^2-3)^5$ **29.** $\dfrac{9x}{(5-2x^2)^{7/4}}$

30. $\dfrac{9x}{(5-2x^2)^{7/4}}$

31. $\dfrac{1}{\sqrt{1 + \sqrt{1 + \sqrt{1 + 8s}}}\sqrt{1 + \sqrt{1 + 8s}}\sqrt{1 + 8s}}$

32. $(x-1)^2(x^2-2)(7x^2 - 4x - 6)$

33. $\dfrac{-2x-3}{2x^2(4x+3)^{1/2}}$ **34.** $\dfrac{-1}{\sqrt{t}(\sqrt{t}-1)^2}$

35. $\dfrac{2x - 6(2x-3y)^2}{1 - 9(2x-3y)^2}$ **36.** $\dfrac{x(1-y^2)}{y(x^2-1)}$

37. $\dfrac{5}{48}$ **38.** $-15{,}972$ **39.** $\dfrac{74}{5}$

40. $-\dfrac{1}{36}$ **41.** $36x^2 - 2x^{-3}$

42. $\dfrac{-16}{(1-8x)^{3/2}}$ **43.** $\dfrac{56}{(1+4x)^3}$

44. $480(6x+5)^2(3x+1)$

45.

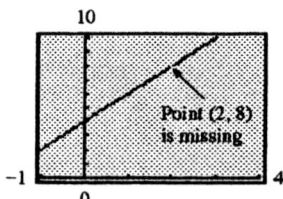

46. An odd number of solutions.

47. **(a)** 30 ft/s   **(b)** 6 ft/s

48. f_2 **49.** -31 **50.** $-\dfrac{8}{27}$ **51.** 5

52. $t = 2$

53. $-k + k^2 t - \dfrac{1}{2}k^3 t^2$

54. 80 ft   **55.** $\dfrac{-2k}{r^3}$ **56.** $\dfrac{a}{\sqrt{v_0^2 + 2as}}$

57. $0.04(0.01t + 1)^2(0.04t + 1)$

58. $\dfrac{\alpha z^2 + \alpha - \beta}{(\alpha(1 - z^2) - \beta)^2}$ **59.** $\dfrac{2R(R+2r)}{3(R+r)^2}$

60. 560,000 m^3/h.   **61.** $-\dfrac{1}{4\pi\sqrt{C}(L+2)^{3/2}}$

62. $\dfrac{aI(2b - I)}{(b-I)^2}$ **63.** $\dfrac{-15}{(0.5t+1)^2}$ **64.** $\dfrac{40V_2^{0.4}}{V_1^{1.4}}$

65.
$$y' = \frac{w}{6EI}(3L^2 x - 3Lx^2 + x^3)$$
$$y'' = \frac{w}{2EI}(L-x)^2$$
$$y''' = \frac{w}{EI}(x - L)$$
$$y^{iv} = \frac{w}{EI}$$

66. -0.0320 g/min^2

67.
$$p = \frac{150}{w} + 2w$$
$$\frac{dp}{dw} = \frac{-150}{w^2} + 2$$

68. $4\pi r - \dfrac{200}{r^2}$

69.
$$A = 4x - x^3$$
$$\frac{dA}{dx} = 4 - 3x^2$$

70. 397 mi/h

71. At $t = 5$ years, $dV/dt = -\$7500$/year (rate of appreciation is decreasing); $\frac{d^2V}{dt^2} = \$1500$/year^2 (rate at which appreciation changes is increasing), (Machinery is depreciating, but depreciation is lessening.)

72. 1.05 mi, 0.50 mi

APPLICATIONS OF THE DERIVATIVE

4.1 Tangents and Normals

1. $4x - y - 2 = 0$

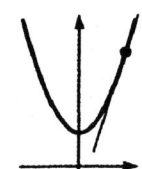

2. $4x - y - 18 = 0$

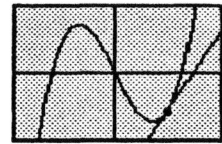

3. $x + 2y - 2 = 0$

4. $3x + 4y - 25 = 0$

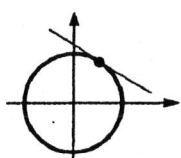

5. $x - 2y + 6 = 0$

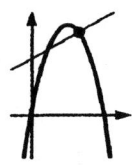

6. $x - 3y + 28 = 0$

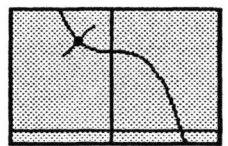

7. $2x - 6y + 7 = 0$

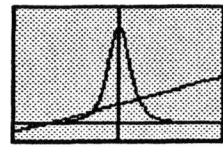

8. $x + 3y - 6 = 0$

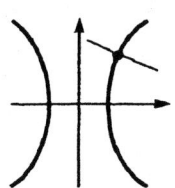

9. $\sqrt{3}x + 8y - 7 = 0,$
$16x - 2\sqrt{3}y - 15\sqrt{3} = 0$

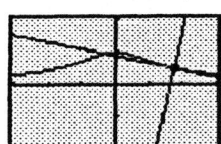

10. $16x - y - 28 = 0,$
$x + 16y - 66 = 0$

11. $2x - 12y + 37 = 0,$
$72x + 12y + 37 = 0$

12. For $x = 2, y = \dfrac{3\sqrt{21}}{5}$

E. of T.L:

$6x + 5\sqrt{21}y - 75 = 0,$

Eq of N.L:

$25\sqrt{21}x - 30y - 32\sqrt{21} = 0.$

For $x = 2, y = -\dfrac{3\sqrt{21}}{5}$

E. of T.L: $6x - 5\sqrt{21}y - 75 = 0,$

Eq of N.L: $25\sqrt{21}x + 30y - 32\sqrt{21} = 0$

13. $y = 2x - 4$

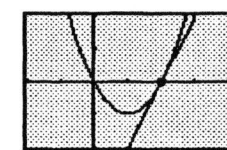

14. $x - y - 4 = 0$

15. $y - 8 = -\dfrac{1}{24}\left(x - \dfrac{3}{2}\right)$; or

$2x + 48y - 387 = 0$

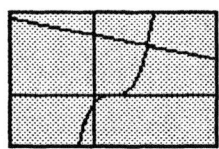

16. $128x - 32y + 97 = 0$

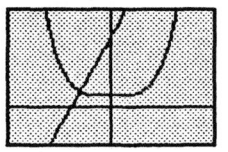

17. $m_{\text{parabola}}(a,b)\cdot m_{ellipse}(a,b) = \dfrac{2}{b}\cdot\dfrac{-2a}{b} = \dfrac{-4a}{b^2}$ and
since $b^2 = 4a$

$$m_{\text{parabola}}(a,b)\cdot m_{ellipse}(a,b) = \dfrac{-4a}{-4a} = -1$$

18. $\dfrac{152}{3}$

19. $3x - 5y - 150 = 0$ **20.** $3x + 4y - 15 = 0$

21. $y + x - 6 = 0$ **22.** $0.40x + y - 1.728 = 0$

23. $x + 2y - 3 = 0, x = 0;\ x - 2y + 3 = 0$

24. $(-6, 8)$ and $(0, -10)$.

4.2   Newtons Method for Solving Equations

1. 3.449489743   **2.** 1.2807764

3. -0.1804604 **4.** -3.4142136

5. 0.5857864   **6.** 0.7983603

7. 0.3488942   **8.** 1.7071068

9. 2.5615528   **10.** 2.3027756

11. -1.2360680 **12.** -1.5615528

13. 0.9175433.   **14.** 1.1347241

15. 0.6180340   **16.** 0.5935135

17. $-1.8557725, 0.6783628$, and 3.1774097

18. 3.2676453   **19.** 1.5874011

20. 0.00962518 should be 0.00961518, possibly a typographical or computational error.

21. 29.5 m   **22.** 2.2143 μF, 3.2143 μF, 4.2143 μF

23. 5.05 ft   **24.** 0.629 cm

4.3   Curvilinear Motion

1. $3.16, 341.6°$ **2.** $0.54, 68.2°$

 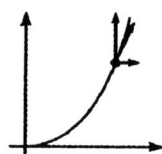

3. $8.07, 352.4°$ **4.** $7.01, -87.3°$

 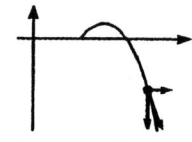

5. $a = 0.$ **6.** $0.26, 128.7°$

7. $20.0, 3.7°$ **8.** $2.00, 268.9°$

9. 9.4 m/s, 302°   **10.** 4.8 ft/s at $\theta = 34°$

11. 1.3 ft/min^2, 288°   **12.** 5.4 m/s^2 at $\theta = 312°$

13. 120 ft/s, 323°; 32 ft/s^2; 270°

14. 9.8 m/s^2 at $\theta = 270°$

15. 276 m/s, 43.5°; 2090 m/s, 16.7°

16. 40.5 m/s, 46.2°

17. 22.1 m/s^2, 25.4°; 20.2 m/s^2, 8.5°

18. 18.4 m/s^2, 67.6°

19. 21.2 mi/min, 296.6°

20. 16.4 km/h at $\theta = 85.8°$

21. $x^2 + y^2 = 1.75^2$; $v_x = 28,800$ in/min, $v_y = -27,100$ in/min

22. 2.6 cm/s at $\theta = 11°$

23. 370 m/s, 19°

24. Acceleration is inversely proportional to the square of the distance to the center of earth.

4.4   Related Rates

1. $0.0900 \; \Omega/s$ **2.** $37{,}500 \; J/s$

3. $330 \; mi/h$ **4.** $0.098 \; \Omega/min$

5. $4.1 \times 10^{-6} \; m/s$ **6.** $-3180 \; mi/h$

7. $\dfrac{dB}{dt} = \dfrac{-3kr\dfrac{dr}{dt}}{\left[r^2 + \left(\dfrac{\ell}{2}\right)^2\right]^{5/2}}$

8. $-67{,}000 \; kPa/s$ **9.** $0.15 \; mm^2/month$

10. $3.25 \; in^2/s$ **11.** $-101 \; mm^3/min$

12. $-3.04 \; ft/s.$ **13.** $-4.6 \; kPa/min$

14. $-39 \; kHz/s$ **15.** $3.18 \times 10^6 \; mm^3/s$

16. $1.3 \times 10^{-4} \; ft/s^3$ **17.** $0.48 \; m/min$

18. $13.3 \; ft/s$ **19.** $-12.0 \; ft/s$

20. $7.0 \; ft/s$ **21.** $820 \; mi/h$

22. $15.4 \; m/s$ **23.** $-8.33 \; ft/s$ **24.** $-0.978 \; cm/s$

4.5   Using Derivatives in Curve Sketching

1. $x > -1$; $f(x)$ increases.
   $x < -1$; $f(x)$ decreases.

2. for $x < 1$, $f(x)$ increases,
   for $x > 1$, $f(x)$ decreases

3. $f(x)$ decreases for $x < -2$, $x > 2$;
   $f(x)$ increases for $-2 < x < 2$

4. increasing for $-\sqrt{3} < x < 0$ and $x > \sqrt{3}$,
   decreasing for $0 < x < \sqrt{3}$ and $x < -\sqrt{3}$

5. $(-1, -1)$ minimum.

6. max $(1, 5)$

7. $(-2, -16)$ rel. min., $(2, 16)$ rel. max.

8. $(0, 0)$ rel. max, $(-\sqrt{3}, -9)$ rel. min.,
   $(\sqrt{3}, -9)$ rel min.

9. concave up for all x

10. $f(x)$ is concave down everywhere, $f(x)$ has no inflection points

11. concave down for $x > 0$; concave up for $x < 0$; $(0, 0)$ is infl. point

12. $x < -1$, concave up, $-1 < x < 1$, concave down, $x > 1$, concave up $(-1, -5)$ infl. point, $(1, -5)$ infl. point

13. 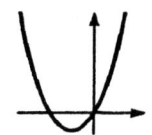   **14.**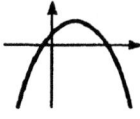

15. 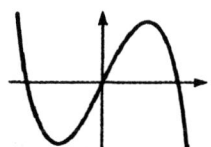   **16.**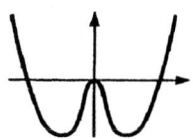

17. concave down for all x, $(3, 18)$ maximum point.

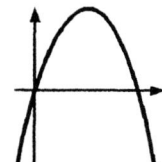

18. concave up for all $x (0, -1)$ rel. minimum.

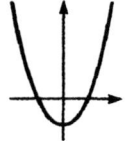

19. $(0, 0)$ min. point, $(-2, 8)$ max. point, $(-1, 4)$ infl. point

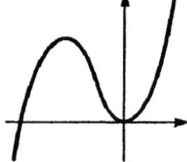

20. $(1,8)$ rel. max $(5,-24)$ rel. min. $(3,-8)$ infl. point, $(0,1)$ y-intercept

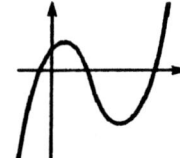

21. $(-1,1)$ is an inflection point. No maximum or minimum points.

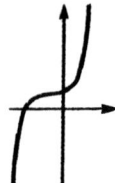

22. $(0,12)$ infl. point, $(-2,28)$ rel. max., $(2,-4)$ rel. min.

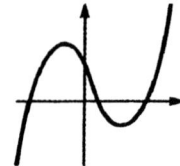

23. $(2,8)$ infl. point, $(1,16)$ max. point, $(3,0)$ min. point

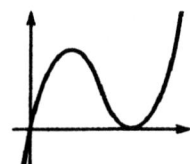

24. min $(1,-27)$, $(2,-16)$ and $(4,0)$ are inflection points

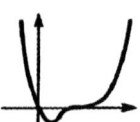

25. $(1,1)$ is a relative maximum, $(0,0)$ and $\left(\frac{2}{3},\frac{16}{27}\right)$ are inflection points

26. $(\sqrt[3]{2},-18\sqrt[3]{4})$ infl. point, $(0,0)$ max., $(2,-48)$ min. point

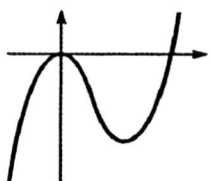

27. $(0,0)$ infl. point, $(-1,4)$ max. point $(1,-4)$ min. point

28. minimum $(-\sqrt[3]{2}, 2-6\sqrt[3]{2})$

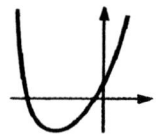

29. Where $y' > 0$, y inc.; $y' < 0, y$ dec. $y'' > 0, y$ conc. up; $y'' < 0, y$ conc. down, $y'' = 0, y$ has infl.

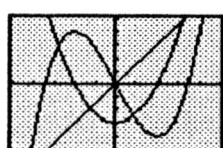

30. Where $y' > 0, y$ inc.; $y' = 0$, y has maximum or minimum, $y' < 0, y$ dec., $y'' > 0, y$ conc. up $y'' = 0, y$ has infl., $y'' < 0, y$ conc. down

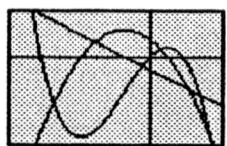

31. $(200, 100)$ max.   **32.**

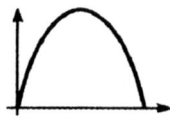   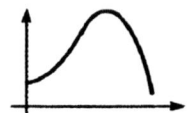

33. Max. at $(0,75)$, $(1,64)$ and $(3,48)$ are inflection points.

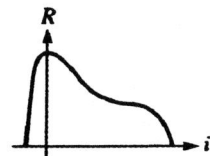

34.

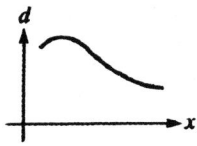

35. $V = 4x^3 - 40x^2 + 96x$; max. $(1.57, 67.6)$

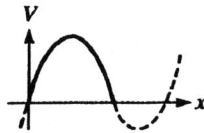

36. $V = \dfrac{64}{3}x - \dfrac{2}{3}x^3$ **37.**

38.   **39.**

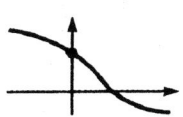   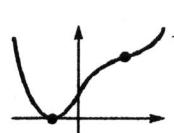

40. $f(x)$ is continuous everywhere
   $f'(x)$ is continuous everywhere except $x = 0$
   $f''(x)$ is continuous everywhere except $x = 0$
   $f(x)$ is concave down everywhere, except $x = 0$
   $f'(x)$ is concave down for $x < 0$ and concave up for $x > 0$
   $f''(x)$ is concave down everywhere except $x = 0$

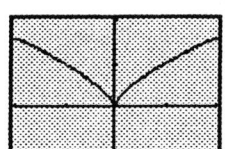

4.6   More on Curve Sketching

1. Inc. $x < 0$, dec. $x > 0$
   Concave up $x < 0$, $x > 0$
   Asym. $x = 0$, $y = 0$

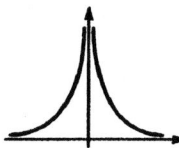

2. symmetry WRT the origin.
   x-axis is a horizontal asymptote.

   y-axis is a vertical asymptote.

   decreasing for all x, except $x = 0$

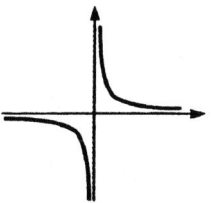

3. Intercepts: $(0,2)$; x-axis is a horizontal asymptote.
   $x = -1$ is a vertical asymptote. $f(x)$ decreasing for all $x, x \neq -1$.
   concave down for $x < -1$. Concave up for $x > -1$.

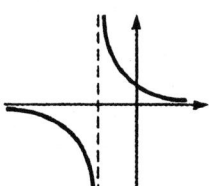

4. Intercepts: $(0,0)$
   $y = 1$ is a horizontal asymptote. Vertical asymptote at $x = 2$. decreasing all for x. Concave down for $x < 2$. Concave up for $x > 2$.

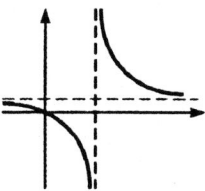

5. x-intercept at $(-\sqrt[3]{2}, 0)$. $x = 0$ is a vertical asymptote. $(-\sqrt[3]{2}, 0)$ is an inflection point. $(1, 3)$ is a relative minimum.

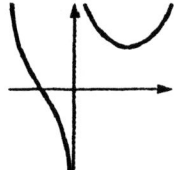

6. Intercepts: $(-\sqrt[3]{4}, 0)$; $y = x$ is an asymptote. $x = 0$ is a vertical asymptote. Concave up for all x. Increases for $x < 0$. decreases for $0 < x < 2$. Increases for $x > 2$.

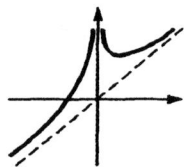

7. Intercepts: $(-1, 0)$ and $(1, 0)$, $y = x$ is an asymptote. $x = 0$ is a vertical asymptote. $f(x)$ concave up for $x < 0$. Concave down for $x > 0$.

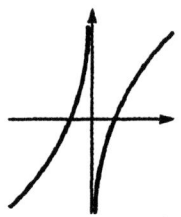

8. Symmetry WRT the origin. $y = 3x$ is an asymptote. $x = 0$ is a vertical asymptote. max. $(-1, -4)$, min. $(1, 4)$; concave up for $x > 0$. concave down for $x < 0$.

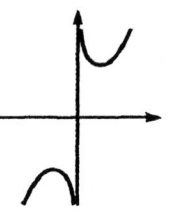

9. The origin is the only intercept. $(-2, -4)$ is a relative maximum point. $(0, 0)$ is a relative minimum point. asym. $x = -1$

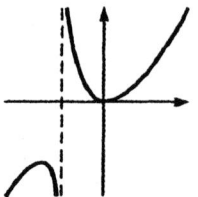

10. Intercepts: $(0, 0)$
Symmetry WRT origin. x-axis is a horizontal asymptote. min. $(-3, -3/2)$, max. $(3, 3/2)$. $(0, 0)$ infl. point $\left(-3\sqrt{3}, -\frac{3\sqrt{3}}{4}\right)$ infl. point, $\left(3\sqrt{3}, \frac{3\sqrt{3}}{4}\right)$ infl. point

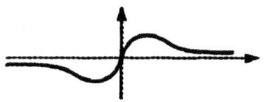

11. Intercepts: $(0, -1)$; $y = 0$ is a horizontal asymptote, vertical asymptotes at $x = -1$ and $x = 1$. max. $(0, -1)$, ??

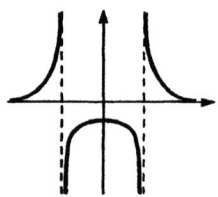

12. Intercepts: $(-1, 0), (1, 0)$, symmetry WRT origin $x = 0$ is vertical asymptote, $(-\sqrt{3}, -0.385)$ min, $(\sqrt{3}, 0.385)$ max. $(-\sqrt{6}, -0.340)$ and $(\sqrt{6}, 0.340)$ inflection points.

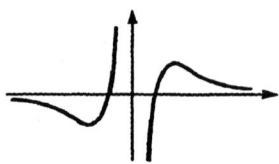

13. $(1,0)$ is an x-intercept. $x = 0$ is an asymptote; $y = 0$ is an asymptote, $(2,1)$ is a relative maximum. $\left(3, \frac{8}{9}\right)$ is an inflection.

14. $x = 0$ is a vertical asymptote. min. $\left(\frac{1}{4}, 3\right)$ concave up for all x.

15. Intercepts: $(0,0), (-1,0), (1,0)$, min $\left(-\frac{\sqrt{2}}{2}, -\frac{1}{2}\right)$, max. $\left(\frac{\sqrt{2}}{2}, \frac{1}{2}\right)$

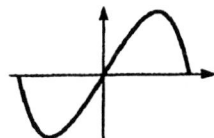

16. Intercepts: $(1,0)$, x-axis is a horizontal asymptote. $x = 0$ and $x = 2$ are vertical asymptotes. decreasing for $x < 0$. Decreasing for $0 < x < 2$. Decreasing for $x > 2$. $(1,0)$ infl. point.

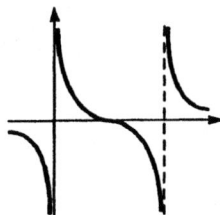

17. Intercept at $x = 0, y = 0$, Asymptotes at $x = -3, x = 3$, $(0,0)$ is an inflection point, $y = 0$ is an asymptote.

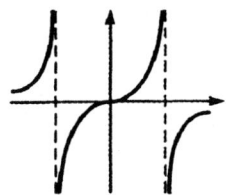

18. Intercepts: $(0,-1), (-2,0), (2,0)$. $y = 1$ is a horizontal asymptote. min. $(0,-1)$, Infl. point $\left(-\frac{2\sqrt{3}}{3}, -\frac{1}{2}\right)$, Infl. point $\left(\frac{2\sqrt{3}}{3}, -\frac{1}{2}\right)$

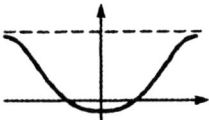

19. C_T is increasing for all C. C_T is concave down for $C \geq 0$, $(0,0)$ is the only intercept, horizontal asymptote at $C_T = 6$.

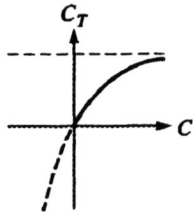

20. e-axis is a horizontal asymptote (positively). $e = 0$ is a vertical asymptote. Decreases for $e > 0$. Concave up for $e > 0$.

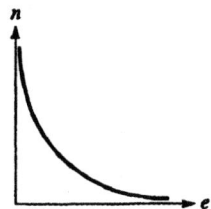

21. R-intercept at $(0,1)$, max, $(0,1)$. Inflection, $(141, 0.82)$, $R = 0$ is a horizontal asymptote

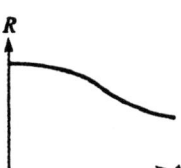

22. Intercepts: $(0,0)$; $P = 0$ is a horizontal asymptote. max $(1,9)$, Infl. point $(2,8)$

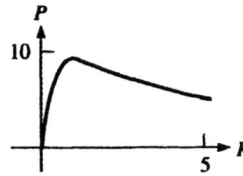

23. $A_T = 2\pi r^2 + \frac{40}{r}$, Vertical asymptote at $r = 0$. min. $(1.47, 40.8)$.

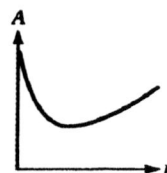

24. $x = 0$ is a vertical asymptote. min $(200, 400)$, concave up for all x.

4.7   Applied Maximum and Minimum Problems

1. 196 ft   **2.** \$800   **3.** $\dfrac{E}{2R}$

4. The fund will run out of money sometime in April of 2028.

5. 35 m^2, \$8300   **6.** 2000 ft   **7.** 1500 Ω

8. $(1.2, 1.2)$ **9.** 12 in by 12 in

10. each resistor is 16 Ω.   **11.** 5 mm by 5 mm

12. 80,000 ft^2 **13.** 1.1 h   **14.** 30 m $\times$ 45 m

15. 8.49 cm   **16.** 18 in $\times$18 in $\times$36 in.

17. 3.00 ft   **18.** $l = 48$ ft, $w = 6.8$ ft, $d = 6.0$ ft

19. 12   **20.** -15 **21.** $0.58L$

22. 5.9 mm from 2.00 nC charge   **23.** 1.33 in.

24. $h = 5.76$ cm and $r = 4.07$ cm

25. 100 m   **26.** 1250 units

27. $w = 1.00$ ft, $d = 1.73$ ft

28. The rocket passes 0.466 km from target.

29. 8.00 mi

30. $S = \sqrt{a^2 + x^2} + \sqrt{b^2 + (c - x)^2}$

31. 59.2 m by 118 m

32. $r = 4.54$ cm, $h = 5.79$ cm

4.8   Differentials and Linear Approximations

1. $(5x^4 + 1)dx$ **2.** $6x\,dx$ **3.** $\dfrac{-10\,dr}{r^6}$

4. $\left(\dfrac{1}{\sqrt{x}} + \dfrac{1}{x^2}\right)dx$ **5.** $48t(3t^2 - 5)^3 dt$

6. $\dfrac{5\,dx}{(4 + 3x)^{2/3}}$ **7.** $\dfrac{-12x\,dx}{(3x^2 + 1)^2}$

8. $\dfrac{1}{2}\sqrt{\dfrac{1 + 2u}{u}}\,\dfrac{1}{(1 + 2u)^2}\,du$

9. $x(1 - x)^2(-5x + 2)dx$

10. $\dfrac{6(1 - 6x)dx}{\sqrt{1 - 4x}}$ **11.** $\dfrac{2\,dx}{(5x + 2)^2}$ **12.** $\dfrac{(3x - 4)dx}{(2x - 1)^{3/2}}$

13. 12.28, 12   **14.** 2.595, 2.55

15. 1.71275, 1.675   **16.** -10.805571, -10.40576

17. -2.4, -2.4730881 **18.** 3810, 3834

19. 0.6257, 0.6264903   **20.** 0.0026553, 0.0026509

21. $L(x) = 2x$ **22.** $L(x) = \dfrac{1}{6}(x - 8) + 4$

23. $L(x) = -2x - 3$ **24.** $L(x) = 1 \cdot (x + 2) - 4$

25. 0.0038 cm^2 **26.** 0.8%   **27.** -31 nm

28. 0.95%   **29.** $\dfrac{dr}{r} = \dfrac{1}{2}\dfrac{d\lambda}{\lambda}$ **30.** $\dfrac{dF}{F} = \dfrac{-2\,dr}{r}$

31. $\dfrac{dA}{A} = 2\dfrac{ds}{s}$ **32.** 16.96

33. $L(x) = -\frac{1}{2}x + \frac{3}{2}$, 1.45

34. 2.0025   **35.** $L(V) = -0.13V + 1.73$

36. $L(R) = \frac{16}{25}(R - 3.2) + 4$

Chapter 4 Review Exercises

1. $5x - y + 1 = 0$

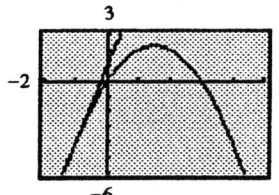

2. $11x - 2y - 20 = 0$

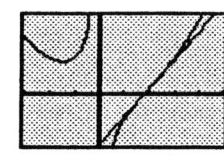

3. $8x + 5y - 50 = 0$

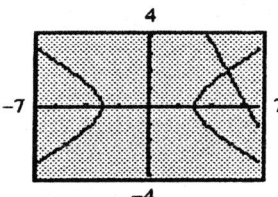

4. $32x - 2y - 191 = 0$

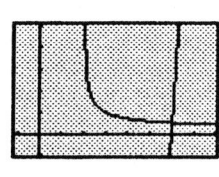

5. $x - 2y + 3 = 0$

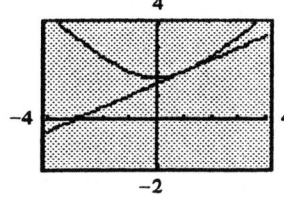

6. $x - 2y + 2 = 0$

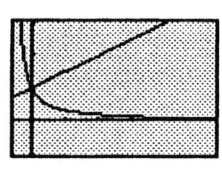

7. 4.19, 72.6°

8. 1.26, 18.4°

9. 2.12   **10.** −0.250 cm/s   **11.** 2.00, 90.9°

12. 0.500 cm/s², 90°   **13.** 0.7458983

14. 2.643804331   **15.** 1.911164287

16. −0.5857864376

17. For all x; the graph is concave up, $(-2, -16)$ is a minimum.

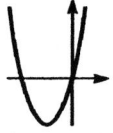

18. Continuous for all x. intercepts $(0, 1)$ and (-1.75). $(-1, 1)$ is a local maximum, $\left(-\frac{1}{3}, \frac{23}{27}\right)$ is a local minimum. $\left(-\frac{2}{3}, \frac{25}{27}\right)$ is an inflection point.

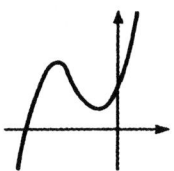

19. Intercepts are $(\pm 3\sqrt{3}, 0)$ and $(0, 0)$, $(3, 54)$ is a local maximum; $(-3, -54)$ is a local minimum, $(0, 0)$ is an inflection point.

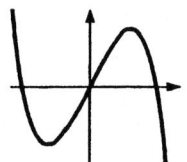

20. Continuous for all x. intercepts $(0, 0)$ and $(6, 0)$. $\left(\frac{3}{2}, \frac{2187}{16}\right)$ is a local maximum. $(3, 81)$ and $(6, 0)$ are inflection points.

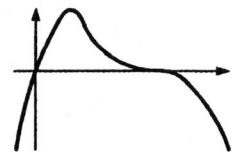

21. Concave up everywhere, $(2, -48)$ is a minimum.

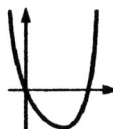

22. Continuous for all x, intercepts $(0, 0)$ and $(1.68, 0)$. $(1, -11)$ is a local minimum, $(-2, 16)$ and $(0, 0)$ are inflection points.

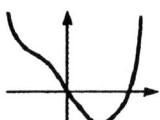

23. $x = \pm 1$ are vertical asymptotes, $(\pm\sqrt{2}, 2)$ are local minimums, concave up for $x < -1$ or $x > 1$.

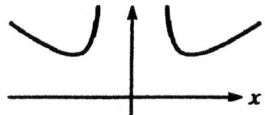

24. Continuous for all x in domain. $x = 0$ is a vertical asymptote. symmetrical with respect to the origin. $(-1, -4)$ is a local maximum, $(1, 4)$ is a local minimum.

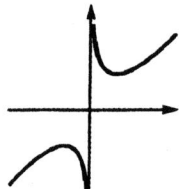

25. $\left(12x^2 - \dfrac{1}{x^2}\right) dx$ **26.** $\dfrac{-4\,dx}{(2x-1)^3}$

27. $\dfrac{(1-4x)dx}{(1-3x)^{2/3}}$ **28.** $2\sqrt{\dfrac{1}{(2-t)^3(2+t)}}\,dt$

29. 0.061   **30.** 0.24   **31.** $L(x) = \dfrac{1}{3}(11x - 4)$

32. $L(x) = -20x - 36$ **33.** 1.85 m^3 **34.** 12 W

35. $\dfrac{R\,dR}{R^2 + X^2}$ **36.** $\dfrac{dV}{V} = 3\dfrac{dr}{r}$

37. $2x - y + 1 = 0$ **38.** $y = -4x - 3$

39. 0.0 m, 6.527 m   **40.** 1.20 ft

41. 8.8 m/s, 336°   **42.** 48.7 km/h, −109.7 km/h

43. −7.44 cm/s   **44.** 0.31 Ω/min

45. 22 m^3/s   **46.** 40,000 ft

47.   **48.**

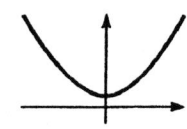   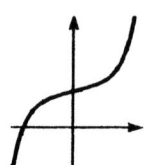

49. −0.567 ft/min   **50.** −0.0185 A/min

51. 38,000 m^2/min   **52.** 7.31 ft/s

53. 5000 cm^2 **54.** $w = 28.3$ ft, $l = 42.4$ ft

55. $L(x) = -1.42x + 113$, $(0, 100)$ is maximum. $(37, 63)$ is an inflection point; intercepts are $(0, 100)$ and $(89, 0)$

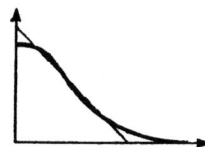

56. Continuous for all t in domain. $(0, 0)$ is the only intercept. x-axis is a horizontal asymptote. $(4, 313)$ is a local maximum. $(8, 278)$ is an inflection point.

57. 710 mi/h   **58.** −0.14 cm^3/min

59. Each capacitor is 6 μF.

60. B is located 159 ft from base of perpendicular from A.

61. 13.5 ft^3 **62.** $r = 1, \theta = 2$ **63.** 2.2 in.

64. $r = h = 1.68$ ft   **65.** 0.318 ft/min

66. 3.0 km from P toward A.

67. $r = 2.09$ cm, $h = 23.0$ cm

68. $y = 0.585x + 2.32$

INTEGRATION

5.1 Antiderivatives

1. 1   **2.** 1   **3.** 3   **4.** 5

5. 6   **6.** 8   **7.** -1 **8.** -2

9. $x^{5/2}$ **10.** $x^{4/3}$ **11.** $\dfrac{3}{2}t^4 + 2t$

12. $2x^6 + x^2$ **13.** $\dfrac{2}{3}x^3 - \dfrac{1}{2}x^2$

14. $\dfrac{1}{3}x^3 - 5x$ **15.** $\dfrac{4}{3}x^{3/2} + 3x$

16. $\dfrac{27}{4}s^{4/3} - 3s$ **17.** $\dfrac{7}{5x^5}$ **18.** $\dfrac{-2}{x^4}$

19. $2v^2 + 3\pi^2 v$ **20.** $\sqrt{x} + 4x$ **21.** $\dfrac{1}{3}x^3 + 2x - \dfrac{1}{x}$

22. $\dfrac{2}{5}x^{5/2} + \dfrac{1}{2x^2}$ **23.** $(2x+1)^6$ **24.** $(R^2+1)^3$

25. $(p^2 - 1)^4$ **26.** $(2x^4 + 1)^5$

27. $\dfrac{1}{40}(2x^4+1)^5$ **28.** $-\dfrac{1}{16}(1-x^2)^8$

29. $(6x+1)^{3/2}$ **30.** $(1-y)^{5/4}$

31. $\dfrac{1}{4}(3x+1)^{4/3}$ **32.** $\dfrac{1}{6}(4x+3)^{3/2}$

5.2 The Indefinite Integral

1. $x^2 + C$ **2.** $x^5 + C$ **3.** $\dfrac{1}{8}x^8 + C$

4. $0.1y^6 + C$ **5.** $\dfrac{4}{5}x^{5/2} + C$ **6.** $\dfrac{9}{2}x^{4/3} + C$

7. $-\dfrac{1}{3x^3} + C$ **8.** $8\sqrt{x} + C$ **9.** $\dfrac{1}{3}x^3 - \dfrac{1}{6}x^6 + C$

10. $-\dfrac{1}{6}(1-3x)^2 + C_1$

    OR:

$$x - \dfrac{3x^2}{2} + C_2, \; C_2 = C_1 - \dfrac{1}{6}$$

11. $3x^3 + \dfrac{1}{2}x^2 + 3x + C$ **12.** $\dfrac{x^4}{4} - \dfrac{4x^3}{3} + 2x^2 + C$

13. $\dfrac{t^3}{6} + \dfrac{2}{t} + C$ **14.** $3x + \dfrac{4}{x} + C$

15. $\dfrac{2}{7}x^{7/2} - \dfrac{2}{5}x^{5/2} + C$ **16.** $\dfrac{6}{5}R^{5/2} - \dfrac{5}{3}R^3 + C$

17. $6x^{1/3} + \dfrac{1}{9}x + C$ **18.** $\dfrac{3}{4}x^{4/3} + \dfrac{5}{6}x^{6/5} + \dfrac{7}{6}x^{6/7} + C$

19. $s + \dfrac{4s^3}{3} + \dfrac{4s^5}{5} + C$ **20.** $\dfrac{3}{5}(x+2)^{5/3} + C$

21. $\dfrac{1}{6}(x^2-1)^6 + C$ **22.** $\dfrac{(x^3-2)^7}{7} + C$

23. $\dfrac{1}{5}(x^4+3)^5 + C$ **24.** $\dfrac{3}{4}(1-2x)^{4/3} + C$

25. $\dfrac{(2\theta^5+5)^8}{80} + C$ **26.** $-\dfrac{6}{7}(1-x^3)^{7/3} + C$

27. $\dfrac{1}{12}(8x+1)^{3/2} + C$ **28.** $\dfrac{-1}{4(0.3+2V)^2} + C$

29. $\dfrac{1}{6}\sqrt{6x^2+1} + C$ **30.** $\dfrac{2}{3}(2x^3+1)^{1/2} + C$

31. $\sqrt{x^2-2x} + C$ **32.** $\dfrac{1}{27}\left(x^3 - \dfrac{3}{2}x^2\right)^9 + C$

33. $y = 2x^3 + 2$ **34.** $y = 4x^2 + x + 1$

35. $y = 5 - \dfrac{1}{18}(1-x^3)^6$ **36.** $y = \dfrac{1}{10}(x^4-6)^5 - 9990$

37. $12y = 83 + (1-4x^2)^{3/2}$

38. $\displaystyle\int (x^3-1)dx$ cannot be integrated by letting $u = x^3 - 1$ and $du = 3x^2 dx$ because there is no $3x^2$ with dx for proper du.

39. $i = 2t^2 - 0.2t^3 + 2$ **40.** $f = 160 - \dfrac{160}{(4+L)^{1/2}}$

41. $f(A) = \sqrt{0.01A + 1} - 1$

42. $p = 600\sqrt{60x - x^2} - 5000$

43. $y = 3x^2 + 2x - 3$ **44.** $y = x^4 + 5$

5.3   The Area Under a Curve

1. 9; 12.15   **2.** 5, 5.6   **3.** 1.92, 2.28

4. 11, 13.695   **5.** 7.625, 8.208

6. 0.17, 0.189375   **7.** 0.464, 0.5995

8. 4.146, 4.540   **9.** 1.92, 1.96

10. 115, 132   **11.** 13.5   **12.** 6   **12.** $\frac{8}{3}$

14. 15   **15.** 9   **16.** $\frac{5}{24}$ **17.** 0.8

18. $\frac{14}{3}$ **19.** 2   **20.** 149

5.4   The Definite Integral

1. 1   **2.** 8   **3.** $\frac{254}{7}$ **4.** $\frac{347}{5}$

5. $6 + 2\sqrt{6} - 2\sqrt{3}$ **6.** 2.67   **7.** 2.53   **8.** $\frac{26}{3}$

9. $-\frac{32}{3}$ **10.** 24   **11.** -1.552 **12.** 10.7

13. $\frac{4}{3}$ **14.** $\frac{38}{3}$ **15.** $-\frac{81}{4}$ **16.** $\frac{5}{8}$

17. 2   **18.** 0.359   **19.** 0.1875   **19.** 2

21. $\frac{88}{3249} = 0.0271$ **22.** 0.00181   **23.** 84

24. $\frac{56}{3}$ **25.** $\frac{364}{3}$ **26.** 8.1   **27.** $\frac{3880}{9}$

28. $\frac{11}{756}$ **29.** 0.0421   **30.** -47.99 **31.** 13.25

32. -0.7034 **33.** 64,000 ft·lb   **34.** $\frac{kR^4}{4}$

35. 86.8 m²   **36.** 817 kN

5.5   Numerical Integration: The Trapezoidal Rule

1. $\frac{11}{2} = 5.50$, $\frac{16}{3} = 5.33$

2. $\frac{35}{54} = 0.6481$, $\frac{2}{3} \approx 0.6667$

3. 7.661, $\frac{23}{3} = 7.667$ **4.** 12.66, $\frac{38}{3} = 12.67$

5. 0.2042   **6.** 0.590   **7.** 18.98

8. 3.28   **9.** 0.5205   **10.** 0.219

11. 21.74   **12.** 13.36   **13.** 45.36

14. 31.70   **15.** 0.177k **16.** 200.054 ft

5.6   Simpson's Rule

1. (a) 6   (b) 6   **2.** (a) 11.1   (b) 12

3. (a) 19.67   (b) 19.67

4. (a) 3.3922   (b) $\frac{1}{3}[5^{3/2} - 1] = 3.3934$

5. 0.2028   **6.** 0.5878   **7.** 19.27

8. 3.2396   **9.** 0.5114   **10.** 0.2187

11. 13.147   **12.** 0.2154   **13.** 44.63

14. 31.60   **15.** 1.191 in   **16.** 1.1380 A

Chapter 5 Review Exercises

1. $x^4 - \frac{1}{2}x^2 + C$ **2.** $5x + x^3 + C$

3. $\frac{2}{7}u^{7/2} + \frac{4}{3}u^{3/2} + C$ **4.** $\frac{x^3}{3} - \frac{x^6}{2} + C$ **5.** $\frac{19}{3}$

6. 2   **7.** $\frac{16}{3}$ **8.** $\frac{17}{3}$ **9.** $3x - \frac{1}{x^2} + C$

10. $2x^{3/2} + x^{1/2} - \frac{x}{4} + C$ **11.** 3   **12.** 0.525

13. $\frac{1}{10(2 - 5n)^2} + C$ **14.** $-\frac{2}{3}\left(1 + \frac{1}{x}\right)^{3/2} + C$

15. $-\frac{6}{7}(7 - 2x)^{7/4} + C$ **16.** $\frac{(y + 1)^3}{3} + C$

17. $\frac{9}{8}(3\sqrt[3]{3} - 1)$ **18.** $\frac{8}{3}$ **19.** $-\frac{1}{30}(1 - 2x^3)^5 + C$

20. $-\frac{9}{80}(1 - 5x^4)^{4/3} + C$

21. $-\frac{1}{(2x - x^3)} + C$ **22.** $-\frac{2}{3}(6 + 9x - x^3)^{1/2} + C$

23. $\dfrac{3350}{3}$ **24.** $\dfrac{43,904}{3}$ **25.** $y = 3x - \dfrac{x^3}{3} + \dfrac{17}{3}$

26. $y = \dfrac{1}{6}(x^2 + 1)^3 - \dfrac{10}{3}$

27. **(a)** $x - x^2 + C_1$

  (b) $x - x^2 + C_2 - \dfrac{1}{4}; \ C_1 = C_2 - \dfrac{1}{4}$

28. **(a)** $\dfrac{3}{2}x^2 + 2x + C_1$

  (b) $\dfrac{3}{2}x^2 + 2x + \dfrac{2}{3} + C_2; \ C_1 = \dfrac{2}{3} + C_2. \ C_1$ and C_2
are not equal.

29. 22   **30.** $\dfrac{48}{5}$ **31.** 0.842   **32.** 46.2

33. 0.811   **34.** 6.58   **35.** 13.6

36. 16.255   **37.** 19.3016   **38.** 19.1020

39. 19.0354   **40.** 19.0354   **41.** 24.68 m^2

42. 24.68 m^2 **43.** 25.81 m^2 **44.** 25.83 m^2

45. $y = k\left(2L^3 x - 6Lx^2 + \dfrac{2}{5}x^5\right)$

46. $Q = \dfrac{k}{12R}(4r^3 R - 3r^4 - R^4) + Q_0$

47. 14.9 m^2 **48.** 66.4 in

APPLICATIONS OF INTEGRATION

6.1 Applications of the Indefinite Integral

1. 80 ft/s
2. -14.0 ft/s
3. $s = 8.00 - 0.25t$
4. 0.84 mm
5. 15 ft/s
6. $v = \dfrac{-1200}{t^2 + 120} + 10$
7. 17,800 m
8. 25 ft
9. 76 ft/s
10. 216 ft
11. 256 ft
12. $s = \dfrac{2}{3}[10(1+0.2t)^{5/2} - 5t - 7]$
13. 0.345 nC
14. 0.015 C
15. 0.017 C
16. 16 μs
17. 120 V
18. 9.9 nV
19. 4.65 mV
20. 21.9 ms
21. 970 rad
22. $\theta = \dfrac{1}{240}[(8t+1)^{5/2} - 20t - 1]$
23. 66.7 A
24. $23°$C
25. $\dfrac{k}{x_1}$
26. $y = \dfrac{k}{6}(x^6 + 2025x^4 - 14,000x^3)$
27. $m = -2\sqrt{t+1} + 1002$, 2.51×10^5 min
28. $r = 53.8\sqrt{\lambda}$

6.2 Areas by Integration

1. 2
2. 4
3. $\dfrac{8}{3}$
4. 27
5. $\dfrac{27}{8}$
6. $\dfrac{4}{3}\sqrt{2}$
7. $\dfrac{32}{3}$
8. $\dfrac{4}{3}$
9. $\dfrac{1}{6}$
10. $\dfrac{41}{3}$
11. $\dfrac{26}{3}$
12. $\dfrac{8}{3}$
13. 3
14. $\dfrac{1}{6}$
15. $\dfrac{15}{4}$
16. 1
17. $\dfrac{7}{6}$
18. $\dfrac{19}{6}$
19. $\dfrac{256}{15}$
20. $\dfrac{7}{6}$
21. $\dfrac{343}{24}$
22. $\dfrac{45}{4}$
23. $\dfrac{65}{6}$
24. $\dfrac{343}{6}$
25. 1
26. 3.25
27. $\dfrac{48}{5}$
28. 8
29. 18.0 J
30. 0.072 C
31. 80.8 km
32. $5000
33. 4 cm^2
34. 77.3 m^2
35. 0.683 m^2
36. 88.0 ft^3

6.3 Volumes by Integration

1. $\dfrac{8}{3}\pi$
2. $\dfrac{8\pi}{3}$
3. $\dfrac{8\pi}{3}$
4. $\dfrac{8\pi}{3}$
5. $\dfrac{8\pi}{3}$
6. 8π
7. 72π
8. $\dfrac{16\pi}{15}$
9. $\dfrac{768\pi}{7}$
10. $\dfrac{2\pi}{15}$
11. $\dfrac{348}{5}\pi$
12. $\dfrac{496\pi}{15}$
13. $\dfrac{16\pi}{3}$
14. $\dfrac{8\pi}{9}(4\sqrt[4]{2} - 1)$
15. $\dfrac{128\pi}{7}$
16. $\dfrac{16\pi\sqrt{8}}{3}$
17. $\dfrac{2}{5}\pi$
18. $\dfrac{1024\pi}{15}$
19. $\dfrac{10\sqrt{5}}{3}\pi$
20. $\dfrac{243\pi}{10}$
21. $\dfrac{1296\pi}{5}$
22. $\dfrac{8\pi}{3}$
23. $\dfrac{16\pi}{3}$
24. $\dfrac{96\pi}{5}$
25. $\dfrac{8}{3}\pi$
26. 8π
27. $\dfrac{1}{3}\pi r^2 h$
28. Use a semi-circle of radius r, centered at origin.
$x^2 + y^2 = r^2$
$y = \pm\sqrt{r^2 - x^2}$
Use the upper branch of the curve, $y = +\sqrt{r^2 - x^2}$.
Rotate half circle about x-axis.
29. 7.56 mm^3
30. 84,100 ft^3
31. 18.3 cm^3
32. 22.6 ft^3

6.4   Centroids

1. 2.9 cm   2. 5.2 cm   3. 1.2 cm

4. −14 cm   5. (−0.5 in, 0.5 in)

6. (0.03 in, 1.18 in)   7. (0.32 in, 0.23 in)

8. (1.32 in, 1.64 in)   9. $\left(0, \frac{6}{5}\right)$ 10. $\left(0, \frac{4a}{3\pi}\right)$

11. $\left(\frac{4}{3}, \frac{4}{3}\right)$ 12. $\left(\frac{8}{5}, \frac{16}{7}\right)$ 13. $\left(\frac{3}{5}, \frac{12}{35}\right)$

14. $\left(\frac{6}{5}, \frac{3}{2}\right)$ 15. $\left(\frac{5}{3}, 4\right)$ 16. $\left(5, \frac{10}{7}\right)$

17. $\left(\frac{7}{8}, 0\right)$ 18. $\left(0, \frac{1}{2}\right)$ 19. $\left(0, \frac{5}{6}\right)$

20. $\left(\frac{5}{3}, 0\right)$ 21. $\left(\frac{2}{3}, 0\right)$ 22. $\left(0, \frac{102}{43}\right)$

23. $\left(\frac{2}{3}b, \frac{1}{3}a\right)$ 24. $\left(0, \frac{3}{8}a\right)$

25. 0.375 cm above center of base.

26. 0.29 in from larger base.

27. 19.3 cm from larger base.

28. 3.25 m above the lower base.

6.5   Moments of Inertia

1. 68 g · cm², 2.9 cm   2. 72 g·cm², 2.4 cm

3. 2530 g·cm², 3.58 cm

4. 2,320,000 g·cm², 35.8 cm

5. $\frac{64}{15}k$ 6. $\frac{15}{2}k$ 7. $\frac{2\sqrt{6}}{3}$

8. $\frac{\sqrt{5}}{5}$ 9. $\frac{1}{6}mb^2$ 10. $\frac{mb^2}{3}$

11. $\frac{4\sqrt{7}}{7}$ 12. $\frac{4\sqrt{15}}{9}$ 13. $\frac{8}{11}\sqrt{55}$

14. $\frac{\sqrt{10}}{6}$ 15. $\frac{64\pi k}{3}$ 16. $\frac{2\sqrt{3}}{3}$

17. $\frac{2}{5}\sqrt{10}$ 18. $\frac{2\sqrt{10}}{5}$ 19. $\frac{3mr^2}{10}$

20. mr^2 21. 0.324 g·cm²   22. 2 kg · m²

23. 31.2 kg · cm²   24. $\frac{1}{3}mL^2$

6.6   Work by A Variable Force

1. 8.0 lb-in   2. 24 lb · in   3. 200 N·mm

4. 3600 lb · in   5. 600 N·mm

6. 1.7×10^{-16} J   7. 9.4×10^{-22} J

8. $−2.16 \times 10^{-8}$ J   9. $99k$ J   10. $0.09k$ ft·lb

11. 10,000 ft·lb   12. 20,000 ft·lb

13. 1800 N·m   14. 12,600 J

15. 3.00×10^5 ft·ton   16. 5.88×10^5 N·m

17. 8.82×10^4 ft·lb   18. 6.62×10^4 ft·lb

19. 1.26×10^6 N·m = 1.26 MJ

20. 4.71×10^5 ft·lb

6.7   Force Due To Liquid Pressure

1. 2340 lb   2. 156,800 N

3. 28,100 lb   4. 14.4 N

5. 20,800 lb   6. 101,000 lb

7. 5320 lb   8. 3640 lb   9. 6500 N

10. 35,900 N   11. 1570 lb

12. 2560 lb

13. 3.92×10^4 N, 1.18×10^5 N buoyant force.

14. 83.2 lb   15. 11,700 lb   16. 600 lb

6.8   Other Applications

1. $\dfrac{38}{3}$ 2. $\dfrac{14}{3}$ 3. 21   4. $\dfrac{14}{3}$

5. $4\pi\sqrt{2}$ 6. 20π 7. $\dfrac{56\pi}{3}$

8. 2291   9. 2.7 A   10. 15.7°C

11. 35.3%   12. $\dfrac{1}{3}\pi r^3$ 13. 109 ft

14. 15.3 km   15. $\pi r\sqrt{h^2 + r^2}$ 16. 9.6 cm^3

Chapter 6 Review Exercises

1. 4.4s 2. 267 m   3. 4.2 s

4. 160 ft   5. 0.44 C   6. 4.33 C

7. 55 V   8. 12.8 μF   9. $y = 20x + \dfrac{1}{120}x^3$

10. 40.8%   11. $\dfrac{2}{3}$ 12. $\dfrac{27}{4}$ 13. 18

14. $\dfrac{1}{15}$ 15. $\dfrac{27}{4}$ 16. $\dfrac{8}{3}$ 17. $\dfrac{48\pi}{5}$

18. $\dfrac{512\pi}{9}$ 19. $\dfrac{512\pi}{5}$ 20. $\dfrac{8\pi}{3}$ 21. $\dfrac{4}{3}\pi ab^2$

22. 24.7 cm^3 23. $\left(\dfrac{40}{21}, \dfrac{10}{3}\right)$ 24. $\left(\dfrac{4}{3}, -\dfrac{2}{3}\right)$

25. $\left(\dfrac{14}{5}, 0\right)$ 26. $\left(0, \dfrac{7}{3}\right)$ 27. $\dfrac{8}{5}k$

28. $\dfrac{2\sqrt{2}}{3}$ 29. 68.7 g·mm^2 30. 0.53 in.

31. 8500 ft·lb   32. 8.47×10^6 mi·lb   33. 1.8 m

34. 10,600 m^3 35. 47 m^3 36. 107 ft^2

37. 10,200 lb   38. 998 lb   39. 0.29 Ω

40. $\dfrac{1}{12}mL^2$

Chapter 7

DIFFERENTIATION OF THE TRIGONOMETRIC AND INVERSE TRIGONOMETRIC FUNCTIONS

7.1 The Trigonometric Functions

1. $15.2°$

2. $301.27°$

3. $315°48'$

4. $24°55'$

5. $\dfrac{\pi}{12}, \dfrac{5\pi}{6}$

6. $\dfrac{\pi}{15}, \dfrac{5\pi}{4}$

7. $\dfrac{5\pi}{12}, \dfrac{11\pi}{6}$

8. $\dfrac{\pi}{5}, \dfrac{7\pi}{4}$

9. $72°, 270°$

10. $54°, 150°$

11. $10°, 315°$

12. $84°, 240°$

13. 0.401

14. 3.115

15. $43.0°$

16. $939.7°$

17. -0.8290

18. -0.9613

19. 1.4663

20. -2.281

21. 0.7071

22. 0.8660

23. 3.732

24. 0.9397

25. -1.732

26. 1.732

27. -0.1161

28. 7.745

29. $0.3141, 2.827$

30. $2.723, 3.561$

31. $2.932, 6.074$

32. $3.185, 6.240$

33. $0.8309, 5.452$

34. $0.4933, 3.635$

35. $2.442, 3.841$

36. $0.2566, 2.885$

37.

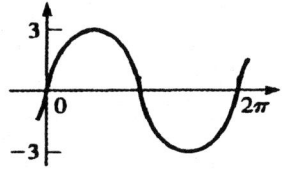

38.

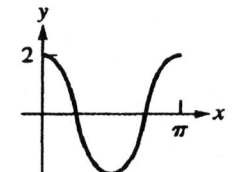

39.

40.

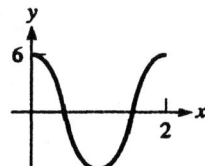

41.

42.

43.

44.

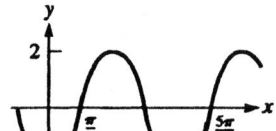

45.

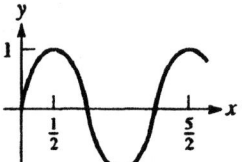

46.

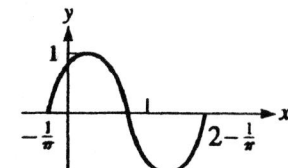

47.

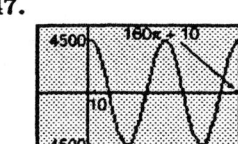

48.

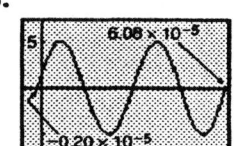

49. Amplitude is 5.

Period $= \dfrac{2\pi}{b} = 16, b = \dfrac{\pi}{8}$.

Displacement $= -\dfrac{c}{b} = -1, c = \dfrac{\pi}{8}$.

$y = 5\sin\left(\dfrac{\pi}{8}x + \dfrac{\pi}{8}\right)$

50. Amplitude is 5.

Period is $\dfrac{2\pi}{b} = 16;\ 16b = 2\pi;\ b = \dfrac{\pi}{8}$.

Displacement is $-\dfrac{c}{b} = 3;\ c = -\dfrac{3\pi}{8}$.

$y = 5\cos\left(\dfrac{\pi}{8}x - \dfrac{3\pi}{8}\right)$

51. Amplitude is $|-0.8| = 0.8$.

Period is $\dfrac{2\pi}{b} = \pi;\ b = 2$.

Displacement is $-\dfrac{c}{b} = 0;\ c = 0$.

$y = -0.8\cos 2x$

52. Amplitude is 0.8.

Period is $\dfrac{2\pi}{b} = \pi;\ b = 2$.

Displacement is $-\dfrac{c}{b} = \dfrac{\pi}{4}$;

$y = 0.8\sin\left(2x - \dfrac{\pi}{2}\right)$

7.2   Basic Trigonometric Relations

1. $\dfrac{\cos\theta}{\sin\theta}\dfrac{1}{\cos\theta} = \dfrac{1}{\sin\theta}$ **2.** $\sin x\dfrac{1}{\tan x} = \sin x\dfrac{\cos x}{\sin x}$

3. $\dfrac{\sin y}{\cos y}\dfrac{1}{\sin y} = \dfrac{1}{\cos y}$ **4.** $\dfrac{\sin x}{1}\dfrac{\cos x}{\sin x} = \cos x$

5. $1 - \sin^2 x - \sin^2 x$

6. $\cos^2\theta\left(1 + \dfrac{\sin^2\theta}{\cos^2\theta}\right) = \cos^2\theta + \sin^2\theta = 1$

7. $\dfrac{\sin x}{1}\dfrac{\sin x}{\cos x} + \dfrac{\cos x}{1} = \dfrac{\sin^2 x + \cos^2 x}{\cos x} = \dfrac{1}{\cos x}$

8. $\dfrac{\sin x}{\cos x} + \dfrac{\cos x}{\sin x} = \dfrac{\sin^2 x + \cos^2 x}{\cos x \sin x} = \dfrac{1}{\cos x \sin x}$

9. $\tan x \cot x + \tan^2 x = 1 + \tan^2 x$

10. $\tan^2 y(\sec^2 y - \tan^2 y) = \tan^2 y(1) = \tan^2 y$

11. $\dfrac{1}{\cos\theta}\left(\dfrac{1}{\cos\theta}\right) - \dfrac{\sin\theta}{\cos\theta}\left(\dfrac{\sin\theta}{\cos\theta}\right) = \dfrac{\cos^2\theta}{\cos^2\theta}$

12. $\dfrac{1 - \cos^2\theta}{\sin^2\theta} = \dfrac{\sin^2\theta}{\sin^2\theta} = 1$

13. $(\sin x\cos y + \cos x\sin y)(\sin x\cos y - \cos x\sin y)$
$\quad = \sin^2 x\cos^2 y - \cos^2 x\sin^2 y$
$\quad = \sin^2 x(1 - \sin^2 y) - (1 - \sin^2 x)(\sin^2 y)$

14. $(\cos x\cos y - \sin x\sin y)(\cos x\cos y + \sin x\sin y)$
$\quad = \cos^2 x\cos^2 y - \sin^2 x\sin^2 y$
$\quad = \cos^2 x(1 - \sin^2 y) - (1 - \cos^2 x)\sin^2 y$
$\quad = \cos^2 x - \cos^2 x\sin^2 y - \sin^2 y + \cos^2 x\sin^2 y$

15. $\cos x\cos y + \sin x\sin y + \sin x\cos y + \cos x\sin y$
$\quad = \cos x(\cos y + \sin y) + \sin x(\cos y + \sin y)$

16. $2\sin x(1 + \cos x) = \dfrac{2\sin x(1 + \cos x)(1 - \cos x)}{(1 - \cos x)}$
$\qquad\qquad\qquad = \dfrac{2\sin x(1 - \cos^2 x)}{1 - \cos x}$

17. $(\cos^2 x + \sin^2 x)(\cos^2 x - \sin^2 x) = 1(\cos^2 x - \sin^2 x)$

18. $\dfrac{2\sin x}{2\sin x\cos x\cos x} = \dfrac{1}{\cos^2 x}$

19. $\dfrac{\sin 3x\cos x + \cos 3x\sin x}{\sin x\cos x} = \dfrac{2\sin 4x}{\sin 2x}$

20. $\dfrac{\sin 3x\cos x - \cos 3x\sin x}{\sin x\cos x} = \dfrac{\sin(3x - x)}{\frac{1}{2}\sin 2x} = \dfrac{\sin 2x}{\frac{1}{2}\sin 2x}$

21. $\dfrac{1 - \cos\alpha}{2\sqrt{\dfrac{1 - \cos\alpha}{2}}} = \sqrt{\dfrac{1 - \cos\alpha}{2}}$

22. $\dfrac{\sin\frac{\alpha}{2}}{\cos\frac{\alpha}{2}} = \dfrac{\pm\sqrt{\frac{1 - \cos\alpha}{2}}}{\pm\sqrt{\frac{1 + \cos\alpha}{2}}}$

23. $2\left(\dfrac{1 - \cos x}{2}\right) + \cos x$

24. $2\left(\dfrac{1 + \cos\theta}{2}\right)\sec\theta = (1 + \cos\theta)\sec\theta$

25. $0 = \cos A\cos B\cos C + \sin A\sin B$

$\cos C = \dfrac{-\sin A\sin B}{\cos A\cos B}$

26. $r^2 - 2rR\cos\theta + R^2\cos^2\theta + R^2\sin^2\theta$
$\quad = r^2 - 2rR\cos\theta + R^2(\cos^2\theta + \sin^2\theta)$
$\quad = r^2 - 2rR\cos\theta + R^2$

27. $i_0\sin(\omega t + \alpha) = i_0[\sin\omega t\cos\alpha + \sin\alpha\cos\omega t]$

28. $T\cos\alpha - \left(T\dfrac{\sin\alpha}{\cos\theta}\right)\sin\theta$

$$= \frac{T\cos\alpha\cos\theta - T\sin\alpha\sin\theta}{\cos\theta}$$

$$= \frac{T(\cos\alpha\cos\theta - \sin\alpha\sin\theta)}{\cos\theta}$$

29. $vi\sin\omega t\sin\left(\omega t - \dfrac{\pi}{2}\right)$

$$= vi\sin\omega t\left[\sin\omega t\cos\frac{\pi}{2} - \cos\omega t\sin\frac{\pi}{2}\right]$$

$$= -vi\sin\omega t\cos\omega t = -\frac{1}{2}vi(2\sin\omega t\cos\omega t)$$

30. $a\left(\dfrac{1}{2}(1+\cos 2\theta)\right) + b\left(\dfrac{1}{2}(1-\cos 2\theta)\right)$

$$- t(2\sin\theta\cos\theta)$$

$$= \frac{a}{2}[1+\cos^2\theta - \sin^2\theta] + \frac{b}{2}[1-\cos^2\theta + \sin^2\theta]$$

$$- t\sin 2\theta$$

$$= \frac{a}{2} + \frac{a}{2}\cos^2\theta - \frac{a}{2}\sin^2\theta + \frac{b}{2} - \frac{b}{2}\cos^2\theta$$

$$+ \frac{b}{2}\sin^2\theta - t\sin 2\theta$$

$$= \frac{a}{2} + \frac{b}{2} + \cos^2\theta\left(\frac{a}{2} - \frac{b}{2}\right) - \sin^2\theta\left(\frac{a}{2} - \frac{b}{2}\right)$$

$$- t\sin 2\theta$$

$$= \frac{1}{2}(a+b) + \left(\frac{a}{2} - \frac{b}{2}\right)(\cos^2\theta - \sin^2\theta) - t\sin 2\theta$$

31. $\sin^2\omega t = \sin^2\left[\left(\dfrac{1}{2}\right)(2\omega t)\right] = \left(\sqrt{\dfrac{1-\cos 2\omega t}{2}}\right)^2$

$$= \frac{1-\cos 2\omega t}{2}$$

32. $2E^2 - 2E^2(\cos\pi\cos\theta + \sin\pi\sin\theta)$

$$= 2E^2 - 2E^2((-1)\cos\theta + (0)\sin\theta)$$

$$= 2E^2 + 2E^2\cos\theta$$

$$= 2E^2(1+\cos\theta)$$

$$= 2E^2\left(2\cos^2\frac{\theta}{2}\right)$$

33. 25.7 ft   **34.** 15.5 rad   **35.** 34.73 m^2

36. 2.58 ft^2

7.3   Derivatives of The Sine and Cosine Functions

1. $\cos(x+2)$

2. $12\cos 4x$

3. $12x^2\cos(2x^3 - 1)$

4. $-15\cos(2-3t)$

5. $-3\sin\left(\dfrac{1}{2}x\right)$

6. $\sin(1-x)$

7. $-6\sin(3x-1)$

8. $-48x\sin(6x^2+5)$

9. $6\pi\sin(3\pi\theta)\cos(3\pi\theta) = 3\pi\sin 6\pi\theta$

10. $72x^3\sin^2(2x^4+1)\cos(2x^4+1)$

11. $-45\cos^2(5x+2)\sin(5x+2)$

12. $\dfrac{4\cos\sqrt{x}\sin\sqrt{x}}{\sqrt{x}}$

13. $\sin 3x + 3x\cos 3x$

14. $2x^2\cos 2x + 2x\sin 2x$

15. $9x^2\cos 5x - 15x^3\sin 5x$

16. $-\theta\sin\left(2\theta + \dfrac{\pi}{4}\right) + 0.5\cos\left(2\theta + \dfrac{\pi}{4}\right)$

17. $2x\cos x^2\cos 2x - 2\sin x^2\sin 2x$

18. $6(\cos x\cos 4x - 4\sin x\sin 4x)$

19. $\dfrac{2\cos 4x}{\sqrt{1+\sin 4x}}$

20. $4(x-\cos^2 x)^3(1+2\sin x\cos x)$

21. $\dfrac{3t\cos\left(3t - \frac{\pi}{3}\right) - \sin\left(3t - \frac{\pi}{3}\right)}{2t^2}$

22. $\dfrac{2\sin 4x - 8x\cos 4x - 12\cos 4x}{\sin^2 4x}$

23. $\dfrac{4x(1-3x)\sin x^2 - 6\cos x^2}{(3x-1)^2}$

24. $\dfrac{-2\cos 3x[3\sin 3x(1+2\sin^2 2x) + 4\cos 3x\sin 2x\cos 2x]}{(1+2\sin^2 2x)^2}$

25. $4\sin 3x(3\cos 3x\cos 2x - \sin 3x\sin 2x)$

26. $4\sin 2x\cos 2x\cos^3 4x - 12\sin 4x\sin^2 2x\cos^2 4x$

27. $2\cos 2t\cos(\sin 2t)$

28. $-0.6\sin(\sin 3\phi)\cos 3\phi$

29. $3\sin^2 x\cos x + 2\sin 2x$

30. $x \cos x$

31. $\dfrac{-\cos s}{\sin^2 s} + \dfrac{\sin s}{\cos^2 s}$

32. $x^2 \sin x$

33. (a) 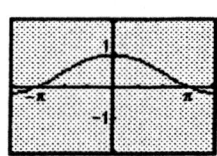   **(b)** See the table.

34. 1

35. (a) 0.5403023, the derivative
    (b) 0.5402602, slope of secant line

36. (a) −0.8414710, Value of derivative.

    (b) −0.8414980, Value of slope of secant line.

37. Resulting curve is $y = \cos x$.

38. Resulting curve is $y = -\sin x$.

39. $\dfrac{2x - y \cos xy}{x \cos xy - 2 \sin 2y}$

40. $\dfrac{\cos 2y + \cos x \cos y}{2x \sin 2y + \sin x \sin y}$

41. $\dfrac{d}{dx} \sin x = \cos x;$

    $\dfrac{d^2}{dx^2} \sin x = -\sin x,$

    $\dfrac{d^3}{dx^3} \sin x = -\cos x;$

    $\dfrac{d^4}{dx^4} \sin x = \sin x$

42. $\dfrac{dy}{dx} = -2 \sin 2x$

    $\dfrac{d^2 y}{dx^2} = -4 \cos 2x = -4y$

43. 0.085   **44.** $L(x) = -x + \dfrac{\pi}{2}$ **45.** −2.36

46. −2.646   **47.** 410 V/s   **48.** 45°

49. −199 cm/s

50. $V_L = -0.024\pi \sin\left(120\pi t + \dfrac{\pi}{6}\right)$

51. −38.5 km   **52.** $\dfrac{Ln^2 \cos \theta}{d(n^2 - \sin^2 \theta)^{3/2}}$

7.4 Derivatives Of The Other Trigonometric Functions

1. $5 \sec^2 5x$ **2.** $9 \sec^2(3x + 2)$

3. $5 \csc^2(0.25\pi - \theta)$ **4.** $-18 \csc^2 6x$

5. $6 \sec 2x \tan 2x$ **6.** $-\dfrac{\sec \sqrt{1-x} \tan \sqrt{1-x}}{2\sqrt{1-x}}$

7. $\dfrac{3 \csc \sqrt{2x+3} \cot \sqrt{2x+3}}{\sqrt{2x+3}}$

8. $\pi \csc(1 - 2\pi t) \cot(1 - 2\pi t)$

9. $30 \tan 3x \sec^2 3x$ **10.** $8x \tan(x^2) \sec^2(x^2)$

11. $-4 \cot^3 \dfrac{1}{2}x \csc^2 \dfrac{1}{2}x$

12. $4x \cot(1 - x^2) \csc^2(1 - x^2)$

13. $2 \tan 4x \sqrt{\sec 4x}$

14. $12 \sec^3(5u) \tan(5u)$

15. $-84 \csc^4 7x \cot 7x$

16. $-8x \csc^2(2x^2) \cot(2x^2)$

17. $\dfrac{t^2}{2} \sec^2(0.5t) + 2t \tan(0.5t)$

18. $3 \sec 4x(4x \tan 4x + 1)$

19. $-4 \csc x^2(2x \cos x \cot x^2 + \sin x)$

20. $\sin x \tan x + \sec x \cos 2x$

21. $\dfrac{\csc x(x \cot x + 1)}{x^2}$

22. $\dfrac{-z \csc^2(0.25z) - 4 \cot(0.25z)}{8z^2}$

23. $\dfrac{2(-4 \sin 4x - 4 \sin 4x \cot 3x + 3 \cos 4x \csc^2 3x)}{(1 + \cot 3x)^2}$

24. $\dfrac{2 \tan 3x(6 \sec^2 3x + 3 \sin x^2 \sec^2 3x - x \tan 3x \cos x^2)}{(2 + \sin x^2)^2}$

25. $\sec^2 x(\tan^2 x - 1)$

26. $-2 \csc 2x(\cot 2x - 2 \csc 2x)$

27. $2 \cos 2\theta \sec^2(\sin 2\theta)$

28. $x \sec^2 x + \tan x + 4 \sec^2 2x \tan 2x$

29. $\dfrac{1 + 2 \sec^2 4x}{\sqrt{2x + \tan 4x}}$

30. $18(1 - \csc^2 3x)^2 \csc^2 3x \cot 3x$

31. $\dfrac{2\cos 2x - \sec y}{x \sec y \tan y - 2}$

32. $\dfrac{3\csc^2(x+y)}{2y \sin y^2 - 3\csc^2(x+y)}$

33. $24\tan 3x \sec^2 3x\, dx$

34. $15\sec^3 2t \tan 2t\, dt$

35. $4\sec 4x(\tan^2 4x + \sec^2 4x)dx$

36. $(2\cot 3x - 6x\csc^2 3x)dx$

37. **(a)** 3.4255188, value of derivative.

(b) 3.4260524, the slope of a secant line.

38. **(a)** 2.8824747; value of derivative.

(b) 2.88302; value of slope of secant line.

39. $2\tan x \sec^2 x = 2\sec x \sec x \tan x$

40. $-2\cot x \csc^2 x = -2\cot x \csc^2 x$

41. -12 **42.** 6.945

43. $2\sec^2 x - \sec x \tan x = \dfrac{2}{\cos^2 x} - \dfrac{1}{\cos x}\cdot\dfrac{\sin x}{\cos x}$

44. $\cos x(\cos x - 3\cos x\sin^2 x)$
$+ 3(\cos^3 x \tan x)\sin x - \cos^2 x$

$\cos^2 x - 3\cos^2 x \sin^2 x + 3\cos^3 x \dfrac{\sin x}{\cos x}\sin x - \cos^2 x$

$\cos^2 x - 3\cos^2 x \sin^2 x + 3\cos^2 x \sin^2 x - \cos^2 x = 0$

45. -8.4 cm/s   **46.** 2.5 A   **47.** 140 ft/s

48. -0.47 m

7.5   The Inverse Trigonometric Functions

1. y is an angle whose tangent is x.

2. y is an angle whose secant is x.

3. y is an angle whose cotangent is $3x$.

4. y is an angle whose cosecant is $4x$.

5. y is twice the angle whose sine is x.

6. y is three times the angle whose tangent is x.

7. y is five times the angle whose cosine is $2x - 1$.

8. y is four times the angle whose sine is $3x + 2$.

9. $\dfrac{\pi}{3}$ **10.** $\dfrac{\pi}{2}$ **11.** $\dfrac{\pi}{4}$ **12.** $\dfrac{\pi}{2}$

13. $-\dfrac{\pi}{3}$ **14.** $-\dfrac{\pi}{6}$ **15.** $\dfrac{\pi}{3}$ **16.** $\dfrac{\pi}{6}$

17. $-\dfrac{\pi}{4}$ **18.** $\dfrac{5\pi}{6}$ **19.** $\dfrac{\pi}{4}$ **20.** $\dfrac{5\pi}{6}$

21. 0   **22.** $\sqrt{2}$ **23.** $\dfrac{1}{2}\sqrt{3}$ **24.** 1

25. $\dfrac{1}{2}\sqrt{2}$ **26.** -2 **27.** -1 **28.** 0.8000

29. $\dfrac{2}{\sqrt{21}}$ **30.** $\dfrac{\sqrt{2}}{4}$ **31.** $\dfrac{2}{\sqrt{3}}$

32. $\dfrac{\sqrt{2}}{2}$ **33.** -1.3090 **34.** 2.286

35. -0.9838 **36.** 0.2773   **37.** 1.4413

38. 0.2135   **39.** 1.4503   **40.** -1.093

41. -1.2389 **42.** 0.63219   **43.** -0.2239

44. -0.3167 **45.** $x = \dfrac{1}{3}\sin^{-1} y$

46. $x = \pi + \cos^{-1} y$ **47.** $x = 4\tan y$

48. $x = 6\sin\dfrac{1}{2}y$ **49.** $x = \dfrac{1}{3}\sec^{-1}\left(\dfrac{y-1}{3}\right)$

50. $x = \dfrac{1}{8}\csc^{-1}\dfrac{5-4y}{2}$ **51.** $x = 1 - \cos(1-y)$

52. $x = \dfrac{1}{3}\cot(2y+5)$ **53.** $\dfrac{x}{\sqrt{1-x^2}}$

54. $\sqrt{1-x^2}$ **55.** $\dfrac{1}{x}$ **56.** x **57.** $\dfrac{3x}{\sqrt{9x^2-1}}$

58. $\dfrac{2x}{\sqrt{1-4x^2}}$ **59.** $2x\sqrt{1-x^2}$ **60.** $\dfrac{1-x^2}{1+x^2}$

61. $t = \dfrac{1}{2\omega}\cos^{-1}\dfrac{y}{A} - \dfrac{\phi}{\omega}$ **62.** $\theta = \tan^{-1}\mu$

63. $t = \dfrac{1}{\omega}\left(\sin^{-1}\left(\dfrac{i}{I_m}\right) - \alpha - \phi\right)$

64. $A\cos 2\pi ft = d$

65. $\dfrac{3}{5}\left(\dfrac{12}{13}\right) + \dfrac{4}{5}\left(\dfrac{5}{13}\right) = \dfrac{56}{65}$

66. $\sin\left(\tan^{-1}\dfrac{1}{3} + \tan^{-1}\dfrac{1}{2}\right)$

$$= \sin\left(\tan^{-1}\dfrac{1}{3}\right)\cos\left(\tan^{-1}\dfrac{1}{2}\right)$$

$$+ \cos\left(\tan^{-1}\dfrac{1}{3}\right)\sin\left(\tan^{-1}\dfrac{1}{2}\right)$$

$$= \dfrac{2}{\sqrt{50}} + \dfrac{3}{\sqrt{50}}$$

$$= \dfrac{1}{\sqrt{2}} = \sin\dfrac{\pi}{4}$$

67. $\dfrac{\pi}{6} + \dfrac{\pi}{3} = \dfrac{\pi}{2}$ **68.** $\dfrac{\pi}{3} + \dfrac{\pi}{6} = \dfrac{\pi}{2}$

69. $\sin^{-1}\left(\dfrac{a}{c}\right)$ **70.** $A = \sin^{-1}\left(\dfrac{a\sin B}{b}\right)$

71. Let y = height to top of pedestal; $\tan\alpha = \dfrac{151+y}{d}$,

$\tan\beta = \dfrac{y}{d}$; $\tan\alpha = \dfrac{151 + d\tan\beta}{d}$

72. $L = 12 + 12 + 8\pi + 3\pi + 16\sin^{-1}\dfrac{5}{13} - 6\sin^{-1}\dfrac{5}{13}$

$$= 24 + 11\pi + 10\sin^{-1}\dfrac{5}{13}$$

7.6 Derivatives Of the Inverse Trigonometric Functions

1. $\dfrac{2x}{\sqrt{1-x^4}}$ **2.** $\dfrac{-2}{\sqrt{2-x^2}}$ **3.** $\dfrac{18x^2}{\sqrt{1-9x^6}}$

4. $\dfrac{-1}{\sqrt{2x-4x^2}}$ **5.** $\dfrac{-1.8}{\sqrt{1-0.25s^2}}$

6. $\dfrac{-1}{\sqrt{1-25t^2}}$ **7.** $\dfrac{1}{\sqrt{(x-1)(2-x)}}$

8. $\dfrac{-6x}{\sqrt{1-(x^2+0.5)^2}}$ **9.** $\dfrac{1}{2\sqrt{x}(1+x)}$

10. $\dfrac{-1}{x^2-2x+2}$ **11.** $\dfrac{-6}{x^2+1}$

12. $\dfrac{48x^3}{1+9x^8}$ **13.** $\dfrac{5x}{\sqrt{1-x^2}} + 5\sin^{-1}x$

14. $\dfrac{-x^2}{\sqrt{1-x^2}} + 2x\cos^{-1}x$

15. $\dfrac{0.8u}{1+4u^2} + 0.4\tan^{-1}2u$

16. $\dfrac{4(x^2+1)}{\sqrt{1-16x^2}} + 2x\sin^{-1}4x$

17. $\dfrac{3\sqrt{1-4x^2}\sin^{-1}2x - 6x + 2}{\sqrt{1-4x^2}(\sin^{-1}2x)^2}$

18. $\dfrac{2r - (1+4r^2)\tan^{-1}(2r)}{\pi r^2(1+4r^2)}$

19. $\dfrac{2(\cos^{-1}2x + \sin^{-1}2x)}{\sqrt{1-4x^2}(\cos^{-1}2x)^2}$

20. $\dfrac{2x\tan^{-1}x - 1}{(\tan^{-1}x)^2}$ **21.** $-\dfrac{24(\cos^{-1}4x)^2}{\sqrt{1-16x^2}}$

22. $\dfrac{6(\sin^{-1}(3t))^3}{\sqrt{1-9t^2}}$ **23.** $\dfrac{4\sin^{-1}(4x+1)}{\sqrt{-4x^2-2x}}$

24. $\dfrac{1}{2\sqrt{(2x-x^2)\sin^{-1}(x-1)}}$ **25.** $\dfrac{-1}{1+t^2}$

26. $\dfrac{2}{\sqrt{1-4x^2}(\cos^{-1}2x)^2}$ **27.** $\dfrac{-2(1+2x)^2}{(1+4x^2)^2}$

28. $\dfrac{1+x}{\sqrt{1-x^2}}$ **29.** $\dfrac{18(4-\cos^{-1}2x)^2}{\sqrt{1-4x^2}}$

30. $\dfrac{2x\sqrt{1-(x+y)^2}-1}{1+\sqrt{1-(x+y)^2}}$ **31.** $\dfrac{-(x^2y^2+2y+1)}{2x}$

32. $\dfrac{-2}{\sqrt{(1-16x^2)(1-\sin^{-1}4x)}}$

33. (a) 1.1547005; value of derivative

    (b) 1.1547390; slope of secant line

34. (a) 0.8; the derivative of $\tan^{-1}x$ at $x = 0.5$.

    (b) 0.79996801; the slope of the secant line passing through points where $x_1 = 0.5000$ and $x_2 = 0.5001$

35. $\dfrac{3(\sin^{-1}x)^2 dx}{\sqrt{1-x^2}}$ **36.** $L(x) = \pi x$

37. 0.41

38. $\sin^{-1}(x^2+1)$ is defined for $x = 0$ only.

39. 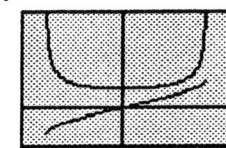   **40.**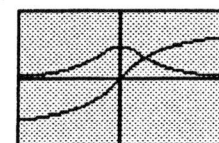

41. $\dfrac{-16x}{(1+4x^2)^2}$

42. Let $\cot^{-1} u = y$; take derivative, substitute

43. Let $\sec^{-1} u = y$, take derivative, substitute

44. Let $\csc^{-1} u = y$, take derivative, substitute

45. $\dfrac{E-A}{\omega m \sqrt{E^2 m^2 - (A-E)^2}}$ **46.** $\dfrac{f}{r\sqrt{f(r-f)}}$

47. $\theta = \tan^{-1}\dfrac{h}{x}$; $\dfrac{d\theta}{dx} = \dfrac{-h}{h^2 + x^2}$

48. $A = \cos^{-1}\dfrac{89 - x^2}{80}$; 0.20 rad/cm

7.7   Applications

1. Points of intersection occur when $\sin x = \cos x$.

$y_1 = \sin x$; $y_2 = \cos x$; $\dfrac{dy_1}{dx} = \cos x$; $\dfrac{dy_2}{dx} = -\sin x$

2. $(\sec x)^2 \geq 1$ **3.** $\dfrac{1}{1+x^2} > 0$

4. max. $\left(\dfrac{\pi}{4}, 1.414\right)$, min. $\left(\dfrac{5\pi}{4}, -1.414\right)$,

infl. pt. $\left(\dfrac{3\pi}{4}, 0\right)$ and $\left(\dfrac{7\pi}{4}, 0\right)$

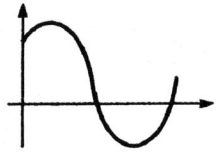

5. The function decreases from $-\frac{\pi}{2}$ to $\frac{\pi}{2}$ $(x \neq 0)$.
Asymptotes at $x = -\frac{\pi}{2}$ and $\frac{\pi}{2}$. Infl. $(0,0)$

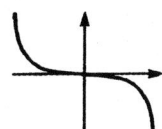

6. $\left(\dfrac{\pi}{3}, \dfrac{3\sqrt{3}}{2}\right)$ max, $\left(\dfrac{5\pi}{3}, \dfrac{-3\sqrt{3}}{2}\right)$ min,

$(\pi, 0), (1.82, 1.46), (4.46, -1.45)$ are inflection points.

7. $8\sqrt{2}x + 8y + 4\sqrt{2} - 5\pi\sqrt{2} = 0$

8. $13x + 2y - 40.97 = 0$

9. 1.9337538 **10.** 1.1655612

11. 10 **12.** -3 **13.** 0.58 ft/s, -1.7 ft/s^2

14. June 21st is longest day with 14.1 hours.
Dec 22nd is shortest day with 10.1 hours.

15. -0.072 lb/s   **16.** 0.657 W/min

17. -98.96 in/s, $270°$ **18.** 2.5 cm/s

19. 3731 in/s^2, $0°$ **20.** 17.4 cm/s^2

21. -0.073 rad/s   **22.** 97.9 ft/s

23. 8.08 ft/s   **24.** 0.036 rad/s

25. 0.020 **26.** $p(t) = -7.923t + 0.0344$

27. 0.19 m   **28.** $30°$

29. $w = 9.24$ in, $d = 13.1$ in   **30.** $60°$ **31.** 14 ft

32. 28.7 ft

Chapter 7 Review Exercises

1. $-12\sin(4x - 1)$

2. $-12x^2 \sec(1 - x^3)\tan(1 - x^3)$

3. $\dfrac{-0.2\sec^3\sqrt{3 - 2v}}{\sqrt{3 - 2v}}$ **4.** $-30\cos(1 - 6x)$

5. $-6\csc^2(3x + 2)\cot(3x + 2)$

6. $-10\pi \cot 5\pi\theta \csc^2 5\pi\theta$

7. $-24x \cos^3 x^2 \sin x^2$

8. $\dfrac{3\sin^2 \sqrt{x} \cos \sqrt{x}}{\sqrt{x}}$

(g)

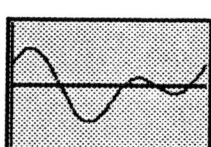

9. $\dfrac{9}{9+x^2}$

10. $\dfrac{-0.4\sqrt{\pi}}{\sqrt{-t(\pi t + 1)}}$

11. $\pm 1, x \neq k\pi$

12. $\dfrac{\cos(\tan^{-1} x)}{1+x^2}$

27. $7.27x + y - 8.44 = 0$

28. $2x + y - 2 - \dfrac{\pi}{4} = 0$

13. $(-2\csc 4x)\sqrt{\csc 4x + \cot 4x}$

14. $-2\cos(\tan x)\sin(\tan x)\sec^2 x$

29. $2\sin x \cos x - 2\cos x \sin x = 0$

15. $8\cos 2x (1 + \sin 2x)^3$

30. $\cos(x + 1)$ **31.** 0.5109734

16. $\pm \sin x$ **17.** $\dfrac{2x(1+4x^2)\tan^{-1} 2x - 2x^2}{(1+4x^2)(\tan^{-1} 2x)^2}$

32. 0.8336061944 **33.** $-0.064°$ C/day

18. $\dfrac{x - \sqrt{1-x^2}\sin^{-1} x}{4x^2 \sqrt{1-x^2}}$

34. $P = -20\sin 2t$ **35.** $-kE_0^2 \cos\dfrac{1}{2}\theta \sin\dfrac{1}{2}\theta$

19. $-\dfrac{2y^2 \cos 2x + \sec^2 x}{2y\sin 2x}$

36. $\dfrac{f}{\sqrt{R^2 - F^2 f^2}}$

37. $45°$

20. $(\sin^{-1} x)^2$ **21.** $\cos^{-1} x$

38. 0.005934 rad/s

22. $\dfrac{-1 - 2\sec^2(xy)\tan(xy)y}{2x\sec^2(xy)\tan(xy)}$

39. $2\pi, 330°$

40. $4\pi^2, 240°$

23. $\dfrac{2y\sin 2x + \sin 2y}{\cos 2x - 2x\cos 2y}$ **24.** $\dfrac{y + 2x^3 y + 2xy^3}{x - x^2 y^2 - x^4}$

41. 0.568 rad/s

25.

42. $11.3°$

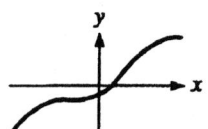

43. -0.0065 rad/s

44. 0.40 cm/s, $72.5°$

45. 7.07 in.

26. (a) no asymptotes

46.

(b) y-intercept is $(0,1)$

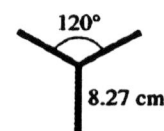

(c) intercepts $\left(\frac{\pi}{4},0\right), \left(\frac{3\pi}{4},0\right), \left(\frac{7\pi}{12},0\right), \left(\frac{11\pi}{12},0\right)$.

(e) $(0.317, 1.76)$ is a local maximum, $(1.25, -1.76)$ is a local minimum, $(2.07, 0.367)$ is a local maximum, $(2.64, -0.369)$ is a local minimum

47. $A = 16\cos\theta(1 + \sin\theta)$, max $\left(\frac{\pi}{6}, 20.8\right)$

(f) inflection points: $\left(\dfrac{\pi}{4},0\right), (1.63, -0.758),$
$\left(\dfrac{3\pi}{4},0\right), (3.08, 0.749)$

48. 5570 cm^3

DIFFERENTIATION OF THE EXPONENTIAL AND LOGARITHMIC FUNCTIONS

8.1 Exponential and Logarithmic Functions

1. $\log_4 256 = 4$

2. $\log_3\left(\dfrac{1}{9}\right) = -2$

3. $16 = 8^{4/3}$

4. $\dfrac{1}{49} = 7^{-2}$

5. $\log_8 2 = \dfrac{1}{3}$

6. $\log_{81} 27 = \dfrac{3}{4}$

7. $16 = (0.5)^{-4}$

8. $3 = 243^{1/5}$

9. $\log_{12} 1 = 0$

10. $\log_{1/2} 4 = -2$

11. $\dfrac{1}{512} = 8^{-3}$

12. $\left(\dfrac{1}{32}\right)^{3/5} = \dfrac{1}{8}$

13. 343   **14.** 8   **15.** 0.2   **16.** $\dfrac{1}{4}$

17.

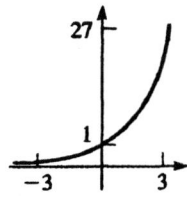

18.

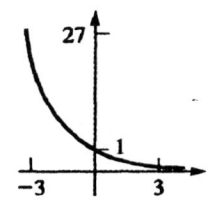

19.

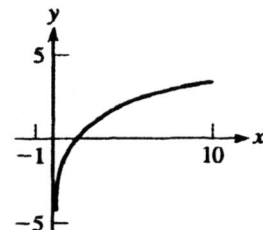

20. Same as the graph for exercise 19.

21. $\log_5 3$

22. $\log_2 3x$

23. $\log_6 x^{5/2}$

24. $\log_7 3^2$

25. $\log_b 4y$

26. $\log_b \dfrac{81}{x}$

27. $\log_2 \dfrac{3x^2}{5}$

28. $\log_4 \dfrac{7a}{t^2}$

29. 1.099

30. -0.1054

31. 1.921

32. 1.933

33. $b_2 = b_1(10)^{0.4(m_1 - m_2)}$

34. $w = w_0 e^{-v/u}$

35. $N = N_0 e^{-kt}$

36. $t = -\dfrac{1}{a}\log_e\left(1 - \dfrac{q}{q_0}\right)$

37.

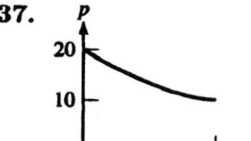

38.

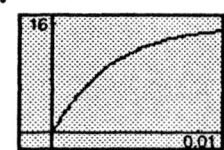

39.

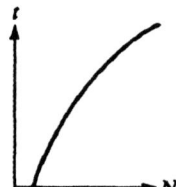

40.

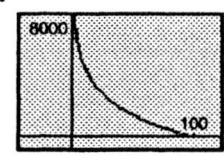

41. 21.7 s

42. $t = -0.1\ln\left(1 - \dfrac{i}{0.6}\right)$

43. 2.3×10^4

44. The final product required raising e to the appropriate power.

45.

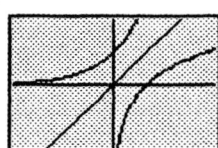

46.

47. $\dfrac{1}{4}(e^u + e^{-u})^2 - \dfrac{1}{4}(e^u - e^{-u})^2$

$\qquad = \dfrac{1}{4}(e^{2u} + 2e^0 + e^{-2u}) - \dfrac{1}{4}(e^{2u} - 2e^0 + e^{-2u})$

$\qquad = 1$

48. $\left[\dfrac{1}{2}(e^{0.25} + e^{-0.25})\right]^2 - \left[\dfrac{1}{2}(e^{0.25} - e^{-0.25})\right]^2$

$\qquad = \dfrac{1}{4}(e^{0.50} + 2e^0 + e^{-0.50}) - \dfrac{1}{4}(e^{0.50} - 2e^0 + e^{-0.50})$

$\qquad = 1$

8.2   Derivative of the Logarithmic Function

1. $\dfrac{2\log e}{x}$

2. $\dfrac{1}{x}\log_2 e$

3. $\dfrac{6}{3x+1}\log_5 e$

4. $\dfrac{6x\log_7 e}{x^2+1}$

5. $\dfrac{-0.6}{1-3x}$

6. $\dfrac{12x}{3x^2-1}$

7. $\dfrac{4\sec^2 2x}{\tan 2x} = 4\sec 2x \csc 2x$

8. $2\cot x$

9. $\dfrac{1}{2x}$

10. $\dfrac{10}{4x-3}$

11. $\dfrac{6(x+1)}{x^2+2x}$

12. $\dfrac{2(6t^2-1)\ln(2t^3-t)}{t(2t^2-1)}$

13. $\dfrac{6(t+2)(t+\ln t^2)}{t}$

14. $x + 2x\ln 2x$

15. $\dfrac{3(2x+1)\ln(2x+1)-6x}{(2x+1)[\ln(2x+1)]^2}$

16. $\dfrac{8(1-\ln x)}{x^2}$

17. $\dfrac{1}{x\ln x}$

18. $-\pi\theta\tan(\pi\theta^2)$

19. $\dfrac{1}{x^2+x}$

20. $\dfrac{3x+2}{2x(x+1)}$

21. $\dfrac{\cos(\ln x)}{x}$

22. $\dfrac{1}{x(1+\ln^2 2x)}$

23. $6\ln 2v + 3\ln^2 2v$

24. $0.4\ln^3 s + 0.1\ln^4 s$

25. $\dfrac{x\sec^2 x + \tan x}{x\tan x}$

26. $\dfrac{1}{\sqrt{x^2-1}}$

27. $\dfrac{x+4}{x(x+2)}$

28. $\dfrac{x+1}{2x\sqrt{x+\ln 3x}}$

29. $\dfrac{\sqrt{x^2+1}}{x}$

30. $\dfrac{2x^2 y - 3y}{3x + xy\cos y}$

31. $\dfrac{x+y-2\ln(x+y)}{x+y+2\ln(x+y)}$

32. $\dfrac{x+1}{x(x+\ln x)}$

33. 0.4999875; slope of secant line. 0.5 value of derivative.

34. 1.99980006; slope of secant line. 2; the value of the derivative.

35. (a)   **(b)** See table.

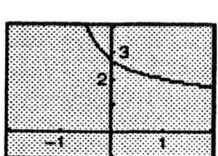

36. $3+2\ln$ **37.** 1.15   **38.** -0.00832

39. $L(x) = 4x - \pi$

40. $\dfrac{-6\ln 2}{x\ln^2 x}dx$

41. 2.73

42. 2.386

43. $x^x(1 + \ln x)$

Eq. (3-15); $\dfrac{d}{dx}u^n$, n is a constant. In x^x both the base and the exponent are variable.

44. Cannot use Eq. (3-15) because exponent of $(\sin x)^x$ is variable.

45. $\dfrac{10}{I}\log e\,\dfrac{dI}{dt}$

46. $k(1+\ln N)$

47. $0.083\ \text{s}^2/\text{ft}$

48. $\dfrac{2ka}{x\sqrt{a^2+x^2}}$

8.3   Derivative of the Exponential Function

1. $(2\ln 3)3^{2x}$

2. $-(\ln 3)3^{1-x}$

3. $6(\ln 4)4^{6x}$

4. $(2x\ln 10)10^{x^2}$

5. $\dfrac{e^{\sqrt{x}}}{2\sqrt{x}}$

6. $0.6\theta e^{\theta^2}$

7. $4e^{2t}(3e^t - 2)$

8. $\dfrac{e^{5x}}{e^{5x} + 1}$

9. $e^{-x}(1 - x)$

10. $10xe^{2x}(x + 1)$

11. $e^{\sin x}(x\cos x + 1)$

12. $2e^x\left(\cos\dfrac{1}{2}x + 2\sin\dfrac{1}{2}x\right)$

13. $8e^{-4s}$

14. $\dfrac{e^{0.5v}(v - 2)}{4v^2}$

15. $e^{-3x}(4\cos 4x - 3\sin 4x)$

16. $2e^{x^2-1}(x\cos 2x - \sin 2x)$

17. $\dfrac{2e^{3x}(12x + 5)}{(4x + 3)^2}$

18. $\dfrac{7(e^{2x} + 2 - 2xe^{2x}\ln 2x)}{x(e^{2x} + 2)^2}$

19. $\dfrac{2xe^{x^2}}{e^{x^2} + 4}$

20. $162e^{6n} + 108e^{4n+2} + 18e^{2n+4}$

21. $16e^{6x}(x\cos x^2 + 3\sin x^2)$

22. $\dfrac{-2e^{6/x}(x^2\sin x + 3\cos x)}{x^2}$

23. $\dfrac{2(1 + 2te^{2t})}{t\sqrt{\ln 2t + e^{2t}}}$

24. $6x(2e^{x^2} + x^2)^2(2e^{x^2} + 1)$

25. $\dfrac{e^{xy}(xy + 1)}{1 - x^2e^{xy} - \cos y}$

26. $\dfrac{8y\ln ye^{-2/x}}{x^2y - 4x^2e^{-2/x}}$

27. $\dfrac{3e^{2x}}{x} + 6e^{2x}\ln x$

28. $e^{2\theta}(-0.4\tan\theta + 0.8\ln(\cos\theta))$

29. $12e^{6x}\cot 2e^{6x}$

30. $6e^{x+1}\sec^2 e^{x+1}$

31. $\dfrac{4e^{2x}}{\sqrt{1 - e^{4x}}}$

32. $\dfrac{3e^{3x}}{1 + e^{6x}}$

33. **(a)** 2.7182818, value of derivative

   (b) 2.7184177, slope of secant line

34. **(a)** $e^2 = 7.3890561$; value of $\dfrac{d}{dx}e^x$ at $x = 2$

   (b) 7.3894256; slope of secant line

35. -0.724

36. -0.06246

37. $\dfrac{2e^{4x}(4x + 7)}{(x + 2)^2}dx$

38. $L(x) = \dfrac{20x}{3} + 2$

39.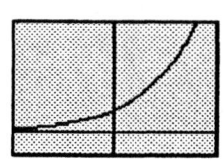

40.

41. $(-xe^{-x} + e^{-x}) + (xe^{-x}) = e^{-x}$

42. $-2e^{-x}\cos x + 2e^{-x}(\cos x - \sin x) + 2e^{-x}\sin x = 0$
   $-2e^{-x}\cos x + 2e^{-x}\cos x - 2e^{-x}\sin x + 2e^{-x}\sin x = 0$

43. $\dfrac{(e^{2x} + 1)2e^{2x} - (e^{2x} - 1)2e^{2x}}{(e^{2x} + 1)^2}$

   $= \dfrac{4e^{2x}}{(e^{2x} + 1)^2}$

   $= \dfrac{(e^{2x} + 1)^2 - (e^{2x} - 1)^2}{(e^{2x} + 1)^2}$

44. $e^y\dfrac{dy}{dx} - (e^x + e^y)\dfrac{dy}{dx} = e^x + e^y - e^x$

   $\dfrac{dy}{dx}(e^y - e^x - e^y) = e^y; \ \dfrac{dy}{dx} = \dfrac{-e^y}{-e^x} = -e^{y-x}$

45. $-0.00164/\text{h}$ **46.** $1.0°\,\text{C/min}$

47. $e^{-66.7t}(999\cos(226t) - 295\sin(226t))$

48. $\dfrac{0.39e^{-0.060t}}{(1 + 0.65e^{-0.060t})^2}$

49. $\dfrac{d}{dx}\dfrac{1}{2}(e^u - e^{-u}) = \left[\dfrac{1}{2}(e^u + e^{-u})\right]\dfrac{du}{dx}$

50. $\dfrac{d}{dx}\dfrac{1}{2}(e^u + e^{-u}) = \left[\dfrac{1}{2}(e^u - e^{-u})\right]\dfrac{du}{dx}$

51. $2x\cosh 2x + \sinh 2x$

52. $\dfrac{d^2\sinh x}{dx^2} = \dfrac{d}{dx}(\cosh x) = \sinh x$

   $\dfrac{d^2\cosh x}{dx^2} = \dfrac{d\sinh x}{dx} = \cosh x$

8.4   Applications

1. Int. $(0,0)$, max. $(0,0)$, not defined for $\cos x < 0$, asym. $x = -\frac{1}{2}\pi, \frac{1}{2}\pi, \ldots$

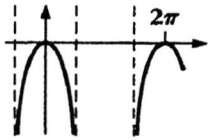

2. x-int $= (1,0)$; $x = 0$ is vertical asymptote; $\left(e, \frac{2}{e}\right)$ is a maximum, $\left(e^{3/2}, \frac{3}{e^{3/2}}\right)$ is an inflection point.

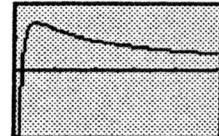

3. Intercepts: $x = 0, y = 0$ (origin). asymptote $y = 0$. max. $\left(1, \frac{1}{e}\right)$, infl. $\left(2, \frac{2}{e^2}\right)$

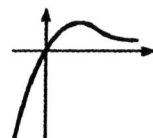

4. Horizontal asymptote $y = 0$. Vertical asymptote at $x = 0$. min. $(1, e)$

5. Int. $(0,0)$, max. $(0,0)$, infl. $(-1, -\ln 2), (1, -\ln 2)$

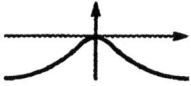

6. $(e, 0)$ is x intercept. Vertical asymptote $x = 0$. decreasing $x > 0$, concave up $x > 0$.

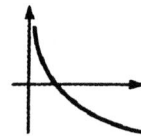

7. $(0, 4)$ intercept. x-axis is a horizontal asymptote. max. $(0, 4)$. $\left(-\frac{\sqrt{2}}{2}, \frac{4}{\sqrt{e}}\right), \left(\frac{\sqrt{2}}{2}, \frac{4}{\sqrt{e}}\right)$ are inflection points.

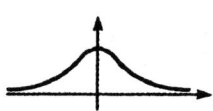

8. Intercepts: $(0, -1)$. max. $(0, -1)$, concave down for all x.

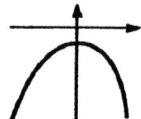

9. Max. $(1, -1)$, asymptote $x = 0$

10. Intercepts: $(0, 0), (\pi, 0)$, etc.
$\left(\frac{\pi}{4}, 0.322\right)$ max.; $\left(\frac{5\pi}{4}, -0.014\right)$ min.

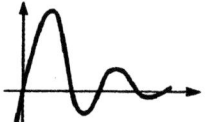

11. Intercepts: $(0, 0)$. Inc for all x. infl. at $(0, 0)$

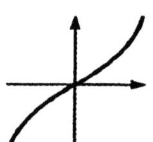

12. Intercepts: $(0, 1)$. min, $(0, 1)$, concave up for all x.

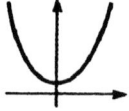

13. $y = x - 1$ **14.** $2x - 5y + 3.54 = 0$

15. $2\sqrt{2}x - 2y + 2\sqrt{2} - 3\pi\sqrt{2} = 0$

16. $x + e^2 y - 1 - e^4 = 0$ **17.** 1.3140968

18. 0.4401655 **19.** -0.303 W/day

20. 0.17 V

21. $\dfrac{p(-a + bT)}{T^2}$

22. $R\left(\dfrac{CE}{RC}\right)e^{-t/RC} + \dfrac{CE}{C}(1 - e^{-t/RC}) = E$

$Ee^{-t/RC} + E - Ee^{-t/RC} = E$

23. $a = k^2 x$

24. 1.5 dm

25. minimum $(0,0)$, $(2\pi, 0)$, $(0,0)$ is an intercept. Asymptotes $x = -\frac{\pi}{2}, \frac{\pi}{2}, \frac{3\pi}{2} \cdots$

26. $Ae^{k/t}(2T - k)dT$

27. 117.6° W 50.2°N, maximum,
101.9° W 41.2° N, minimum,
86.2° W 47.7° N, maximum,
70.5° W 43.0° N, minimum

28. 169 h

29. $v = -e^{-0.5t}(1.4\cos 6t + 2.3\sin 6t)$, -2.03 cm/s

30. -0.81 km/min

31. $\dfrac{1}{\sqrt{e}} = 0.607$

32. $\dfrac{1}{e}$ units^2

Chapter 8 Review Exercises

1. $\dfrac{6x}{x^2 + 1}$

2. $\dfrac{-15}{1 - 5x}$

3. $2e^{2(x-3)}$

4. $\dfrac{-e^{\sqrt{1-x}}}{2\sqrt{1-x}}$

5. $-4t \cot t^2$

6. $\dfrac{2x\cos x^2}{3 + \sin x^2}$

7. $\dfrac{2\cos x \ln(3 + \sin x)}{3 + \sin x}$

8. $\dfrac{2\cos x}{3 + \sin x}$

9. $12e^{\sin 2\theta}\cos 2\theta$

10. $9e^{\sec 3x}\sec 3x \tan 3x$

11. $x^2(x + 3)e^x$

12. $2(4x + 1)e^{4x}$

13. $\dfrac{2(1 + e^{-x})}{x - e^{-x}}$

14. $\cot 2\phi$

15. $\dfrac{-\cos x(2e^{3x}\sin x + 3e^{3x}\cos x + 2\sin x)}{(e^{3x} + 1)^2}$

16. $\dfrac{3(1 - \ln(3x + 1))}{2(3x + 1)^2}$

17. $x(1 + 2\ln x)$

18. $\dfrac{3t^2(2t + 1)}{t^3 + 3} + 2\ln(t^3 + 3)$

19. $\dfrac{2e^{2x}(x^2 - x + 1)}{(x^2 + 1)^2}$

20. $\dfrac{2x + 3 - x\ln x^2}{x(2x + 3)^2}$

21. $3e^{-\theta}\sec 2\theta(2\tan 2\theta - 1)$

22. $e^{3x}\left(\dfrac{1}{x} + \ln x\right)$

23. $\dfrac{y(1 - 2x\ln y)}{x^2 - y}$

24. $2x(e^{\cos^2 x})^2(1 - 2x\sin x \cos x)$

25. $1.73x + 3.00y - 0.48 = 0$

26. $2x + 2.57y - 4.30 = 0$

27. Intercepts: $(0,0)$, $x = -1$ is an asymptote, $x > -1, y'' < 0$, conc. down

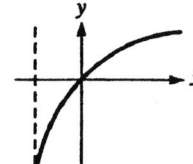

28. Intercepts: $(1,0)$, $(e^{-2}, 4e^{-2})$ maximum, (e^{-1}, e^{-1}) is an inflection point.

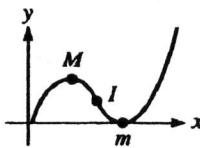

29. -0.7034674

30. 4.965114232

31. 0.429

32. 2.28, $126.9°$

33. 4.55 mi/min

34. \$67.65/year

35. $n = 8x\dfrac{\ln 8}{\ln x}$

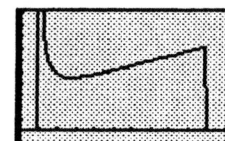

36. $\dfrac{kL}{x(x + L)}$ **37.** 0.0007 ppm

38. $L(t) = -8.32(t - 5.00) + 140$

39. $e^{-0.1t}(75.3\cos 120\pi t - 301.6\sin 120\pi t)$

40. 2,100,000/year

41. 2.00 m wide; 1.82 m high

42. $\dfrac{di}{dt} = -\dfrac{R}{L}i$

43. Find the derivative and substitute.

44. 5.5 in.

Chapter 9

INTEGRATION BY STANDARD FORMS

9.1 The General Power Formula

1. $\frac{1}{5}\sin^5 x + C$ **2.** $\frac{1}{6}\cos^6 x + C$

3. $-\frac{0.8}{3}(\cos x)^{3/2} + C$ **4.** $6\sin^{4/3} x + C$

5. $\frac{4}{3}\tan^3 x + c$ **6.** $\frac{1}{4}\sec^4 x + C$

7. $\frac{1}{8}$ **8.** 2.559 **9.** $\frac{1}{4}(\sin^{-1} x)^4 + C$

10. $-2(\cos^{-1} 2t)^5 + C$ **11.** $\frac{1}{2}(\tan^{-1} 5x)^2 + C$

12. $\frac{1}{8}(\sin^{-1} 4x)^2 + C$ **13.** $\frac{1}{3}[\ln(x+1)]^3 + C$

14. $0.1(3 + 2\ln u)^4 + C$ **15.** 0.179 **16.** 0

17. $\frac{1}{4}(4 + e^x)^4 + C$ **18.** $\frac{4}{3}(1 - e^{-x})^{3/2} + C$

19. $\frac{1}{3}(1 - e^{-2r})^{3/2} + C$ **20.** $-\frac{1}{30}(1 + 3e^{-2x})^5 + C$

21. $\frac{1}{10}(1 + \sec^2 x)^5 + C$ **22.** $\frac{4}{5}(e^x + e^{-x})^{5/4} + C$

23. $\frac{1}{6}$ **24.** 0.449 **25.** 1.102

26. 0.6035 **27.** $y = \frac{1}{3}(\ln x)^3 + 2$

28. $y = \frac{1}{6}(1 + \tan 2x)^3 - 0.6745$

29. $\frac{1}{3}mnv^2$ **30.** πI **31.** $q = (1 - e^{-t})^3$

32. 36.6 km

9.2 The Basic Logarithmic Form

1. $\frac{1}{4}\ln|1 + 4x| + C$ **2.** $-\frac{1}{4}\ln|1 - 4x| + C$

3. $-\frac{1}{3}\ln|4 - 3x^2| + C$ **4.** $\frac{8}{3}\ln|1 + u\sqrt{u}| + C$

5. 0.462 **6.** $\frac{1}{2}\ln 41 = 1.857$

7. $-0.2\ln|\cot 2\theta| + C$ **8.** $-7\ln|\cos x| + C$

9. 0.693 **10.** 0.223 **11.** $\ln|1 - e^{-x}| + C$

12. $-\frac{5}{3}\ln|1 - e^{3x}| + C$ **13.** $\ln|x + e^x| + C$

14. $3\ln(e^t + 2) + C$ **15.** $\frac{1}{4}\ln|1 + 4\sec x| + C$

16. $\ln|1 - \cos^2 x| + C$ **17.** 0.402

18. $2\ln 6 = 3.58$ **19.** $0.5\ln|\ln r| + C$

20. $\frac{1}{2}\ln|1 + 2\ln x| + C$ **21.** $\ln|2x + \tan x| + C$

22. $\frac{1}{2}\ln|x^2 + \sin 2x| + C$ **23.** $-2\sqrt{1 - 2x} + C$

24. $\frac{-2}{1 + x^2} + C$ **25.** $\ln|x| - \frac{2}{x} + C$

26. $3v - 2\ln|v| + C$ **27.** 0.0744

28. $\frac{1}{3}\ln\frac{7}{2} = 0.418$ **29.** 1.10 **30.** $9\ln 2 = 6.238$

31. $\pi\ln 2 = 2.18$ **32.** $\frac{4\pi}{3}(\ln 11.5 - \ln 1) = 10.2$

33. $y = \ln\frac{3.5}{3 + \cos x} + 2$ **34.** $4\ln 2 = 2.7726$

35. 335 million **36.** $T = \frac{91.809}{r - 1}$

37. $i = \frac{E}{R}(1 - e^{-Rt/L})$ **38.** $v = 20(1 - e^{-t})$

39. 1.41 m **40.** $p = -\frac{3}{\pi}\ln(2 + \cos \pi t) + C$

9.3 The Exponential Form

1. $e^{7x} + C$

2. $e^{x^4} + C$

3. $\frac{1}{2}e^{2x+5} + C$

4. $-\frac{1}{2}e^{-4x} + C$

5. 28.2

6. 2190

7. $2e^{x^3} + C$

8. $-\frac{1}{2}e^{-x^2} + C$

9. $2e^2 - 2e = 9.34$

10. $1 - \frac{1}{e^2} \approx 0.8647$

11. $2e^{2\sec\theta} + C$

12. $e^{\tan x} + C$

13. $\frac{2}{3}(1 + e^y)^{3/2} + C$

14. $\frac{1}{2}e^{2x} - 2x - \frac{1}{2}e^{-2x} + C$

15. $6 - \frac{3}{2}(e^6 - e^2) = -588.06$

16. $\frac{3}{2}(e^2 - e^1) = 7.01$

17. $-\frac{4}{e^{\sqrt{x}}} + C$

18. $\frac{-4}{e^{\sin x}} + C$

19. $e^{\tan^{-1} x} + C$

20. $\frac{1}{2}e^{\sin^{-1} 2x} + C$

21. $-\frac{1}{3}e^{\cos 3x} + C$

22. $e^{r^2} + C$

23. 0

24. 0.5662

25. $3e^2 - 3e^0 = 19.2$

26. $e^b - e^a$

27. $\pi(e^4 - e^1) = 163$ units^3

28. $y = 2(\sqrt{e^{x+3}} - e^2)$

29. $\frac{1}{8}(e^8 - 1) = 372$

30. $0.573k$

31. $\ln b \int b\,du = b^u + C_1$

32. $\frac{7}{\ln 2} = 10.10$

33. $q = EC(1 - e^{-t/RC})$

34. $\frac{a}{T}(1 - e^{-I_0 T})$

35. $s = -e^{-2t} - 0.6e^{-5t}$

36. $F = \frac{6}{\pi}(e^{\sin \pi t} - e^{-1})$

9.4 Basic Trigonometric Forms

1. $\frac{1}{2}\sin 2x + C$

2. $4\cos(2 - x) + C$

3. $0.1\tan 3\theta + C$

4. $-\frac{1}{2}\csc 2x + C$

5. $2\sec\frac{1}{2}x + C$

6. $-\cot e^x + C$

7. 0.6365

8. 1.567

9. $\frac{3}{2}\ln\left|\sec\phi^2 + \tan\phi^2\right| + C$

10. $\frac{2}{3}\ln|\csc 3x - \cot 3x| + C$

11. $\cos\left(\frac{1}{x}\right) + C$

12. $\frac{3}{4}\ln|\csc 4x - \cot 4x| + C$

13. $\frac{1}{2}\sqrt{3}$

14. -0.861

15. $\frac{1}{5}\sec 5x + C$

16. $-2\ln|\cos x| + C$

17. $\frac{1}{2}\ln|\sec 2x + \tan 2x| + C$

18. $\dfrac{-5(\ln(\cos u))^2}{2} + C$

19. $\frac{1}{2}(\ln|\sin 2x| + \sin 2x) + C$

20. $\tan x + \cot x + C$

21. $\csc x - \cot x - \ln|\csc x - \cot x| + \ln|\sin x| + C$

22. $\ln|x + \tan x| + C$

23. $\frac{\pi}{9} + \frac{1}{3}\ln 2 = 0.580$

24. 1.865

25. 0.693

26. 2

27. $\pi\sqrt{3} = 5.44$

28. 2.644

29. $\theta = 0.10\cos 2.5t$

30. $\sin 377t$ and $\cos 377t$ are 90° out of phase.

31. 0.7726 m

32. $W = \sec x + 2\ln|\sec x + \tan x| - 1$

9.5 Other Trigonometric Forms

1. $\frac{1}{3}\sin^3 x + C$

2. $-\frac{1}{6}\cos^6 x + C$

3. $-\frac{1}{2}\cos 2x + \frac{1}{6}\cos^3 2x + C$

4. $3\sin x - \sin^3 x + C$

5. $2\sin(2\theta) + C$

6. $-\frac{1}{7}\cos^7 x + \frac{1}{9}\cos^9 x + C$

7. $\dfrac{64 - 43\sqrt{2}}{24} = 0.1329$

8. $\dfrac{203}{12}$

9. $\frac{1}{2}x - \frac{1}{4}\sin 2x + C$ 10. $\frac{1}{2}x + \frac{1}{8}\sin 4x + C$

34. (a) $\frac{1}{2}\sec^2 x + C_1$

11. $\frac{1}{3}(9\phi + 4\sin 3\phi + \sin 3\phi \cos 3\phi) + C$

(b) $\int \frac{1}{2}\tan^2 x + C_2,\ C_2 = \frac{1}{2} + C_1$

12. $\frac{1}{2} - \frac{1}{16}\sin 8 = 0.4382$

35. $\frac{4}{3}$ 36. $\tan\theta - \theta + C$

13. $\frac{1}{2}\tan^2 x + \ln|\cos x| + C$

37. $V_{rms} = \sqrt{\dfrac{1}{1/60.0}\displaystyle\int_0^{1/60.0}(340\sin 120\pi t)^2\,dt}$

14. $-3\cot^2 y - 6\ln|\sin y| + C$

$\qquad\quad = 240\text{ V}$

15. $\frac{3}{4}$ 16. $-\frac{1}{16}\csc^4 4x + C$

38. $i_{rms} = \sqrt{\dfrac{wi_0^2}{2\pi}\displaystyle\int_0^{2\pi/\omega}\frac{1}{2}(1 - \cos 2\omega t)\,dt}$

17. $\frac{1}{6}\tan^3 2x - \frac{1}{2}\tan 2x + x + C$

$\qquad\quad = \sqrt{\dfrac{wi_0^2}{4\pi}\left(t - \dfrac{1}{2\omega}\sin 2\omega t\right)\Big|_0^{2\pi/\omega}}$

18. $-\frac{4}{3}\cot^3 x + 4\cot x + 4x + C$

$\qquad\quad = \sqrt{\dfrac{wi_0^2}{4\pi}\left(\dfrac{2\pi}{\omega}\right)} = \sqrt{\dfrac{i_0^2}{2}} = \dfrac{i_0}{\sqrt{2}}$

19. $\dfrac{\sin^3 s}{3} + C$

20. $2(\tan x)^{1/2}\left(\dfrac{1}{3}\tan x + \dfrac{1}{7}\tan^3 x\right) + C$

39. $\dfrac{Aa}{2} + \dfrac{A}{2b\pi}\sin ab\pi\cos 2bc\pi$ 40. $kb\pi$

21. $x - \frac{1}{2}\cos 2x + C$

9.6   Inverse Trigonometric Forms

22. $\frac{1}{2}(\tan 2x - \cot 2x) + C$

23. $\frac{1}{4}\cot^4 x - \frac{1}{3}\cot^3 x + \frac{1}{2}\cot^2 x - \cot x + C$

1. $\sin^{-1}\dfrac{x}{2} + C$ 2. $\sin^{-1}\dfrac{x}{7} + C$

24. $\dfrac{\sin^3 u}{3} + \dfrac{\sin^4 u}{2} + \dfrac{\sin^5 u}{5} + C$

3. $\frac{1}{8}\tan^{-1}\dfrac{x}{8} + C$ 4. $\tan^{-1}\dfrac{p^3}{2} + C$

25. 1.347 26. $2(\sqrt{3}-2)-2\left(\dfrac{1}{\sqrt{3}} - \dfrac{2}{\sqrt{3}}\right) = 0.6188$

5. $\frac{1}{4}\sin^{-1} 4x + C$ 6. $\sin^{-1}\dfrac{2}{3} = 0.7297$

27. $\frac{1}{5}\tan^5 x + \frac{2}{3}\tan^3 x + \tan x + C$

7. 0.8634 8. $\dfrac{1}{14}\left(\tan^{-1}\dfrac{6}{7} - \tan^{-1}\dfrac{2}{7}\right) = 0.0307$

28. $\frac{1}{6}\tan^6 x - \frac{1}{4}\tan^4 x + \frac{1}{2}\tan^2 x + \ln|\cos x| + C$

9. 0.415 10. $\sin^{-1}\sqrt{x} + C$

29. $\frac{1}{2}\pi^2 = 4.935$ 30. 0.150 units^3

11. $\dfrac{4}{9}\ln|9x^2 + 16| + C$ 12. $-\dfrac{\sqrt{25 - 16y^2}}{4} + C$

31. 0.414 32. $\ln|2 + \sqrt{3}| = 1.317$

13. 2.356 14. $2(\tan^{-1} 1) = 1.5708$

33. $\displaystyle\int \sin x \cos x\,dx = \dfrac{1}{2}\sin^2 x + C_1$

15. $\sin^{-1} e^x + C$ 16. $\sin^{-1}(\tan x) + C$

$\qquad\qquad = -\dfrac{1}{2}\cos^2 x + C_2,$

17. $\tan^{-1}(x + 1) + C$ 18. $2\tan^{-1}(x + 4) + C$

$\quad C_2 = C_1 + \dfrac{1}{2}$

19. $4\sin^{-1}\left(\dfrac{x+2}{2}\right)+C$ **20.** $0.3\sin^{-1}(s-1)+C$

21. -0.714 **22.** $\tan^{-1}2-\tan^{-1}(-2)=2.214$

23. $2\sin^{-1}\dfrac{x}{2}+\sqrt{4-x^2}+C$

24. $\dfrac{3}{2}\tan^{-1}2x-\dfrac{1}{4}\ln\left|1+4x^2\right|+C$

25. **(a)** Inverse tangent, $\int\frac{du}{a^2+u^2}$ where $u=3x$, $du=3\,dx, a=2$; numerator cannot fit du of denominator. Positive $9x^2$ leads to inverse tangent form.

(b) $\displaystyle\int\frac{du}{u}\,u=4+9x; du=9\,dx$ logarithmic.

(c) $\displaystyle\int u^{-1/2}du=4+9x^2; du=18x\,dx$

     general power.

26. **(a)** Logarithmic, $\dfrac{du}{u}$ where $u=4-9x^2$;

     $du=-18x\,dx$.

(b) General power

(c) Logarithmic

27. **(a)** General power, $\displaystyle\int u^{-1/2}du$ where $u=4-9x^2$. $du=-18x\,dx$; numerator can fit du of denominator. Square root becomes $-1/2$ power. Does not fit inverse sine form.

(b) Inverse sine; $\displaystyle\int\frac{du}{\sqrt{a^2-u^2}}, a=2; u=3x$;

     $du=3\,dx$

(c) Logarithmic; $\displaystyle\int\frac{du}{u}, u=4-9x; du=-9\,dx$

28. **(a)** Inverse tangent $\dfrac{du}{a^2+u^2}$ where $u=3x$,

     $du=3\,dx, a=2$;

(b) General power

(c) Logarithmic

29. $\tan^{-1}2=1.11$ **30.** $\dfrac{\pi}{6}$ **31.** $k\tan^{-1}\left(\dfrac{x}{d}\right)+C$

32. 291 m^3 **33.** $\sin^{-1}\dfrac{x}{A}=\sqrt{\dfrac{k}{m}}\,t+\sin^{-1}\dfrac{x_0}{A}$

34. $s=t^2-8.49\tan^{-1}0.707t$ **35.** $0.22k$

36. $\dfrac{\pi}{2}$

Chapter 9 Review Exercises

1. $-\dfrac{1}{2}e^{-2x}+C$ **2.** $-\dfrac{1}{4}e^{\cos 2x}+C$

3. $-\dfrac{1}{\ln 2x}+C$ **4.** $\dfrac{125}{2}-5\sqrt{10}$

5. $4\ln 2=2.773$ **6.** $\ln|2+\tan x|+C$

7. $\dfrac{2}{35}\tan^{-1}\dfrac{7x}{5}+C$ **8.** $\dfrac{1}{2}\sin^{-1}2x+C$

9. 0 **10.** $\dfrac{1}{6}[2\sqrt{2}-1]$ **11.** $\dfrac{1}{2}\ln 2=0.3466$

12. 1 **13.** $-\cos t+\dfrac{2\sin^3 t}{3}+C$

14. $2\sqrt{\cos x}\left(\dfrac{1}{5}\cos^2 x-1\right)+C$ **15.** $\tan^{-1}e^x+C$

16. $\dfrac{\sec^4 3x}{12}+C$ **17.** $\dfrac{1}{9}\tan^3 3x+\dfrac{1}{3}\tan 3x+C$

18. $\dfrac{1}{2}\tan\theta-\dfrac{\theta}{2}+C$ **19.** $\dfrac{3}{\sqrt{e}}-2=-0.1804$

20. $-8e^{-\sqrt{x}}-2\sqrt{x}+C$ **21.** $\dfrac{3}{4}\tan^{-1}\dfrac{x^2}{2}+C$

22. $4(\tan^{-1}\sqrt{3}-\tan^{-1}1)=1.047$

23. $\dfrac{1}{4}\ln 3$ **24.** $\sin^{-1}\dfrac{e^x}{3}+C$

25. $2\ln|x+e^{2x}|+C$ **26.** $\ln|\tan x-x|+C$

27. $\sin^{-1}\dfrac{x+2}{3}+C$ **28.** $\dfrac{369}{4}$ **29.** $\dfrac{\pi}{4}=0.7845$

30. $\dfrac{1}{4}\left[\dfrac{3}{2}x-\sin 2x+\dfrac{1}{8}\sin 4x\right]+C$

31. $\dfrac{1}{2}\sin e^{2x}+C$ **32.** $3\tan^{-1}(x+3)+C$

33. $3\sin 1=2.524$ **34.** $\dfrac{\pi}{4}$

35. $\dfrac{1}{2}x^2-2x+3\ln|x+2|+C$ **36.** $-\dfrac{\ln 2}{\ln x}+C$

37. $\dfrac{(e^x+1)^3}{3}+C_1=\dfrac{1}{3}e^{3x}+e^{2x}+e^x+C_2; C_2=C_1+\dfrac{1}{3}$

38. $\dfrac{1}{2} + \ln x + \dfrac{1}{2}(\ln x)^2 + C_1$, $\ln x + \dfrac{1}{2}(\ln x)^2 + C_2$,

$C_2 = C_1 + \dfrac{1}{2}$

39. $\displaystyle\int \dfrac{1}{1 + \sin x}\, dx = \int \dfrac{1 - \sin x}{1 - \sin^2 x}\, dx = \int \dfrac{1 - \sin x}{\cos^2 x}\, dx$

$$= \int \sec^2 x\, dx - \int \sec x \tan x\, dx$$

$$= \tan x - \sec x + C$$

40. $y = -\dfrac{(2 - e^x)^3}{3} + \dfrac{13}{3}$ **41.** $y = \dfrac{1}{3}\tan^3 x + \tan x$

42. 38.17   **43.** $\ln 3 = 1.10$

44. $\Delta S = a \ln T + bT + \dfrac{1}{2}cT^2 + C$

45. $v = 64(1 - e^{-0.5t})$ **46.** $\dfrac{60}{\pi} = 19.1$ units

47. $\sqrt{2}$ **48.** $\dfrac{A}{a}(e^a - e^{-a})$ **49.** $\dfrac{2k}{3}$

50. The results are the same.

51. 3.47 cm^3 **52.** $\dfrac{2}{\pi}\ln 2 = 0.441$ in.

METHODS OF INTEGRATION

10.1   Integration By Parts

1. $\cos\theta + \theta\sin\theta + C$

2. $-\dfrac{1}{2}x\cos 2x + \dfrac{1}{4}\sin 2x + C$

3. $\dfrac{1}{2}xe^{2x} - \dfrac{1}{4}e^{2x} + C$ **4.** $3e^x(x-1) + C$

5. $x\tan x + \ln|\cos x| + C$

6. $\dfrac{\pi}{4}\sqrt{2} - \ln\left|\sqrt{2}+1\right| = 0.229$

7. $2x\tan^{-1}x - 2\ln\sqrt{1+x^2} + C$

8. $s(\ln s - 1) + C$ **9.** $-\dfrac{32}{3}$

10. $\dfrac{2}{15}(x+1)^{3/2}(3x-2) + C$

11. $\dfrac{1}{2}x^2\ln x - \dfrac{1}{4}x^2 + C$ **12.** $\dfrac{1}{3}x^3\ln 4x - \dfrac{1}{9}x^3 + C$

13. $\dfrac{\phi}{2}\sin(2\phi) - \dfrac{1}{4}(2\phi^2 - 1)\cos(2\phi) + C$

14. 1.597 **15.** $\dfrac{1}{2}(e^{\pi/2} - 1) = 1.91$

16. $-\dfrac{1}{5}e^{-x}(\sin 2x + 2\cos 2x) + C$

17. $1 - \dfrac{3}{e^2} = 0.594$ **18.** 0.6009 **19.** 0.1104

20. Exercise 3: First choice:

$u = x \qquad dv = e^{2x}\,dx$

$$\int xe^{2x}\,dx = \dfrac{x}{2}e^{2x} - \dfrac{1}{4}e^{2x} + C$$

Second choice:

$u = e^{2x} \qquad dv = x\,dx$

$$\int xe^{2x}\,dx = \dfrac{x^2}{2}e^{2x} - \int \dfrac{x^2}{2}(2e^{2x}\,dx)$$

$\int \dfrac{x^2}{2}(2e^{2x}\,dx)$ cannot be integrated, the first

choice is necessary.

Exercise 15: First choice:

$u = e^x \qquad dv = \cos x\,dx$

$$\int e^x\cos x\,dx = \dfrac{1}{2}e^x(\sin x + \cos x)$$

Second choice:

$u = \cos x \qquad dv = e^x\,dx$

$$\int e^x\cos x\,dx = \dfrac{1}{2}e^x(\sin x + \cos x).$$

Either choice will work.

21. $\dfrac{\pi}{2} - 1 = 0.571$ **22.** $3.54k$ **23.** 0.756

24. $y = \dfrac{k}{15}((1+x^2)^{3/2}(3x^2 - 2) + 2)$

25. $s = \dfrac{1}{3}[(t^2 - 2)(t^2 + 1)^{1/2} + 2]$ **26.** 70.3 m^3

27. $q = \dfrac{1}{5}[e^{-2t}(\sin t - 2\cos t) + 2]$

28. $\bar{x} = \lim_{b\to\infty} 3.2 - \lim_{b\to\infty} \dfrac{0.4(b^2 + 8)}{e^{b^2/8}} = 3.2\text{ nm}$

10.2   Integration By Substitution

1. $\dfrac{2}{15}(x+1)^{3/2}(3x-2) + C$

2. $\dfrac{2}{5}(x+3)^{3/2}(x-2) + C$

3. $\dfrac{1}{15}(2x+1)^{3/2}(3x-1) + C$

4. $-\dfrac{2}{5}(3-x)^{3/2}(x+2) + C$

5. $\dfrac{2}{3}(x+3)^{1/2}(x-6) + C$

6. $\dfrac{1}{3}(2x+7)^{1/2}(x-7) + C$

7. $\dfrac{2}{15}(x-2)^{1/2}(3x^2 + 8x + 32) + C$

8. 40 **9.** $\dfrac{1696}{105}$

10. $-\dfrac{2}{5}(1-x)^{1/2}(3x^2 + 4x + 8) + C$

11. $\dfrac{3}{28}(x-1)^{4/3}(4x+3)+C$

12. $-\dfrac{3}{7}(8-x)^{4/3}(x+6)+C$

13. $\dfrac{2}{7}(2x+3)^{3/4}(x-2)+C$

14. $\dfrac{3}{40}(x-4)^{5/3}(5x+12)+C$

15. $\dfrac{3081}{40}$ **16.** $\dfrac{5}{162}$ **17.** $\dfrac{928}{315}=2.946$

18. $\dfrac{96}{7}(2\sqrt[3]{2}+3)=75.7$ **19.** $\dfrac{30{,}024\pi}{35}=2695$

20. 2418   **21.** 38.5 ft·lb

22. $35.0\times10^{-15}\,$C   **23.** $\dfrac{-2}{15}(1-x)^{3/2}(2+3x)+C$

24. $\dfrac{3}{2}(x+3)^{1/3}(x-9)+C$

10.3   Integration By Trigonometric Substitution

1. $\dfrac{-\sqrt{1-x^2}}{x}-\sin^{-1}x+C$ **2.** $\dfrac{4}{45}$

3. $2\ln\left|x+\sqrt{x^2-4}\right|+C$

4. $\sqrt{x^2-25}-5\sec^{-1}\left(\dfrac{x}{5}\right)+C$

5. $-\dfrac{2\sqrt{z^2+9}}{3z}+C$ **6.** $\dfrac{3}{2}\ln\left|\dfrac{2-\sqrt{4-x^2}}{x}\right|+C$

7. $\dfrac{x}{\sqrt{4-x^2}}+C$ **8.** $2\sqrt{9+p^2}(p^2-18)+C$

9. 0.017   **10.** $\ln 2-\dfrac{3}{5}=0.0931$

11. $5\ln\left|\sqrt{x^2+2x+2}+x+1\right|+C$

12. $\ln\left|x+1+\sqrt{x^2+2x}\right|+C$ **13.** 0.03997

14. $8\sin^{-1}\left(\dfrac{x}{4}\right)+\dfrac{1}{2}x\sqrt{16-x^2}+C$

15. $2\sec^{-1}e^x+C$ **16.** $3\dfrac{\tan u}{\sqrt{4-\tan^2 u}}+C$

17. π **18.** $\dfrac{2\sqrt 2-\sqrt 5}{\sqrt{10}}=0.187$

19. power rule simpler.   **20.** $\dfrac{2}{5}ma^2$ **21.** 2.68

22. 9.42 m^2 **23.** $kQ\left(\ln\left|\dfrac{\sqrt{a^2+b^2}+a}{\sqrt{a^2+b^2}-a}\right|\right)$

24. 37.8 cm^3

10.4   Integration by Partial Fractions: Nonrepeated Linear Factors

1. $\ln\dfrac{(x+1)^2}{|x+2|}+C$ **2.** $\ln\dfrac{x^2}{|x+1|}+C$

3. $\dfrac{1}{4}\ln\left|\dfrac{x-2}{x+2}\right|+C$

4. $\dfrac{17}{2}\ln|2p-1|-8\ln|p-1|+C$

5. $x+\ln\dfrac{|x|}{(x+3)^4}+C$

6. $\dfrac{x^2}{2}-3x+\ln\dfrac{(x+2)^8}{|x+1|}+C$ **7.** 1.057

8. $\dfrac{5\ln 13}{4}-\dfrac{5\ln 5}{4}-\ln 3+\ln 1=0.09578$

9. $\ln\dfrac{x^2\,|x-5|^3}{|x+1|}+C$

10. $\ln\left|\dfrac{(x+2)^2(x-3)^3}{x+4}\right|+C$

11. $\dfrac{1}{4}\ln\left|\dfrac{x^4(2x+1)^3}{2x-1}\right|+C$

12. $\dfrac{\ln\dfrac{32}{27}}{2}=0.08495$ **13.** 2.674

14. $\dfrac{17}{12}\ln|x-2|-\dfrac{19}{4}\ln|x+2|+\dfrac{4}{3}\ln|x+1|+2x+C$

15. $\dfrac{1}{60}\ln\left|\dfrac{(V+2)^3(V-3)^2}{(V-2)^3(V+3)^2}\right|+C$

16. $\ln\left|\dfrac{(x-4)^3(x+3)x^2}{x-1}\right|+C$

17. 1.322   **18.** $\ln\dfrac{2\sqrt 5}{4}=0.1116$

19. $2\pi\ln\dfrac{6}{5}=1.146$ **20.** $\bar{x}=2.738$

21. $y = \ln \dfrac{|x|\,(x+5)^2}{36}$

22. 1.792 C

23. 0.1633 N·cm

24. $\dfrac{1}{2}\ln\left|\dfrac{x-4}{2(x-2)}\right|$

10.5 Integration by Partial Fractions: Other Cases

1. $2\ln\left|\dfrac{x-2}{x}\right| + \dfrac{3}{x-2} + C$

2. $\ln\left|\dfrac{T-1}{T}\right| + \dfrac{1}{T} + C$

3. $\ln\left|\dfrac{x-1}{x+1}\right| + \dfrac{2}{x} + C$

4. 3.172

5. $-\dfrac{5}{4}$

6. $-\dfrac{3x+2}{6(x+2)^3} + C$

7. $\dfrac{-1}{x-3} - \dfrac{2}{x+1} + \ln|x+1| + C$

8. $\ln\left|\dfrac{x+1}{x-1}\right| - \dfrac{2x}{(x+1)(x-1)} + C$

9. 1.491

10. $\tan^{-1} v + \ln|v-2| + C$

11. $\dfrac{3}{2}\tan^{-1}\left(\dfrac{x+2}{2}\right) - \dfrac{2}{x} + C$

12. $\dfrac{\sqrt{2}}{2}\tan^{-1}\dfrac{\sqrt{2}x}{2} + 2\ln|x-1| + C$

13. $\dfrac{\ln(4x^2+1)}{4} + \ln(x^2+6x+10) + \tan^{-1}(x+3) + C$

14. $\dfrac{3}{2}\ln\dfrac{20}{13} + \ln\dfrac{12}{5} = 1.522$

15. $\ln(r^2+1) + \dfrac{1}{r^2+1} + C$

16. $\tan^{-1} x + \dfrac{x}{x^2+1} - \dfrac{1}{2}\ln(x^2+1) + \ln|x+1| + C$

17. $2 - \ln\dfrac{81}{16} = 0.3781$

18. $\ln\dfrac{13}{3} = 1.466$

19. $\pi\ln\dfrac{25}{9} = 3.210$

20. $\dfrac{\pi}{72} = 0.0436$

21. 0.919 m

22. $190\mu A$

23. 1.369

24. $y = \dfrac{13}{6}\tan^{-1}\dfrac{2x}{3} - \dfrac{4}{x} + 9 - \dfrac{13}{6}\tan^{-1}\dfrac{2}{3}$

10.6 Integration by Use of Tables

1. $\dfrac{3}{25}[2+5x-2\ln|2+5x|] + C$

2. $4\left[\dfrac{1}{1+x} + \ln(1+x)\right] + C$

3. $\dfrac{3544}{15} = 236.3$

4. $\dfrac{1}{4}\ln\dfrac{x-2}{x+2} + C$

5. $\dfrac{y}{4\sqrt{y^2+4}} + C$

6. $\dfrac{5}{24}$

7. $\dfrac{1}{2}\sin x - \dfrac{1}{10}\sin 5x + C$

8. $6x\sin^{-1} 3x + 2\sqrt{1-9x^2} + C$

9. $\sqrt{4x^2-9} - 3\sec^{-1}\left(\dfrac{2x}{3}\right) + C$

10. $\dfrac{1}{3}(9x^2+16)^{3/2} + 16\sqrt{9x^2+16}$
$\qquad - 64\ln\left(\dfrac{4+\sqrt{9x^2+16}}{3x}\right) + C$

11. $\dfrac{1}{20}\cos^4 4x\sin 4x + \dfrac{1}{5}\sin 4x - \dfrac{1}{15}\sin^3 4x + C$

12. $\dfrac{1}{10}\tan 2\phi - \dfrac{1}{5}\phi + C$

13. $3r^2\tan^{-1} r^2 - \dfrac{3}{2}\ln(1+r^4) + C$

14. $\dfrac{5}{16}e^{4x}(4x-1) + C$

15. $\dfrac{1}{4}(8\pi - 9\sqrt{3}) = 2.386$

16. $-\dfrac{1}{8}\ln\dfrac{4x-3}{4x+3} + C$

17. $-\ln\left(\dfrac{1+\sqrt{4x^2+1}}{2x}\right) + C$

18. $\sqrt{4+x^2} - 2\ln\left(\dfrac{2+\sqrt{x^2+4}}{x}\right) + C$

19. $-8\ln\left(\dfrac{1+\sqrt{1-4x^2}}{2x}\right) + C$

20. $\dfrac{1}{1+4x} - \ln\left(\dfrac{1+4x}{x}\right) + C$

21. 0.0208

22. $\dfrac{1}{27}(26e^6 - 2) = 388$

23. $\frac{1}{3}(\cos x^3 + x^3 \sin x^3) + C$

24. $-\frac{1}{3}\cos^3 t(3\sin^2 t + 2) + C$

25. $\frac{x^2}{\sqrt{1-x^4}} + C$　　**26.** $-\ln\left(\frac{1-4x}{x}\right) + C$

27. 4.892　　**28.** Division by zero, undefined.

29. $\frac{1}{4}x^4\left(\ln x^2 - \frac{1}{2}\right) + C$　　**30.** $\frac{1}{5}\sec^{-1}\frac{u^2}{3} + C$

31. $\frac{-3x^3}{\sqrt{x^6-1}} + C$

32. $-\frac{1}{30}(8-3x^4)(4+x^4)^{3/2} + C$

33. $\frac{1}{4}[2\sqrt{5} + \ln(2+\sqrt{5})] = 1.479$

34. $\frac{3k\pi}{8}(3e^4 + 1)$　　**35.** πab

36. 5.0×10^{-6} V　　**37.** 208 lb

38. 47.1 min　　**39.** 187,000 m³

40. $\frac{kqQx}{b\sqrt{x^2+b^2}} + C$

10.7　Improper Integrals

1. $\frac{1}{3}$　　**2.** $+\infty$ (divergent)　　**3.** Divergent

4. $\frac{1}{2}$　　**5.** Divergent　　**6.** $+\infty$ (divergent)

7. $\frac{1}{2}$　　**8.** $\frac{1}{4}$　　**9.** 1　　**10.** $+\infty$ (Divergent)

11. Divergent　　**12.** $\frac{\pi}{2}$　　**13.** 6

14. $+\infty$ (Divergent)　　**15.** Divergent

16. $\frac{\pi}{2}$　　**17.** Divergent　　**18.** 0　　**19.** Divergent

20. 2　　**21.** $\ln(2+\sqrt{3})$　　**22.** $+\infty$ (Divergent)

23. 0　　**24.** $+\infty$ (Divergent)

25. (a) Divergent　　(b) π

26. Area (to right) is undefined.

27. $\sqrt{3}$　　**28.** $+\infty$ (Volume is undefined)

29. 2.53×10^7 mi·lb　　**30.** $\frac{2\,kim}{a}$

31. As $b \to +\infty$, $\sin b$ takes on all values from -1 to $+1$.

32. (a) 0　　(b) $-\infty + \infty$ (divergent)

Chapter 10 Review Exercises

1. $-\frac{1}{2}x\cot 2x + \frac{1}{4}\ln|\sin 2x| + C$

2. $\frac{1}{2}(x^2+1)\tan^{-1}x - \frac{1}{2}x + C$

3. $\frac{2}{15}(3x+8)(x-4)^{3/2} + C$

4. $\frac{2}{3}\sqrt{2x+5}(2x+5) + C$

5. $\frac{1}{2}\ln|2x + \sqrt{4x^2-9}| + C$

6. $\frac{9}{2}\sin^{-1}\frac{x}{3} - \frac{1}{2}x\sqrt{9-x^2} + C$

7. $\ln\left|\frac{(x-5)^3}{(x+5)^2}\right| + C$　　**8.** $\ln\left|\frac{(x-1)^3}{x(2x+1)}\right| + C$

9. $\ln|x-1| - \frac{1}{(x-1)^2} + C$

10. $2\ln|x| + \tan^{-1}\frac{x}{3} + C$

11. Divergent　　**12.** $2\sqrt{2}$

13. $\frac{3}{4}(x+3)^{1/3}(x-9) + C$

14. $x\tan x + \ln|\cos x| - \frac{x^2}{2} + C$

15. $\frac{2x}{\sqrt{4x^2+1}} + C$　　**16.** $\frac{2}{x} + \ln|3x+1| + C$

17. $2\tan^{-1}x - \frac{1}{2}\sqrt{2}\tan^{-1}\frac{1}{2}x\sqrt{2} + C$

18. $-\frac{1}{15}(3x^2+8)(4-x^2)^{3/2} + C$

19. $6\ln 2 - 2 = 2.159$　　**20.** $\frac{26}{15}$

21. $\ln\left|\frac{(x+1)(x+2)}{(x-1)(x-2)}\right| + C$

22. $-\left(\frac{4}{x} + \ln|x+3| + \frac{2}{x-3}\right) + C$

23. $\dfrac{144}{5}$ **24.** $1 - \dfrac{\pi}{4}$ **25.** 4

26. $\ln 5 - \dfrac{4}{5} = 0.809$ **27.** 11.18   **28.** $\dfrac{506}{15}$

29. $4\pi(e^2 - 1) = 80.29$

30. $\dfrac{502\pi}{15}$ **31.** 48.3 N·cm   **32.** $\dfrac{1}{2}I^2 L$

33. (1.65, 0.244)   **34.** 644 ft^2 **35.** 1.10 m^2

36. Assume $k = 1$. $R_y = 1.86$

INTRODUCTION TO PARTIAL DERIVATIVES AND DOUBLE INTEGRALS

11.1 Functions Of Two Variables

1. $V = \pi r^2 h$

2. $V = \frac{1}{3}\pi r^2 h$

3. $A = \frac{1}{2}bh$

4. $d = \sqrt{l^2 + w^2}$

5. $A = \frac{2V}{r} + 2\pi r^2$

6. $R = \sqrt{F_1^2 + F_2^2 + 1.732F_1F_2}$

7. $V = \frac{1}{4}\pi h(4r^2 - h^2)$

8. $T = F + 100h$

9. 24 **10.** 18 **11.** -2 **12.** 12

13. $2 - 3y + 4y^2$ **14.** $27 - 27t + 9t^2 - t^3$

15. $6xt + xt^2 + t^3$ **16.** $-4y^4 - 4y^3$

17. $\dfrac{p^2 + pq + pk - p + 2q^2 + 4kq + 2k^2 + 5q + 5k}{p + q + k}$

18. $z\tan^{-1}(x^2 - xz)$

19. $2hx - 2kx - 2hy + h^2 - 2hk - 4h$

20. $8y - 6z^2 - 8z + 4$ **21.** 0

22. $-x^3 - 2x^2 + x + 2$ **23.** $81z^6 - 9z^5 - 2z^3$

24. $-8t^2 + \frac{15}{2}t + \frac{1}{2}$ **25.** $x \neq 0, y \geq 0$

26. There are no values of x and y which are not permissable.

27. $y \leq 1$ **28.** $y \neq 0, x \neq 1$ **29.** 18 V

30. 9 ft/s^2 **31.** 150 Pa **32.** 38.4 W

33. For a, b, T with the same sign: circle if $a = b$, ellipse if $a \neq b$.
For a and b with different signs: hyperbola.

34. $\frac{1}{3}$ **34.** 1.03 A, 1.23 A **36.** 6.67 cm

37. $A = \dfrac{pw - 2w^2}{2}$, 3850 cm^2

38. $V = \pi r^2 h + \frac{4}{3}\pi r^3$, 773 ft^3

39. $L = \dfrac{(1.28 \times 10^5)r^4}{\ell^2}$ **40.** $f = \dfrac{0.16}{\sqrt{LC}}$

11.2 Curves and Surfaces In Three Dimensions

1.
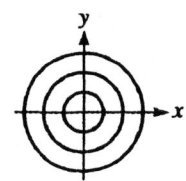

2.
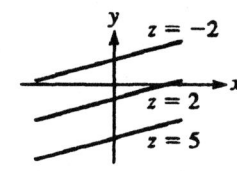

3.
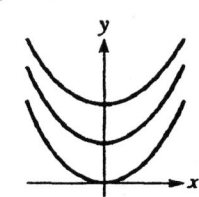

4.
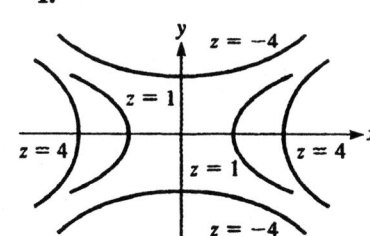

5.
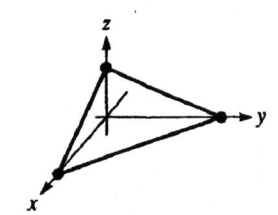

6.
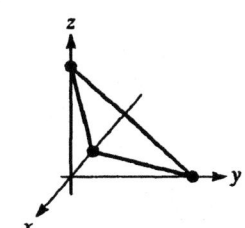

7.

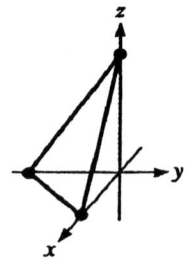

8.

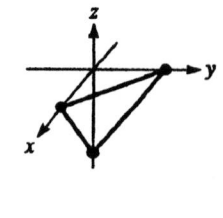

17.

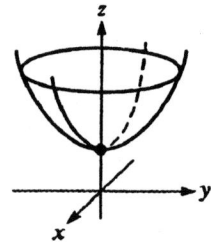

18.

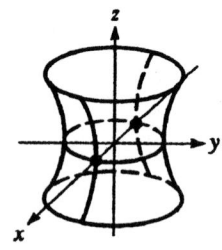

9.

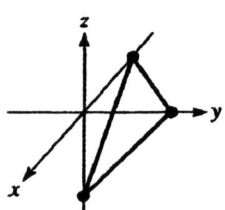

10.

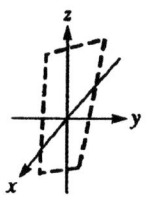

19.

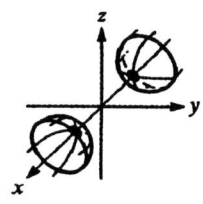

20.

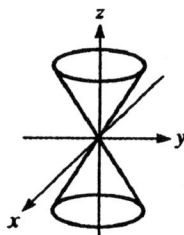

11.

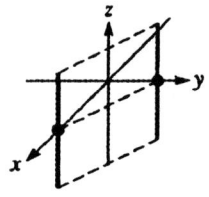

12.

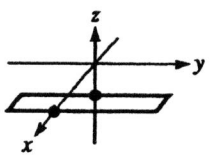

21.

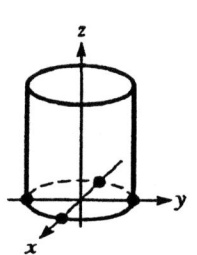

22.

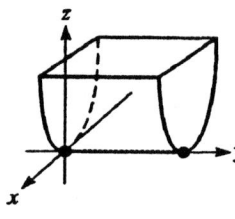

13.

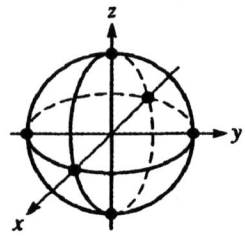

14.

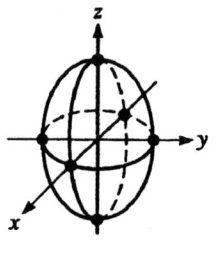

23.

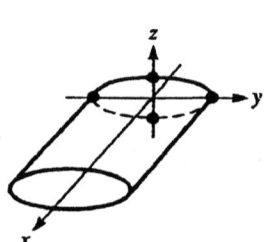

24.

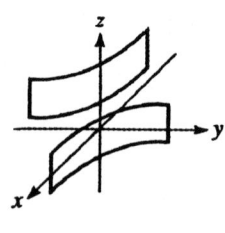

15.

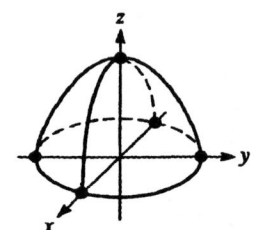

16.

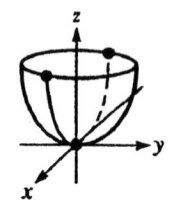

25.

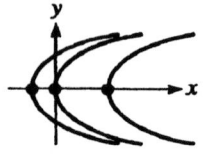

26.

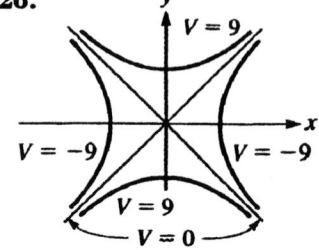

27.

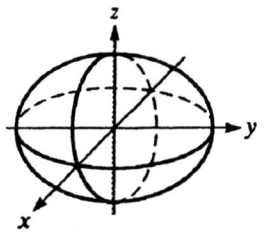

28.

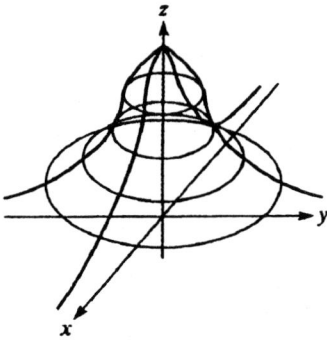

29.

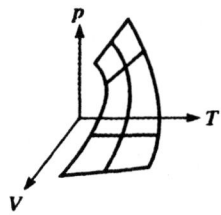

30.

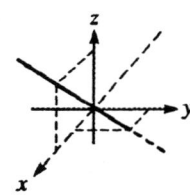

31.

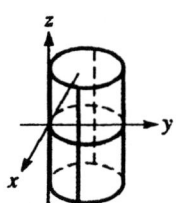

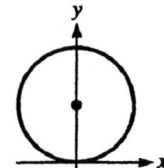

32.

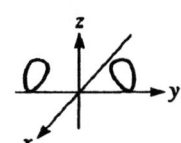

11.3   Partial Derivatives

1. $\dfrac{\partial z}{\partial x} = 5 + 8xy,$

$\dfrac{\partial z}{\partial y} = 4x^2$

2. $\dfrac{\partial z}{\partial x} = 6xy^3 - 3,$

$\dfrac{\partial z}{\partial y} = 9x^2y^2 + 4$

3. $\dfrac{\partial z}{\partial x} = \dfrac{2x}{y} - 2y,$

$\dfrac{\partial z}{\partial y} = -\dfrac{x^2}{y^2} - 2x$

4. $\dfrac{\partial f}{\partial x} = \dfrac{-2y}{(x-y)^2},$

$\dfrac{\partial f}{\partial x} = \dfrac{2x}{(x-y)^2}$

5. $\dfrac{\partial f}{\partial x} = e^{2y},$

$\dfrac{\partial f}{\partial y} = 2xe^{2y}$

6. $\dfrac{\partial z}{\partial x} = -6y \sin 2x,$

$\dfrac{\partial z}{\partial y} = 3 \cos 2x$

7. $\dfrac{\partial f}{\partial x} = \dfrac{-\sin x}{1 - \sec 3y},$

$\dfrac{\partial f}{\partial y} = \dfrac{3(2 + \cos x) \sec 3y \tan 3y}{(1 - \sec 3y)^2}$

8. $\dfrac{\partial f}{\partial x} = -\dfrac{2x \tan^{-1} y}{(2 + x^2)^2},$

$\dfrac{\partial f}{\partial y} = \dfrac{1}{(2 + x^2)(1 + y^2)}$

9. $\dfrac{\partial \phi}{\partial r} = \dfrac{1 + 3rs}{\sqrt{1 + 2rs}},$

$\dfrac{\partial \phi}{\partial s} = \dfrac{r^2}{\sqrt{1 + 2rs}}$

10. $\dfrac{\partial w}{\partial u} = \dfrac{v^2(2 - 3u)}{\sqrt{1 - u}},$

$\dfrac{\partial w}{\partial v} = 2uv\sqrt{1 - u}$

11. $\dfrac{\partial z}{\partial x} = 4(2x + y^3)(x^2 + xy^3)^3,$

$\dfrac{\partial z}{\partial y} = 12xy^2(x^2 + xy^3)^3$

12. $\dfrac{\partial f}{\partial x} = 10(2xy - x^2)^4(y - x),$

$\dfrac{\partial f}{\partial y} = 10x(2xy - x^2)^4$

13. $\dfrac{\partial z}{\partial x} = y \cos xy,$

$\dfrac{\partial z}{\partial y} = x \cos xy$

14. $\dfrac{\partial y}{\partial x} = \dfrac{t}{t^2 + x^2},$

$\dfrac{\partial y}{\partial t} = -\dfrac{x}{t^2 + x^2}$

15. $\dfrac{\partial y}{\partial r} = \dfrac{2r}{r^2 + s},$

$\dfrac{\partial y}{\partial s} = \dfrac{1}{r^2 + s}$

16. $\dfrac{\partial u}{\partial x} = e^{x+2y},$

$\dfrac{\partial u}{\partial y} = 2e^{x+2y}$

17. $\dfrac{\partial f}{\partial x} = \dfrac{12\sin^2 2x \cos 2x}{1-3y}$,

$\dfrac{\partial f}{\partial y} = \dfrac{6\sin^3 2x}{(1-3y)^2}$

18. $\dfrac{\partial f}{\partial x} = \dfrac{3y^2 - 3x^2 - 2x\ln y}{(x^2+y^2)^2}$,

$\dfrac{\partial f}{\partial y} = \dfrac{x^2 + y^2 - 6xy^2 - 2y^2\ln y}{y(x^2+y^2)}$

19. $\dfrac{\partial z}{\partial x} = \dfrac{3y + x^2 y - 2x\sqrt{1-x^2 y^2}\sin^{-1}xy}{(3+x^2)^2\sqrt{1-x^2 y^2}}$,

$\dfrac{\partial z}{\partial y} = \dfrac{x}{(3+x^2)\sqrt{1-x^2 y^2}}$

20. $\dfrac{\partial z}{\partial x} = \dfrac{-[y(x+y)\sec^2 xy + 2(1-\tan xy)]}{2y\sqrt{1-\tan xy}(x+y)^2}$,

$\dfrac{\partial z}{\partial y} = \dfrac{-[xy(x+y)\sec^2 xy + 2(x+2y)(1-\tan xy)]}{2y^2(x+y)^2\sqrt{1-\tan xy}}$

21. $\dfrac{\partial z}{\partial x} = \cos x - y\sin xy$,

$\dfrac{\partial z}{\partial y} = -x\sin xy + \sin y$

22. $\dfrac{\partial t}{\partial r} = 2(rs^2 + 1)e^{rs^2} - 2\sec^2(2r+s)$,

$\dfrac{\partial t}{\partial s} = 4r^2 s e^{rs^2} - \sec^2(2r+s)$

23. $\dfrac{\partial f}{\partial x} = e^x(\cos xy - y\sin xy) - 2e^{-2x}\tan y$,

$\dfrac{\partial f}{\partial y} = -xe^x\sin xy + e^{-2x}\sec^2 y$

24. $\dfrac{\partial u}{\partial x} = -\dfrac{1}{x-y} - e^{-x}(\sin y - \cos 2y)$,

$\dfrac{\partial u}{\partial y} = \dfrac{2x-y}{y(x-y)} + e^{-x}(\cos y + 2\sin 2y)$

25. -8 **26.** 0 **27.** $\dfrac{41}{4}$ **28.** $2e$

29. $\dfrac{\partial^2 z}{\partial x^2} = -6y, \dfrac{\partial^2 z}{\partial y^2} = 12xy$,

$\dfrac{\partial^2 z}{\partial x\partial y} = \dfrac{\partial^2 z}{\partial x\partial y} = 6y^2 - 6x$

30. $\dfrac{\partial^2 f}{\partial x^2} = \dfrac{-y}{(x+2y)^2}$,

$\dfrac{\partial^2 f}{\partial y^2} = \dfrac{4x+4y}{(x+2y)^2}$,

$\dfrac{\partial^2 f}{\partial y\partial x} = \dfrac{x}{(x+2y)^2}$,

$\dfrac{\partial^2 f}{\partial x\partial y} = \dfrac{x}{(x+2y)^2}$

31. $\dfrac{\partial^2 z}{\partial x^2} = e^x\sin y, \dfrac{\partial^2 z}{\partial y^2} = \dfrac{2x}{y^3} - e^x\sin y$,

$\dfrac{\partial^2 z}{\partial x\partial y} = \dfrac{\partial^2 z}{\partial y\partial x} = -\dfrac{1}{y^2} + e^x\cos y$

32. $\dfrac{\partial^2 f}{\partial x^2} = \dfrac{2(3x^2-1)(2+\cos y)}{(1+x^2)^3}$,

$\dfrac{\partial^2 f}{\partial y^2} = \dfrac{-\cos y}{1+x^2}$,

$\dfrac{\partial^2 f}{\partial x\partial y} = \dfrac{\partial^2 f}{\partial y\partial x} = \dfrac{2x\sin y}{(1+x^2)^2}$

33. $-4, -4$

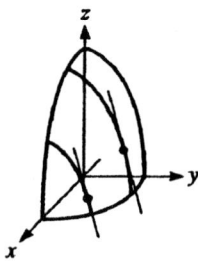

34. $\dfrac{\partial w}{\partial r} = \dfrac{2h}{\sqrt{2rh-h^2}}$,

$\dfrac{\partial w}{\partial h} = \dfrac{2(r-h)}{\sqrt{2rh-h^2}}$

35. $\dfrac{R_2^2}{(R_1+R_2)^2}$

36. $\dfrac{\partial z}{\partial y} = 0$

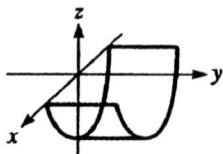

37. $114\ \text{cm}^2$

38. $M\left[\dfrac{2mg}{(M+m)^2}\right] + m\left[\dfrac{-2Mg}{(M+m)^2}\right] = 0$

39. 0.807

40. $f_s\dfrac{\partial f_o}{\partial v_s} = \dfrac{f_0^2}{v+v_o}$,

$f_0\dfrac{\partial f_0}{\partial v_0} = \dfrac{f_o^2}{v+v_o}$

41. $3.75\ 10^{-3}\ 1/\Omega$ **42.** 5

43. $\dfrac{k_2 + 2k_3 FT}{L_o + k_1 F + k_2 T + k_3 FT^2}$

44. $\dfrac{\partial f}{\partial T} = \dfrac{1800}{\sqrt{65}L}\dfrac{1}{2\sqrt{T}}$, 0.231 Hz/N **45.** $-\dfrac{nRT}{V^2}$

46. $\left(\dfrac{\partial V}{\partial T}\right)\left(\dfrac{\partial T}{\partial p}\right)\left(\dfrac{\partial p}{\partial V}\right) = -\left(\dfrac{nR}{p}\right)\left(\dfrac{V}{nR}\right)\left(\dfrac{pV}{V^2}\right)$

$= -1$

47. $-5e^{-t}\sin 4x = \dfrac{1}{16}(-80e^{-t}\sin 4x)$

48. $\dfrac{\partial^2 y}{\partial t^2} = -32\sin 2x\cos 4t$,

$\dfrac{\partial^2 y}{\partial x^2} = -8\sin 2x\cos 4t$,

$\dfrac{\partial^2 y}{\partial t^2} = 4\dfrac{\partial^2 y}{\partial x^2}$

11.4 Certain Applications of Partial Derivatives

1. $dz = (4x+3)dx - 2y\,dy$

2. $dz = (y - 6xy)dx + (x - 3x^2 + 3y^2)dy$

3. $dz = e^y dx + (xe^y - 2y)dy$

4. $dz = \left(3x^2 - \dfrac{y}{x}\right)dx - \ln x\,dy$

5. $dz = (y - 22x^2)(y - 2x^2)^4 dx$
$+ 5x(y - 2x^2)^4 dy$

6. $dz = \dfrac{-y^3 dx + (2y - 5xy^2)dy}{\sqrt{1 - 2xy}}$

7. $dz = (y\cos xy + y\sin x)dx + (x\cos xy - \cos x)dy$

8. $dz = (\tan 2y - 3x^2)dx + 2x\sec^2 2y\,dy$

9. $dz = \dfrac{dx}{1 - \sin y} + \dfrac{(6y\sin y - 6y + x\cos y - 3y^2\cos y)dy}{(1 - \sin y)^2}$

10. $dz = \dfrac{\sec x^2}{(x-y)^2}\left[(2x(x-y)\tan x^2 - 1)dx + dy]\right]$

11. $dz = \dfrac{-2xy^2 dx}{x^4 + y^2} + \left(\dfrac{yx^2}{x^4 + y^2} + \tan^{-1}\dfrac{y}{x^2}\right)dy$

12. $dz = 2e^{2xy}\left[y\ln(x^2 + y^2) + \dfrac{y}{x^2 + y^2}\right]dx$
$+ 2e^{2xy}\left[x\ln(x^2 + y^2) + \dfrac{y}{x^2 + y^2}\right]dy$

13. Min. $(1,3,0)$ **14.** Min. $(-3,3,-8)$

15. Min. $(-1,2,-1)$ **16.** Min. $(1,0,-3)$

17. no. max. or min. **18.** Min. $\left(\dfrac{1}{2},4,6\right)$

19. Min. $(2,0,0)$, Min. $(-2,\pi,0)$

20. Neither max or min. **21.** 9.60×10^4 rad/min^2

22. -0.30 A **23.** 1.3% **24.** 0.325 A

25. 4.5% **26.** 15.1 ft^3

27. $\ell = 1$ m, $w = 1$ m, $h = 1$ m

28. Max. for $\ell = w = h = 3.27$ ft

29. base 4.00 m by, 4.00 m, height 2.00 m

30. $\left(\dfrac{12}{7},\dfrac{18}{7},-\dfrac{6}{7}\right)$ **31.** Min. at $(1,0)$; $P = 17$ Pa

32. $T_{\text{coldest}} = -0.25°$C at $(0.5, 0.00)$

33. $T_{\text{warmest}} = 0°$C at $(0.67, 1.33)$

34. The area is a maximum for $x = 3$ in. and an angle of $120°$ $(\theta = 60°)$ between the bottom and the edges.

35. $6xt - 6yt$

36. $\dfrac{dz}{dt} = \dfrac{2y\sqrt{t+1} + \sqrt{t}}{2\sqrt{t}\sqrt{t+1}(x+y^2)}$

37. 0 **38.** -4 **39.** -5.0×10^{-5} A/s

40. 28 ft^3/s

11.5   Double Integrals

1. $\dfrac{28}{3}$ 2. $2 - \ln 3 = 0.9014$ 3. $\dfrac{1}{3}$ 4. $\dfrac{4}{3}$

5. $\dfrac{127}{14}$ 6. $-\dfrac{14}{5}$ 7. $\dfrac{1}{3}$ 8. $\dfrac{844}{15}$

9. $\dfrac{\pi - 6}{12}$ 10. $\dfrac{208\sqrt{3}}{105}$ 11. 1   12. 2

13. 495.2   14. $\dfrac{1}{2} - \dfrac{\sqrt{3}}{4} = 0.0670$ 15. $\dfrac{74}{5}$

16. $-\dfrac{\pi}{6} + \dfrac{\sqrt{3}}{2} - 1 = -0.658$ 17. $\dfrac{32}{3}$ 18. 18

19. 8π 20. 8π 21. $\dfrac{28}{3}$ 22. $\dfrac{6}{7}$

23. 18   24. $\dfrac{569}{13,440}$ 25. 300 cm^2

26. $16\pi = 50.3$ in^3

27.

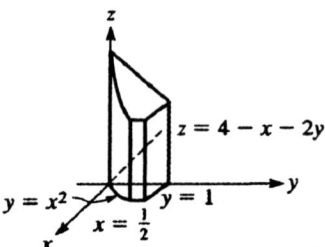

28.

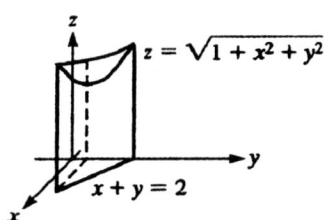

11.6   Centroids and Moments of Inertia By Double Integration

1. $\left(\dfrac{2}{3}, \dfrac{2}{3}\right)$ 2. $\left(\dfrac{3}{4}, \dfrac{12}{5}\right)$ 3. $\left(\dfrac{9}{8}, \dfrac{18}{5}\right)$

4. $\left(\dfrac{14}{9}, \dfrac{14}{9}\right)$ 5. $\dfrac{4}{3}, \dfrac{4}{3}$

6. $I_y = \dfrac{64}{15}I_x, \; I_x = \dfrac{256}{7}$

7. 1.34   8. $\sqrt{\dfrac{10}{3}} = 1.83$ 9. $\left(\dfrac{3}{4}, \dfrac{7}{10}\right), 0.775$

10. $\sqrt{\dfrac{\frac{243}{20}}{\frac{9}{2}}} = 1.64$ 11. $\left(\dfrac{a}{3}, \dfrac{b}{3}\right)$ 12. $\left(\dfrac{4a}{3\pi}, \dfrac{4a}{3\pi}\right)$

13. $\dfrac{1}{3}mb^2$ 14. $\dfrac{ma^2}{6}$ 15. $\dfrac{4}{3}\sqrt{3} = 2.31$

16. $\sqrt{\dfrac{2}{3}} = 0.816$ 17. $\left(3, \dfrac{5}{6}\right)$

18. The centroid is on the center line 3.6 ft from top.

19. $\dfrac{a^4}{12}$ 20. $\left(-1, \dfrac{1}{4}\right)$

Chapter 11 Review Exercises

1. $\dfrac{\partial z}{\partial x} = 15x^2y^2 - 2y^4,$
$\dfrac{\partial z}{\partial y} = 10x^3y - 8xy^3$

2. $\dfrac{\partial z}{\partial x} = 2\sqrt{y} - 2xy;$
$\dfrac{\partial z}{\partial y} = \dfrac{x}{\sqrt{y}} - x^2$

3. $\dfrac{\partial z}{\partial x} = \dfrac{x}{\sqrt{x^2 - 3y^2}},$
$\dfrac{\partial z}{\partial y} = \dfrac{-3y}{\sqrt{x^2 - 3y^2}}$

4. $\dfrac{\partial u}{\partial r} = \dfrac{-(r + 3s)}{(r - 3s)^3},$
$\dfrac{\partial u}{\partial s} = \dfrac{6r}{(r - 3s)^3}$

5. $\dfrac{\partial z}{\partial x} = \dfrac{2 - 2x^2y + 6xy^2}{(x^2y + 1)^2},$
$\dfrac{\partial z}{\partial y} = \dfrac{-(3 + 2x^3)}{(x^2y + 1)^2}$

6. $\dfrac{\partial z}{\partial x} = (y^2 + xy + 2)^3(y^2 + 5xy + 2),$
$\dfrac{\partial z}{\partial y} = 4x(y^2 + xy + 2)^3(2y + x)$

7. $\dfrac{\partial u}{\partial x} = 2xy \cot(x^2 + 2y),$
$\dfrac{\partial u}{\partial y} = 2y \cot(x^2 + 2y) + \ln \sin(x^2 + 2y)$

8. $\dfrac{\partial q}{\partial p} = \ln(r+1) - \dfrac{r}{r+1}$,

$\dfrac{\partial q}{\partial r} = \dfrac{pr}{(r+1)^2}$

9. $\dfrac{\partial z}{\partial x} = \dfrac{1}{2\sqrt{(x+y)(1-x-y)}}$,

$\dfrac{\partial z}{\partial y} = \dfrac{1}{2\sqrt{(x+y)(1-x-y)}}$

10. $\dfrac{\partial z}{\partial x} = ye^{xy}[2\cos(2x-y) + y\sin(2x-y)]$,

$\dfrac{\partial z}{\partial y} = e^{xy}[(1+xy)\sin(2x-y) - y\cos(2x-y)]$

11. $\dfrac{\partial^2 z}{\partial x^2} = 6y$, $\dfrac{\partial^2 z}{\partial y^2} = -6y$,

$\dfrac{\partial^2 z}{\partial x \partial y} = 6x + 2$

12. $\dfrac{\partial^2 z}{\partial x^2} = 6y^2(x-2)$,

$\dfrac{\partial^2 z}{\partial y^2} = -\dfrac{x}{2}(2y+1)^{-3/2}(2) + 2(x-2)^3$,

$\dfrac{\partial^2 z}{\partial y \partial x} = \dfrac{\partial^2 z}{\partial x \partial y} = \dfrac{1}{\sqrt{2y+1}} + 6y(x-2)^2$

13. 12   14. 5.071   15. $\dfrac{21}{2}$ 16. $\dfrac{3}{2}$

17. $\dfrac{1}{4}(e^2 - 3) = 1.097$ 18. $\dfrac{1}{8} - \dfrac{\sqrt{2}}{4} = -0.23$

19. $\dfrac{1}{6}$ 20. $\dfrac{\pi}{2}\ln 3 = 1.73$

21.

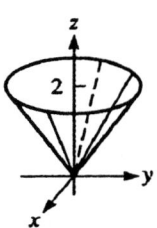

22. $2y - \sqrt{2}z + 2 = 0$ 23. 0.113

24. $dz = \dfrac{x\,dx + 4y\,dy}{\sqrt{x^2 + 4y^2}}$ 25. $z = e^2 x$

26.

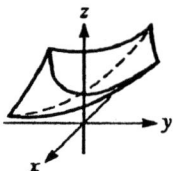

27. 1.48   28. 0.222

29. $\dfrac{\partial v}{\partial r} = \dfrac{ER}{(r+R)^2}$ 30. $\beta = \dfrac{bT^3 + 2cp}{T(apT^2 + bT^3 - pc)}$

$\dfrac{\partial v}{\partial R} = \dfrac{-rE}{(r+R)^2}$

31. 0.982   32. 4.96×10^6 Pa

33. $\dfrac{2\pi\sqrt{\ell/g}}{2\ell} = \dfrac{\pi}{\sqrt{g\ell}}$

34. $\dfrac{\partial V}{\partial r} = \dfrac{2}{3}\pi r h \dfrac{r}{r} = 2\left(\dfrac{1}{3}\pi r^2 h\right)\dfrac{1}{r} = \dfrac{2V}{r}$

35. 1.25 cm

36. The maximum possible error in the impedance is 2%.

37. $\left(\dfrac{3}{2}, 3\right)$

38. Minimum for $x = y = z = 2$ in., a cube.

39. $\dfrac{292}{15}$ 40. $\dfrac{7}{2}$ 41. $32\left(\pi - \dfrac{2}{3}\right) = 79.20$

42. $\dfrac{20}{3}$ 43. $\left(\dfrac{14}{9}, \dfrac{8}{9}\right)$ 44. $\left(\dfrac{3}{2}, \dfrac{12}{5}\right)$

45. 1.83   46. $\dfrac{459}{70} = 2.56$ 47. -12 W/min

48. 2550 J/s

POLAR AND CYLINDRICAL COORDINATES

12.1 Polar Coordinates

1.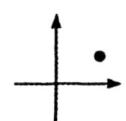

2.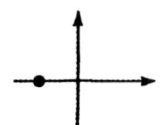

3.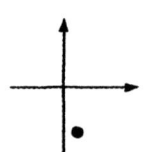

4.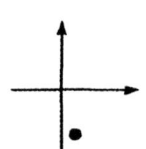

5.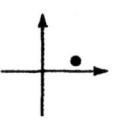

6.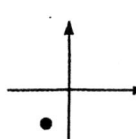

7.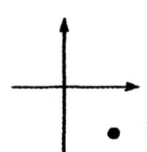

8.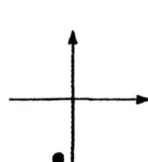

9.

10.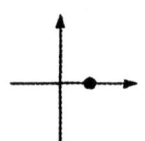

11.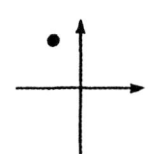

12.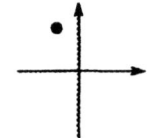

13. $\left(2, \frac{\pi}{6}\right)$ **14.** $\left(\sqrt{2}, \frac{5\pi}{4}\right)$ **15.** $\left(1, \frac{7\pi}{6}\right)$

16. $(6.40, 2.47)$ **17.** $\left(-4, -4\sqrt{3}\right)$

18. $(4, 0)$ **19.** $(2.76, -1.17)$ **20.** $(-0.54, -0.84)$

21. $r = 3\sec\theta$ **22.** $\theta = \frac{\pi}{4}$ **23.** $r = \frac{3}{\cos\theta + 2\sin\theta}$

24. $r = 0.9$ **25.** $r = 4\sin\theta$

26. $r^2 = 0.01\sec 2\theta$ **27.** $r^2 = \frac{4}{1 + 3\sin^2\theta}$

28. $r = 0, r = \frac{4\cos\theta}{\sin^2\theta}$

29. $x^2 + y^2 - y = 0$, circle

30. $x^2 + y^2 = 4x$, circle

31. $x = 4$, straight line

32. $y = -2$, straight line

33. $x - 3y = 2$, straight line

34. $y = e^x$, natural exponential

35. $x^2 + y^2 - 4x - 2y = 0$, circle

36. $\sqrt{3}y + x = 6$, line

37. $x^4 + y^4 - 4x^3 + 2x^2y^2 - 4xy^2 - 4y^2 = 0$

38. $x^4 + 2x^2y^2 + 2x^2y + y^4 + 2y^3 - x^2 = 0$

39. $(x^2 + y^2)^2 = 2xy$

40. $(x^2 + y^2)^2 = 16x^2 - 16y^2 = 16(x^2 - y^2)$

41. $B_x = -\frac{k\sin\theta}{r}, B_y = \frac{k\cos\theta}{r}$

42. $r^2 = \frac{k^2}{k^2\cos^2\theta + \sin^2\theta}$

43. $x^2 + y^2 - ay - bx = 0$

44. $0.98x^2 + y^2 + 1340x - 2.3 \times 10^7 = 0$

12.2 Curves in Polar Coordinates

1.
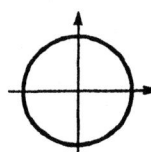

2.
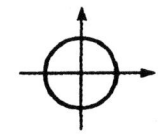

3.
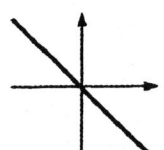

4.
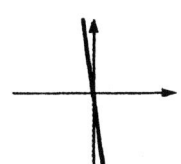

5.
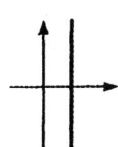

6.
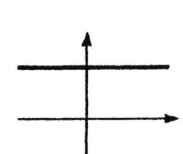

7.
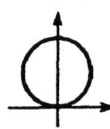

8.
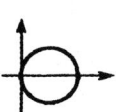

9.
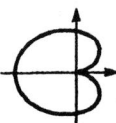

10.
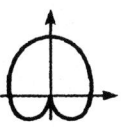

11.
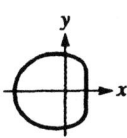

12.
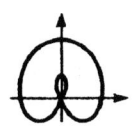

13.

14.
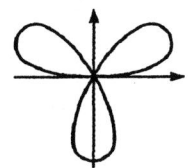

15.

16.
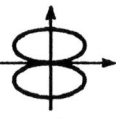

17.
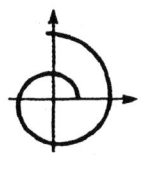

18.
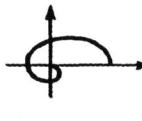

19.

20.
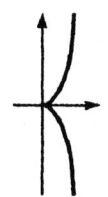

21.
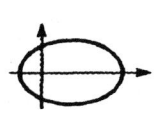

22.
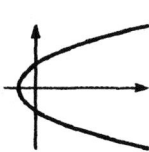

23.
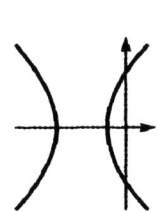

24.
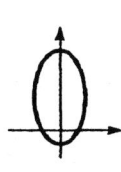

25.
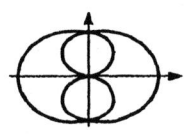

26.
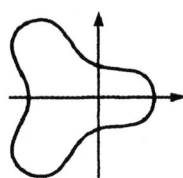

27.
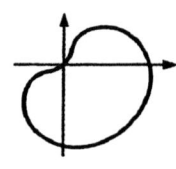

28.
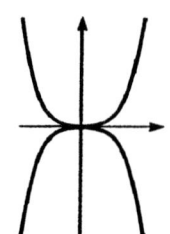

29.
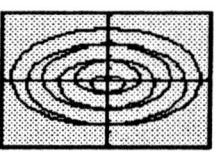

30.
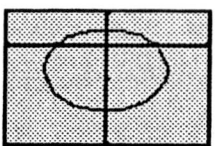

31.
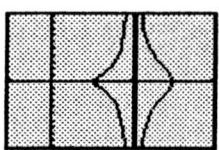

32.
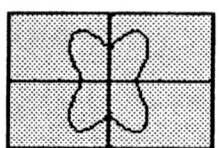

33.
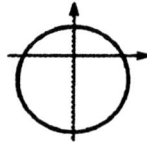

34.
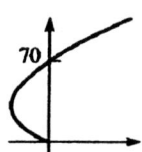

35.
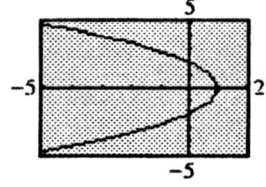

36.
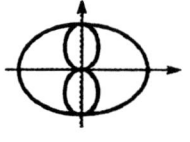

12.3 Applications of Differentiatives and Differentiation In Polar Coordinates

1. 9.49   2. 5   3. 1.85   4. 0.271

5. 4.00 ft/s   6. 17.9 ft/s   7. 2.00 ft/s

8. 4.00 ft/s   9. 8.25 ft/s   10. 14.1 ft/s

11. 1.54 ft/s   12. 3.61 ft/s   13. π 14. 6π

---

15. $\dfrac{1}{2}$ **16.** $2\sqrt{3}$ **17.** π

18. $\dfrac{1}{3}(4\pi - 3\sqrt{3})$ **19.** $\dfrac{1}{8}(e^{2\pi} - 1) = 66.8$

20. $\dfrac{3\pi}{2}$ **21.** π **22.** $\dfrac{9\pi}{2}$ **23.** $\dfrac{9}{2}\pi$

24. 4   **25.** $\dfrac{1}{4}(8 + \pi) = 2.79$ **26.** $1 - \dfrac{\pi}{4}$

27. $\dfrac{\pi}{2} - 1 = 0.571$ **28.** $\dfrac{1}{3}(8\pi + 3\sqrt{3})$

29. 4.98 ft/s, 8.67 ft/s   **30.** 2.83 m/s, 2.83 m/s

31. 119 cm^2 **32.** $\dfrac{\pi + 2}{8}$

33. $\dfrac{dy}{dx} = \dfrac{dy/dr}{dx/dr} = \dfrac{r' \tan\theta + r}{r' - r \tan\theta}$

34. $\dfrac{\sqrt{3}}{3}$ **35.** 4   **36.** $\pi\sqrt{2}$

12.4 Cylindrical Coordinates

1. **(a)** $(0, 2, 4)$ **(b)** $\left(\dfrac{3\sqrt{2}}{2}, \dfrac{-3\sqrt{2}}{2}, 5\right)$

2. **(a)** $(2, 2\sqrt{3}, 2)$ **(b)** $\left(\dfrac{-3\sqrt{3}}{2}, \dfrac{3}{2}, 2\right)$

3. **(a)** $\left(10, \tan^{-1} \dfrac{4}{3}, 5\right)$ **(b)** $\left(4\sqrt{2}, \dfrac{\pi}{4}, -3\right)$

4. **(a)** $\left(17, \tan^{-1} \dfrac{15}{8}, -6\right)$ **(b)** $\left(\sqrt{7}, \tan^{-1} \dfrac{-2}{\sqrt{3}}, 1\right)$

5. **(a)** $r = 2$ describes a cylinder with z-axis as axis
   (b) plane $\theta = 2$ for all r and z

6. **(a)** plane with $\theta = -2$
   (b) plane parallel to xy-plane and 2 units below the pole

7. **(a)** $r = 2\sec\theta$, plane 2 units in front of yz-plane
   (b) $z = 2$, plane 2 units above xy-plane

8. **(a)** $\theta = \dfrac{\pi}{4}$, plane   **(b)** $r = 2$, cylinder

9. $r = 4$

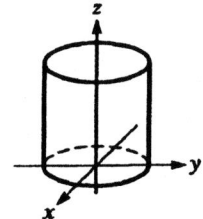

10. $r^2 = 4z$

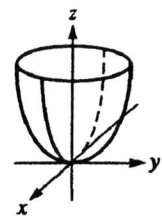

19. $y = 3$

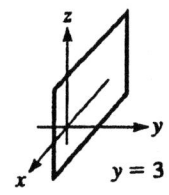

20. $y = x + 1$

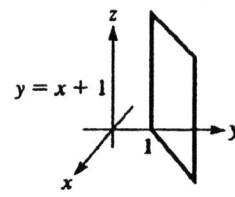

11. $r^2 + 4z^2 = 4$

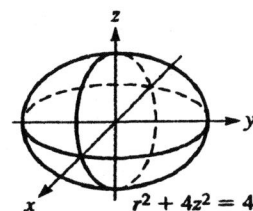

12. $r = 2 \sec \theta$

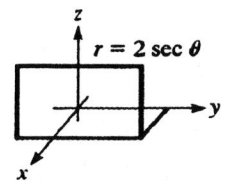

21. $\dfrac{\pi}{2}$

22. $\dfrac{32}{9}$

23. 205 m^3

24. Surfaces $z = 0$, $z = r^2$, and $r = 2 \cos \theta$ in the first octant.

Chapter 12 Review Exercises

1. $\theta = \tan^{-1} 2 = 1.11$

2. $r^2 \sin 2\theta = 1$

3. $r^2 \cos 2\theta = 16$

4. $r^2 + 6r \sin \theta - 7 = 0$

5. $(x^2 + y^2)^3 = 16x^2 y^2$

6. $(x^2 + y^2)^3 = y$

7. $3x^2 + 4y^2 - 8x - 16 = 0$

8. $x^2 - 4y - 4 = 0$

13. $9z = 4r^2$

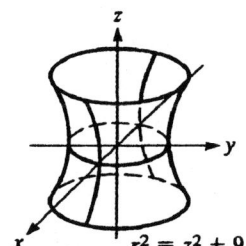

14. $r^2 = z^2 + 9$

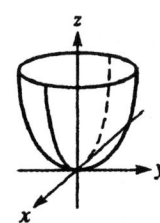

9.

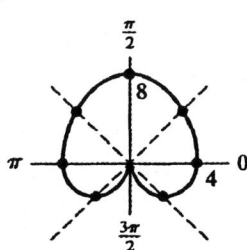

10.

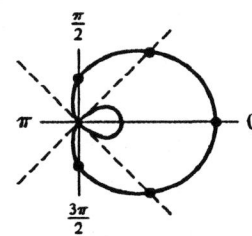

15. $x^2 + y^2 = 4z$

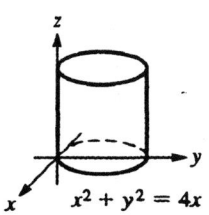

16. $x^2 + y^2 = 4x$

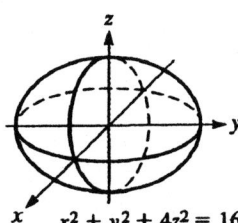

17. $x^2 + y^2 + 4z^2 = 16$

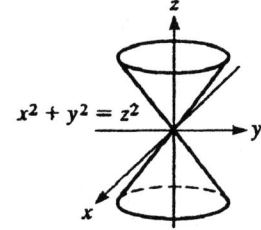

18. $x^2 + y^2 = z^2$

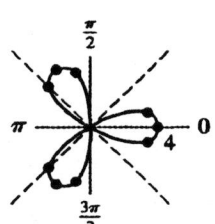

11.

12.

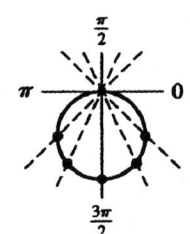

13.

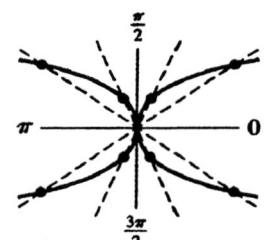

14.

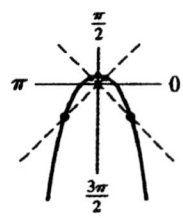

23.

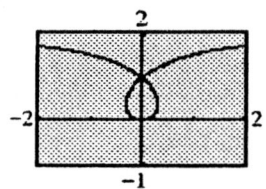

24.

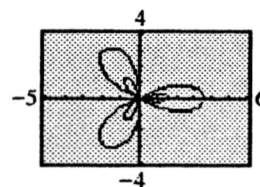

25. $\pi + 2$ **26.** 2   **27.** $\dfrac{19\pi}{2}$ **28.** 1

29. 4.502   **30.** $\pi - \dfrac{3\sqrt{3}}{2}$ **31.** $\dfrac{\pi^3}{48}$

32. $\dfrac{1}{4}(e^{4\pi} - 1)$

33. (a) $(13, \tan^{-1} 2.4, 3)$ **(b)** $(3\sqrt{2}, \tan^{-1}(-1), 2)$

34. (a) $(4\sqrt{3}, 4, 3)$ **(b)** $(0, -5, 4)$ **35.** 4

15.

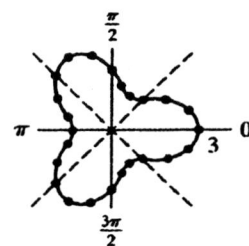

16.

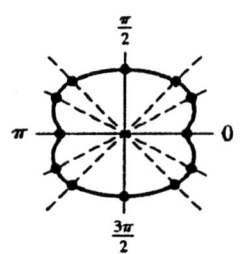

36.

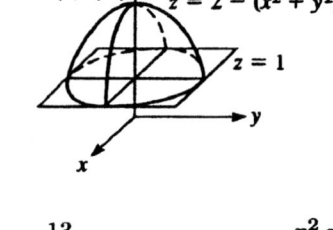

17.

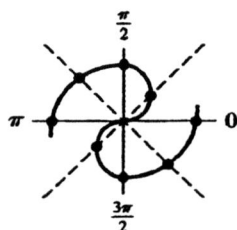

18.

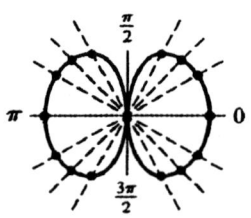

37. $\dfrac{13}{4}$ **38.** $\dfrac{r^2\cos^2\theta}{3.7^2} + \dfrac{r^2\sin^2\theta}{3.6^2} = 1$

39. $E_r = \left(\dfrac{2a}{r^2} + b\right)\cos\theta,\; E_\theta = \left(\dfrac{a}{r^3} - b\right)\sin\theta$

40. 14.1 cm^3

19.

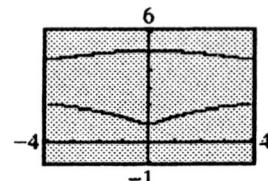

20.

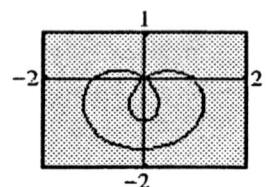

41.

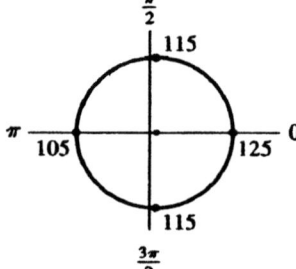

42.   9.507 mi^2

43.   81.9 ft^2

21.

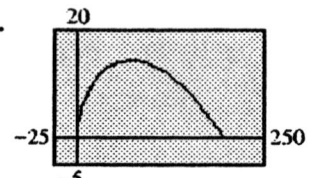

22.

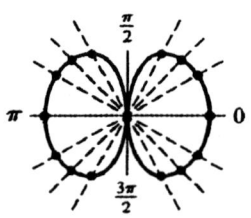

44.

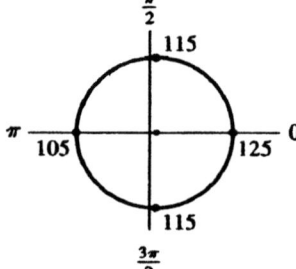

EXPANSION OF FUNCTIONS IN SERIES

13.1 Infinite Series

1. $1, 4, 9, 16 \ldots$

2. $\dfrac{2}{3}, \dfrac{2}{9}, \dfrac{2}{27}, \dfrac{2}{81}$

3. $\dfrac{1}{2}, \dfrac{1}{4}, \dfrac{1}{3}, \dfrac{1}{5}$

4. $1, 1, \dfrac{2}{3}, \dfrac{10}{7}$

5. (a) $-\dfrac{2}{5}, \dfrac{4}{25}, \dfrac{8}{125}, \dfrac{16}{625},$

  (b) $-\dfrac{2}{5} + \dfrac{4}{25} - \dfrac{8}{125} + \dfrac{16}{625} - \cdots$

6. (a) $\dfrac{3}{2}, \dfrac{5}{6}, \dfrac{7}{12}, \dfrac{9}{20},$

  (b) $\dfrac{3}{2} + \dfrac{5}{6} + \dfrac{7}{12} + \dfrac{9}{20} + \cdots$

7. (a) $1, 0, -1, 0$

  (b) $1 + 0 - 1 + 0 - \cdots$

8. (a) $\dfrac{1}{6}, \dfrac{1}{12}, \dfrac{1}{20}, \dfrac{1}{30}$

  (b) $\dfrac{1}{6} + \dfrac{1}{12} + \dfrac{1}{20} + \dfrac{1}{30} + \cdots$

9. $a_n = \dfrac{1}{n+1}$

10. $a_n = \dfrac{1}{2^n}$

11. $a_n = \dfrac{1}{(n+1)(n+2)}$

12. $a_n = \left(-\dfrac{2}{3}\right)^n$

13. $1; 1.125; 1.1620370; 1.776620; 1.1856620.$
Convergent to 1.2.

14. $1; 3; 8; 18; 35$
Divergent

15. $1; 1.5; 2.1666667; 2.9166667; 3.7166667.$
Divergent

16. $0.3333333; 0.2222222; 0.2592593; 0.2469136$
$0.2510288.$
Convergent to 0.25

17. $0, 1, 2.4142, 4.1463, 6.1463,$ divergent.

18. $1; 1.3333333; 1.5; 1.6; 1.6666667.$
Convergent 1.7

19. $0.75; 0.8888889; 0.9375000; 0.9600000;$
$0.9722222.$
Convergent to 1.

20. $0.3333333; 0.7333333; 1.1619048; 1.6063492;$
$2.0608947.$
Divergent

21. Divergent

22. Convergent. $S = 2$

23. Convergent. $S = \dfrac{3}{4}$

24. Divergent

25. $S = 100$, convergent

26. Convergent. $S = \dfrac{16}{3}$

27. Convergent. $S = \dfrac{4096}{9}$

28. Convergent. $S = 64$

29. (a) 1   (b) Diverges

30. (a) It appears the value is approaching 1.

  (b) Diverges

31. 1

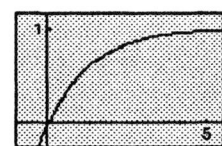

32.

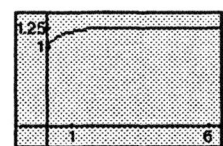

33. (a) diverges

  (b) $y = 2100(1.05^x - 1)$

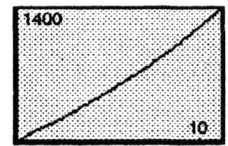

34. 656 nm, 486 nm, 434 nm, 365 nm

35. $r = x, \ S = \dfrac{1}{1-x}$

36. $S = \dfrac{1}{1-(-x)} = \dfrac{1}{1+x}$

13.2 Maclaurin's Series

1. $1 + x + \frac{1}{2}x^2 + \cdots$ **2.** $x - \frac{1}{6}x^3 + \frac{1}{120}x^5 - \cdots$

3. $1 - \frac{1}{2}x^2 + \frac{1}{24}x^4 - \cdots$ **4.** $x - \frac{1}{2}x^2 + \frac{1}{3}x^3 - \cdots$

5. $1 + \frac{1}{2}x - \frac{1}{8}x^2 + \cdots$ **6.** $1 + \frac{1}{3}x + \frac{2}{9}x^2 + \cdots$

7. $1 - 2x + 2x^2 - \cdots$ **8.** $1 + \frac{1}{2}x^2 + \frac{1}{24}x^4 + \cdots$

9. $1 - 8\pi^2 x^2 + \frac{32\pi^4 x^4}{3} - \cdots$

10. $x + x^2 + \frac{1}{3}x^3 + \cdots$ **11.** $1 + x + x^2 + \cdots$

12. $1 - 2x + 3x^2 - \cdots$ **13.** $-2x - 2x^2 - \frac{8}{3}x^3 - \cdots$

14. $1 + \frac{3}{2}x + \frac{3}{8}x^2 - \cdots$ **15.** $1 - x^2 + \frac{1}{3}x^4 - \cdots$

16. $4x - 8x^2 + \frac{64}{3}x^3 - \cdots$ **17.** $x - \frac{1}{3}x^3 + \cdots$

18. $1 - \frac{1}{2}x^4 + \cdots$ **19.** $x + \frac{1}{3}x^3 + \cdots$

20. $1 + \frac{x^2}{2} + \cdots$ **21.** $-\frac{1}{2}x^2 - \frac{1}{12}x^4 - \cdots$

22. $x + x^2 + \cdots$ **23.** $x^2 - \frac{1}{3}x^4 + \cdots$

24. $1 - x^2 + \cdots$

25. **(a)** No, not defined when $x = 0$.

  (b) No, not defined when $x = 0$.

26. **(a)** Maclaurin's expansion not possible; derivatives undefined for $x = 0$.

  (b) Maclaurin's expansion is possible; $f(x)$ and its derivatives are defined at $x = 0$.

27. **(a)** $e^x = 1 + x + \frac{1}{2}x^2 + \cdots$

  (b) $e^{x^2} = 1 + x^2 + \frac{1}{2}x^4 + \cdots$

28. $1 + nx + n(n-1)\frac{x^2}{2} + n(n-1)(n-2)\frac{x^3}{6} + \cdots$

29. $f(x) = 1 + 3x + \frac{9}{2}x^2 + \frac{9}{2}x^3 + \cdots$. $L(x) = 1 + 3x$

30. $\frac{4x^2}{2!} + \frac{24x^4}{4!} = 2x^2 + x^4$

31. $e^{-0.001t} = 1 - 0.001t + (5 \times 10^{-7})t^2 - \cdots$

32. $\dfrac{ab^2 + as^2 + bs^2}{a}$

13.3 Certain Operations with Series

1. $1 + 3x + \frac{9}{2}x^2 + \frac{9}{2}x^3 + \cdots$

2. $1 - 2x + 2x^2 - \frac{4}{3}x^3 + \cdots$

3. $\frac{1}{2}x - \frac{x^3}{2^3 3!} + \frac{x^5}{2^5 5!} - \frac{x^7}{2^7 7!} + \cdots$

4. $x^4 - \frac{1}{6}x^{12} + \frac{1}{120}x^{20} - \frac{1}{5040}x^{28} + \cdots$

5. $x - 8x^3 + \frac{32}{3}x^5 - \frac{256}{45}x^7 + \cdots$

6. $1 - \frac{1}{2}x^4 - \frac{1}{8}x^8 - \frac{1}{16}x^{12} - \cdots$

7. $x^2 - \frac{1}{2}x^4 + \frac{1}{3}x^6 - \frac{1}{4}x^8 + \cdots$

8. $-2x^3 - x^4 - \frac{2x^5}{3} - \frac{x^6}{2} - \cdots$

9. 0.3103   **10.** 0.3886   **11.** 0.1901

12. -0.00748 **13.** $2(1 + x^2 + x^4 + x^6 + \cdots)$

14. $x + \frac{x^3}{3!} + \frac{x^5}{5!} + \frac{x^7}{7!} + \cdots$

15. $x + x^2 + \frac{1}{3}x^3 + \cdots$

16. $x + \frac{1}{3}x^3 + \frac{2}{15}x^5 + \cdots$

17. $\frac{d}{dx}1\left(x - \frac{x^3}{3!} + \frac{x^5}{5!} - \cdots\right) = \frac{x^2}{2} + \frac{x^4}{24} - \cdots$

18. $\frac{d}{dx}e^x = 0 + 1 + \frac{2x}{2!} + \frac{3x^2}{6} + \frac{4x^3}{24} + \cdots$

$$= 1 + x + \frac{x^2}{2!} + \frac{x^3}{3!} + \cdots = e^x$$

19. $\int \cos x\, dx = x - \frac{x^3}{3!} + \frac{x^5}{5!} - \frac{x^7}{7!} + \cdots$

20. $\int -\frac{dx}{(1-x)} = -\int dx - \int x\, dx - \int x^2 dx$

$$= -x - \frac{x^2}{2} - \frac{x^3}{3}$$

$$= \ln(1 - x)$$

21. $\int_0^1 e^x dx = 1.7182818,$

$\int_0^1 \left(1 + x + \dfrac{x^2}{2} + \dfrac{x^3}{6}\right) dx = 1.7083333$

22. 1   **23.** 0.003099   **24.** 1.53

25. 0.199968

26. 189,000 m³ as compared to 187,000 m³

27. $\tan\theta = \dfrac{b}{a} = \dfrac{X_L - X_C}{R}$

$\theta = \tan^{-1}\dfrac{X_L - X_C}{R}$

28. $c(6at - 6a^2t^2 - 33a^3t^3 + 35a^4t^4)$

29.   **30.**

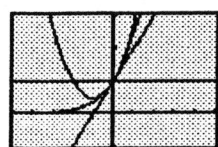   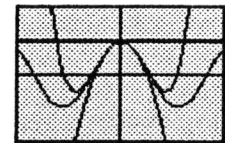

31.   **32.**

   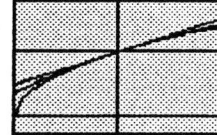

13.4   Computations by Use of Series Expansions

1. 1.22, 1.2214028

2. 0.9901, 0.9900990099

3. 0.09983333, 0.0998334

4. 0.99875; 0.9987503

5. 2.7180556; 2.7182818

6. 0.6068, 0.6065307

7. 0.9986292, 0.9986295

8. 0.0697565, 0.0697565

9. 0.3349333; 0.3364722

10. −0.051293, −0.0512933

11. 0.3546130, 0.3546129

12. 0.91824, 0.9182333

13. −0.0139975; −0.0139975

14. 0.052025, 0.0520230

15. 1.20736, 1.20803

16. 0.98569072, 0.98569039

17. 1.0523528   **18.** 0.8903

19. 0.9874462   **20.** 1.0442

21. 8.3×10^{-8} **22.** 0.000001

23. 3.1×10^{-7} **24.** 0.002

25. 3.146   **26.** 3.142

27. 1.59 years

28. (a) 2.007 s   (b) 2.011 s

29. $i = \dfrac{E}{L}\left(t - \dfrac{Rt^2}{2L}\right)$ **30.** −2.22 cm

31. 18 m   **32.** 1.54%

13.5   Taylor Series

1. 3.32   **2.** 2.013   **3.** 2.049

4. 1.87   **5.** 0.5150   **6.** 0.4695

7. 0.49288   **8.** 1.9628

9. $e^{-2}\left[1 - (x-2) + \dfrac{(x-2)^2}{2!} - \cdots\right]$

10. $\dfrac{\sqrt{2}}{2}\left[1 - \left(x - \dfrac{\pi}{4}\right) - \dfrac{1}{2}\left(x - \dfrac{\pi}{4}\right)^2 + \cdots\right]$

11. $\dfrac{1}{2}\left[\sqrt{3} + \left(x - \dfrac{\pi}{3}\right) - \dfrac{\sqrt{3}}{2!}\left(x - \dfrac{\pi}{3}\right)^2 - \cdots\right]$

12. $\ln 3 + \dfrac{1}{3}(x-3) - \dfrac{1}{18}(x-3)^2 + \cdots$

13. $2 + \dfrac{1}{12}(x-8) - \dfrac{1}{288}(x-8)^2 + \cdots$

14. $\dfrac{1}{2} - \dfrac{1}{4}(x-2) + \dfrac{1}{8}(x-2)^2 - \cdots$

15. $1 + 2\left(x - \dfrac{\pi}{4}\right) + 2\left(x - \dfrac{\pi}{4}\right)^2 + \cdots$

16. $-\dfrac{1}{2}\left(x-\dfrac{\pi}{2}\right)^2 - \dfrac{1}{12}\left(x-\dfrac{\pi}{2}\right)^4 - \dfrac{1}{45}\left(x-\dfrac{\pi}{2}\right)^6 - \cdots$

17. 23.1308   **18.** 1.131   **19.** 3.0496

20. 0.486392   **21.** 2.0247

22. 1.036   **23.** 0.87462   **24.** 0.7432

25. Use the indicated method.

26. $L(x) = x - 1;\ (x-1) - \dfrac{(x-1)^2}{2}$

27. 0.5150408, 0.5150388, 0.5150381

28. $\ln 2 - \dfrac{1}{2L}(x-L) + \dfrac{3}{8L^2}(x-L)^2$

29.

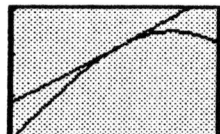

The series gives a good approximation near $x = \frac{\pi}{3}$ and deteriorates as x moves away from $x = \frac{\pi}{3}$.

30. Graph in part (b) will fit the graph of part (a) well for x close to $x = 8$.

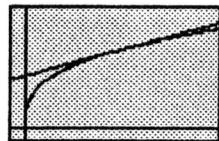

31. Graph of part (b) will fit the graph of part (a) well for values of x close to $x = 2$.

32. Graph of part (b) will fit the graph of part (a) well for values of x close to $x = \dfrac{\pi}{4}$.

13.6 Introduction to Fourier Series

1. $f(x) = \dfrac{1}{2} - \dfrac{2}{\pi}\sin x - \dfrac{2}{3\pi}\sin 3x - \cdots$

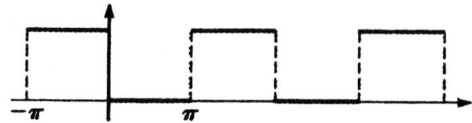

2. $f(x) = \dfrac{1}{2} + \dfrac{2}{\pi}\sin x + \dfrac{2}{3\pi}\sin(3x) + \cdots$

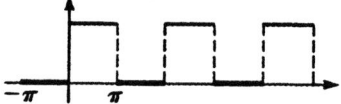

3. $f(x) = \dfrac{3}{2} + \dfrac{2}{\pi}\sin x + \dfrac{2}{3\pi}\sin 3x + \cdots$

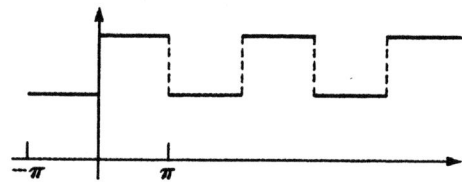

4. $f(x) = \dfrac{1}{4} + \dfrac{1}{\pi}\left(\cos x - \dfrac{1}{3}\cos 3x + \cdots \right.$
$\left. + \sin x + \sin 2x + \sin 3x + \cdots\right)$

5. $f(x) = \dfrac{\pi}{4} - \dfrac{2}{\pi}\left(\cos x + \dfrac{1}{9}\cos 3x + \cdots\right)$
$+ \left(\sin x - \dfrac{1}{2}\sin 2x + \cdots\right)$

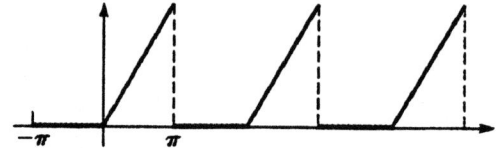

6. $f(x) = 2\left(\sin x - \dfrac{1}{2}\sin 2x + \dfrac{1}{3}\sin 3x - \cdots\right)$

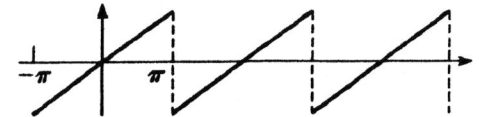

7. $f(x) = -\dfrac{1}{4} - \dfrac{1}{\pi}\cos x + \dfrac{1}{3\pi}\cos 3x - \cdots$

$\qquad + \dfrac{3}{\pi}\sin x - \dfrac{1}{\pi}\sin 2x + \dfrac{1}{\pi}\sin 3x - \cdots$

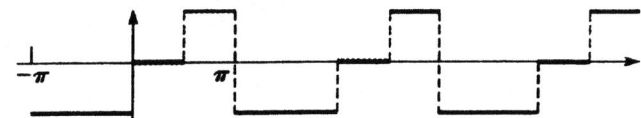

8. $f(x) = \dfrac{\pi^2}{3} - 4\left(\cos x - \dfrac{1}{4}\cos 2x + \dfrac{1}{9}\cos 3x - \cdots\right)$

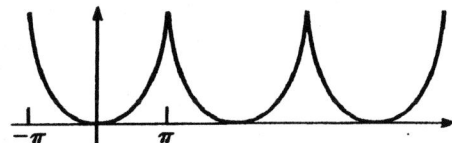

9. $f(x) = \dfrac{\pi}{2} - \dfrac{4}{\pi}\cos x - \dfrac{4}{9\pi}\cos 3x - \cdots$

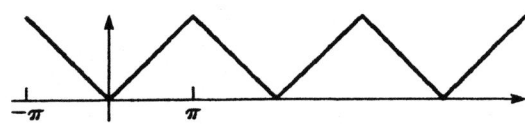

10. $f(x) = \dfrac{\pi^2}{6} + 2\left(-\cos x + \dfrac{1}{4}\cos 2x - \cdots\right)$

$\qquad + \dfrac{\pi^2 - 4}{\pi}\sin x - \dfrac{\pi}{2}\sin 2x + \cdots$

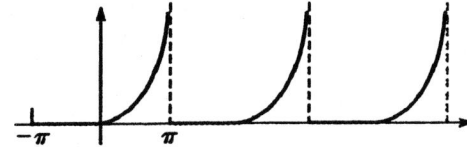

11.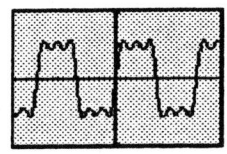

12.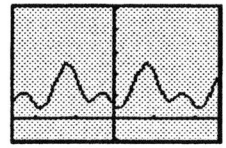

13.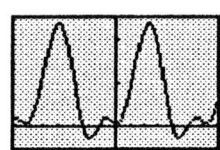

14.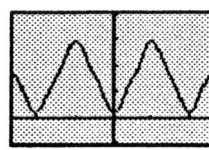

15. $f(t) = \dfrac{2}{\pi} - \dfrac{4}{3\pi}\cos 2t - \dfrac{4}{15\pi}\cos 4t - \cdots$

16. $f(t) = \dfrac{25\pi}{2} - \dfrac{100}{\pi}\cos(2t) + \dfrac{200}{\pi}\sin t - \dfrac{200}{9\pi}\sin(3t) + \cdots$

13.7   More About Fourier Series

1. neither   **2.** odd   **3.** even

4. neither   **5.** even   **6.** neither

7. odd   **8.** even

9. $\dfrac{5}{2} + \dfrac{2}{\pi}\left(\cos x - \dfrac{\cos 3x}{3} + \dfrac{\cos 5x}{5} - \cdots\right)$

10. $\dfrac{4}{\pi}\left(\sin x + \dfrac{1}{3}\sin 3x + \dfrac{1}{5}\sin 5x - \cdots\right) + \dfrac{1}{2}$

11. $-1 + \dfrac{4}{\pi}\left(\sin\dfrac{\pi x}{4} + \dfrac{\sin\frac{3\pi x}{4}}{3} + \cdots\right)$

12. $\dfrac{1}{6} + \dfrac{2}{\pi}\left(\cos x - \dfrac{1}{3}\cos(3x) + \dfrac{1}{5}\cos(5x) - \cdots\right)$

13. $f(x) = \dfrac{5}{2}$

$\qquad - \dfrac{10}{\pi}\left(\sin\dfrac{\pi x}{3} + \dfrac{1}{3}\sin\dfrac{3\pi x}{3} + \dfrac{1}{5}\sin\dfrac{5\pi x}{3} + \cdots\right)$

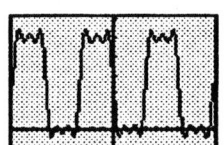

14. $f(x) = \dfrac{4}{\pi}\left(\sin\dfrac{\pi x}{2} + \dfrac{1}{3}\sin\dfrac{3\pi x}{2} + \dfrac{1}{5}\sin\dfrac{5\pi x}{2} + \cdots\right)$

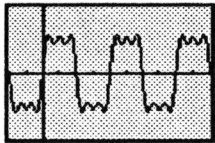

15. $f(x) = 1 + \dfrac{4}{\pi}\left(\cos\dfrac{\pi x}{2} - \dfrac{1}{3}\cos\dfrac{3\pi x}{2} + \dfrac{1}{5}\cos\dfrac{5\pi x}{2} - \cdots\right)$

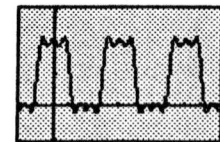

16. $f(x) = \dfrac{1}{4} + \dfrac{1}{\pi}\left(\cos\dfrac{\pi x}{2} - \dfrac{1}{3}\cos\dfrac{3\pi x}{2}\right.$

$\left. + \dfrac{1}{5}\cos\dfrac{5\pi x}{2} - \dfrac{1}{7}\cos\dfrac{7\pi x}{2} + \cdots\right)$

$+ \dfrac{1}{\pi}\left(\sin\dfrac{\pi x}{2} + \sin\pi x + \dfrac{1}{3}\sin\dfrac{3\pi x}{2}\right.$

$\left. + \dfrac{1}{5}\sin\dfrac{5\pi x}{2} + \dfrac{1}{7}\sin\dfrac{7\pi x}{2} + \cdots\right)$

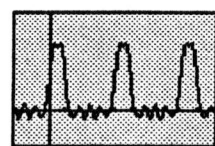

17. $f(x) = 2 - \dfrac{16}{\pi^2}\left(\cos\dfrac{\pi x}{4} + \dfrac{1}{9}\cos\dfrac{3\pi x}{4} + \cdots\right)$

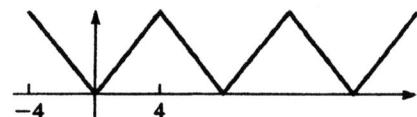

18. $f(x) = \dfrac{e-1}{2} - \dfrac{e+1}{\pi^2+1}\cos\pi x + \dfrac{e-1}{4\pi^2+1}\cos 2\pi x$

$- \dfrac{e+1}{9\pi^2+1}\cos 3\pi x + \cdots$

$+ \dfrac{\pi(1+e)}{\pi^2+1}\sin\pi x + \dfrac{2\pi(1-e)}{4\pi^2+1}\sin 2\pi x$

$+ \dfrac{3\pi(1+e)}{9\pi^2+1}\sin 3\pi x + \cdots$

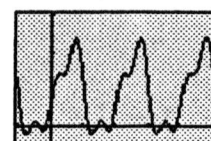

19. $f(x) = \dfrac{4}{\pi}\left(\sin\dfrac{\pi x}{4} + \dfrac{1}{3}\sin\dfrac{3\pi x}{4} + \dfrac{1}{5}\sin\dfrac{5\pi x}{4} + \cdots\right)$

20. $f(x) = \dfrac{1}{2} + \dfrac{2}{\pi}\left(\cos\dfrac{\pi x}{4} - \dfrac{1}{3}\cos\dfrac{3\pi x}{4} + \dfrac{1}{5}\cos\dfrac{5\pi x}{4} - \cdots\right)$

21. $f(x) = \dfrac{4}{3} - \dfrac{16}{\pi^2}\left(\cos\dfrac{\pi x}{2} - \dfrac{1}{4}\cos\pi x + \dfrac{1}{9}\cos\dfrac{3\pi x}{2} - \cdots\right)$

22. $f(x) = \left(\dfrac{-32}{\pi^3} + \dfrac{8}{\pi}\right)\sin\dfrac{\pi}{2} - \dfrac{4}{\pi}\sin\pi$

$+ \left(\dfrac{-32}{27\pi^3} + \dfrac{8}{3\pi}\right)\sin\dfrac{3\pi x}{2} - \cdots$

23. $f(t) = 2 + \dfrac{8}{\pi}\left(\cos\dfrac{\pi t}{2} - \dfrac{1}{3}\cos\dfrac{3\pi t}{2} + \cdots\right.$

$\left. + \sin\dfrac{\pi t}{2} + \sin\pi t + \dfrac{1}{3}\sin\dfrac{3\pi t}{2} + \cdots\right)$

24. $i(t) = \dfrac{e^2-1}{e}\left(\dfrac{1}{2} - \dfrac{1}{\pi^2+1}\cos\pi t + \dfrac{1}{4\pi^2+1}\cos 2\pi t\right.$

$- \dfrac{1}{9\pi^2+1}\cos 3\pi t + \cdots$

$- \dfrac{\pi}{\pi^2+1}\sin\pi t + \dfrac{2\pi}{4\pi^2+1}\sin 2\pi t$

$\left. - \dfrac{3\pi}{9\pi^2+1}\sin 3\pi t + \cdots\right)$

Chapter 13 Review Exercises

1. $\dfrac{1}{2} - \dfrac{1}{4}x + \dfrac{1}{48}x^3 - \cdots$ 　　　**2.** $e\left(1 - \dfrac{x^2}{2} + \dfrac{x^4}{6} - \cdots\right)$

3. $2x^2 - \dfrac{4}{3}x^6 + \dfrac{4}{15}x^{10} - \cdots$ 　　**4.** $1 + 2x + 3x^2 + \cdots$

5. $1 + \dfrac{1}{3}x - \dfrac{1}{9}x^2 + \cdots$ 　　　　**6.** $x^2 - x^4 + x^6 - \cdots$

7. $x + \dfrac{1}{6}x^3 + \dfrac{3}{40}x^5 + \cdots$ 　　　**8.** $1 + x + x^2 + \cdots$

9. 0.82 　　**10.** 0.0953 　　**11.** 1.09

12. 0.0610485 　　**13.** 0.9214 　　　**14.** 0.8507

15. -0.2015 　　　　　　　　　**16.** 0.9905481

17. 0.95299 　　　**18.** 4.02 　　　**19.** 12.1655

20. 0.6820 　　　**21.** 0.259 　　　**22.** 0.1001109

23. $\dfrac{1}{2} + \dfrac{1}{2}\sqrt{3}\left(x - \dfrac{\pi}{3}\right) - \dfrac{1}{4}\left(x - \dfrac{\pi}{3}\right)^2 + \cdots$

24. $\dfrac{1}{2}\ln\dfrac{1}{2} - \left(x - \dfrac{\pi}{4}\right) - \left(x - \dfrac{\pi}{4}\right)^2 - \cdots$

25. $f(x) = \dfrac{\pi-2}{4} - \dfrac{2}{\pi}\left(\cos x + \dfrac{1}{9}\cos 3x + \cdots\right)$

$+ \dfrac{\pi-2}{\pi}\sin x - \dfrac{1}{2}\sin 2x + \cdots$

26. $\dfrac{-2}{3} - \dfrac{4}{\pi^2}\left(\cos \pi x - \dfrac{1}{4}\cos 2\pi x + \dfrac{1}{9}\cos 3\pi x - \ldots\right)$

27. $f(x) = \pi + \dfrac{4}{\pi}\left(\sin \dfrac{\pi x}{4} + \dfrac{1}{3}\sin\dfrac{3\pi x}{4} + \cdots\right)$

28. $1 + \dfrac{1}{\pi} + \dfrac{1}{2}\sin x - \dfrac{2}{\pi}\left(\dfrac{1}{3}\cos 2x + \dfrac{1}{15}\cos 4x + \ldots\right)$

29. $f(x) = \dfrac{1}{2} + \dfrac{2}{\pi}\left(\cos x - \dfrac{1}{3}\cos 3x + \cdots\right)$

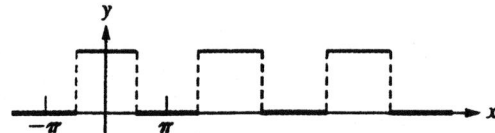

30. $f(x) = \dfrac{\pi}{4} - \dfrac{2}{\pi}\left(\cos x + \dfrac{1}{9}\cos 3x + \cdots\right)$
$\qquad - \left(\sin x - \dfrac{1}{2}\sin 2x + \ldots\right)$

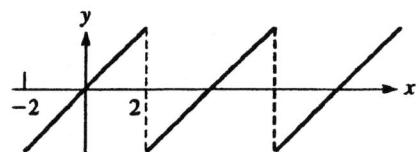

31. $f(x) = \dfrac{4}{\pi}\left(\sin \dfrac{\pi x}{2} - \dfrac{1}{2}\sin \pi x + \dfrac{1}{3}\sin\dfrac{3\pi x}{2} - \cdots\right)$

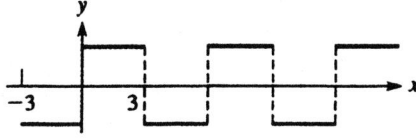

32. $f(x) = \dfrac{8}{\pi}\left(\sin\dfrac{\pi x}{3} + \dfrac{1}{3}\sin \pi x + \cdots\right)$

33. 256

34. The first five partial sums are
$\dfrac{1}{4} = 0.25, \dfrac{15}{28} = 0.5357, \dfrac{117}{140} = 0.8357,$
$\dfrac{2081}{1820} = 1.1434, \dfrac{10,599}{7280} = 1.4559$
divergent

35. $(x+h) - \dfrac{(x+h)^3}{3!} + \cdots - (x-h) + \dfrac{(x-h)^3}{3!} - \cdots$
$\qquad = 2h - \dfrac{6x^2 h}{3!} + \cdots = 2h\left(1 - \dfrac{x^2}{2} + \cdots\right)$

36. $2x - \dfrac{2}{3}x^3 + \dfrac{1}{20}x^5 - \ldots$

37. $4x - 2x^2 + \dfrac{4x^3}{3} - x^4 + \cdots$

38. $2\sin x \cos x = 2x - \dfrac{4}{3}x^3 + \dfrac{4}{15}x^5 - \cdots = \sin 2x$

39. $1 - x^2 + \dfrac{1}{3}x^4 - \dfrac{2}{45}x^6 + \cdots$

40. 0.3012

41. $1 + \dfrac{1}{2}x^2 + \dfrac{5}{24}x^4 + \cdots$

42. $\sin^2 x + \cos^2 x = x^2 - \dfrac{1}{3}x^4 + 1 - x^2 + \dfrac{1}{3}x^4 = 1$

43. $f(x) = \dfrac{2}{\pi} - \dfrac{4}{\pi}\left(\dfrac{1}{3}\cos 2x + \dfrac{1}{15}\cos 4x + \dfrac{1}{35}\cos 6x + \cdots\right)$

44. $f(x) = \dfrac{e^\pi + 1}{\pi}\sin x - \dfrac{4}{5\pi}(e^\pi - 1)\sin 2x$
$\qquad + \dfrac{3}{5\pi}(e^\pi + 1)\sin 3x - \dfrac{8}{17\pi}(e^\pi - 1)\sin 4x + \ldots$

45. 0.0025   **46.** $0.00302k$

47. $x - \dfrac{x^3}{3} + \dfrac{x^5}{5} - \dfrac{x^7}{7} + \cdots$

48. $0.17t - 0.0083t^3 - 0.00011t^5$

49. $N_0\left[1 - \lambda t + \dfrac{\lambda^2 t^2}{2} - \dfrac{\lambda^3 t^3}{6} + \cdots\right]$

50. 3 km

51. $2x + \dfrac{2}{3}x^3 + \dfrac{2}{5}x^5 + \dfrac{2}{7}x^7$

52. $\dfrac{m}{M} = k^2 w^2 + \dfrac{k^4 w^4}{3} + \cdots$

53. $N_0(1 + e^{-kt} + e^{-2kt} + \cdots)$

54. $x = R - \sqrt{R^2 - y^2}$
$\qquad x = \dfrac{1}{2R}y^2 + \dfrac{1}{8R^3}y^4 + \dfrac{1}{16R^5}y^6 + \cdots$

55. $f(t) = \dfrac{1}{2\pi} + \dfrac{1}{\pi}\left(\dfrac{1}{2}\cos t - \dfrac{1}{3}\cos 2t + \cdots\right)$

$\qquad + \dfrac{1}{4}\sin t + \dfrac{2}{3\pi}\sin 2t + \cdots$

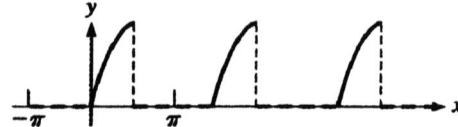

56. $F(t) = \dfrac{1}{4} - \dfrac{2}{\pi^2}\left(\cos t + \dfrac{1}{9}\cos 3t + \cdots\right)$

$\qquad + \dfrac{1}{\pi}\left(\sin t - \dfrac{1}{2}\sin 2t + \cdots\right)$

FIRST—ORDER DIFFERENTIAL EQUATIONS

14.1 Solutions of Differential Equations

1. particular solution

2. general solution

3. general solution

4. particular solution

5. $e^x - (e^x - 1) = 1$; $5e^x - 5(e^x - 1) = 1$

6. $\dfrac{2x}{x^4} = 2x \cdot \dfrac{1}{x^4} = 2xy^2$

7. $-12\cos 2x + 4(3\cos 2x) = 0$,
   $-4c_1\sin 2x - 4c_2\cos 2x + 4(c_1\sin 2x + c_2\cos 2x) = 0$

8. $y'' = 8e^{2x} = 2(4e^{2x}) = 2y'1$ 9. $2x = 2x$

10. $\dfrac{dy}{dx} = 1 - 3x^2$ 11. $2x + 3 - 3 = 2x$

12. $xy' = x(2cx) = 2(cx^2) = 2y$

13. $-2ce^{-2x} + 1 + 2\left(ce^{-2x} + x - \dfrac{1}{2}\right) = 2x$

14. $3x^2 + 1 - 3x^2 = 1$

15. $-\dfrac{1}{2}\cos x + \dfrac{9}{2}\cos x = 4\cos x$

16. $4c_2 e^{2x} + 4xe^{2x} + e^{2x} + 4c_1 e^{2x} + 4c_2 xe^{2x} + 2x^2 e^{2x}$
    $- 4c_2 e^{2x} - 4xe^{2x} - 8c_1 e^{2x} - 8c_2 xe^{2x} - 4x^2 e^{2x}$
    $+ 4c_1 e^{2x} + 4c_2 xe^{2x} + 2x^2 e^{2x}$
    $= e^{2x}$

17. $x^2\left[\dfrac{-c^2}{(x-c)^2}\right] + \left(\dfrac{cx}{x-c}\right)^2 = 0$

18. $3cx^3 - 2x^2 - 3cx^3 + 3x^2 = x^2$

19. $x\left(\dfrac{-c_1}{x^2}\right) + c_1 x^{-1} = 0$

20. $-4c_1\sin 2x - 4c_2\cos 2x + 2e^x + 4c_1\sin 2x$
    $+ 4c_2\cos 2x + 8e^x$
    $= 10e^x$

21. $\cos x - \sin x + e^{-x} + \sin x + \cos x - e^{-x}$
    $= 2\cos x$

22. $x + x\ln x - cx - x(1 + \ln x - c) = 0$

23. $e^{-x} + \dfrac{12}{5}\cos 2x + \dfrac{24}{5}\sin 2x - e^{-x}$
    $+ \dfrac{6}{5}\sin 2x - \dfrac{12}{5}\cos 2x = 6\sin 2x$

24. $12x^3 - \dfrac{c_2}{x} + 4x^3 + \dfrac{c_2}{x} = 16x^3$

25. $\cos x\left[\dfrac{1 - (x + c)(\sec x)}{\sec x + \tan x}\right] + \sin x$
    $= 1 - \dfrac{(x + c)}{\sec x + \tan x}$

26. $2xy\left(\dfrac{c - 2x}{2y}\right) + x^2 = y^2$

27. $(c)^2 + x(c)$; $c^2 + cx$

28. $x^4\left(-\dfrac{c}{x^2}\right)^2 - x\left(-\dfrac{c}{x^2}\right) = y$

14.2 Separation of Variables

1. $y = c - x^2$ 2. $4y^3 + 3x^4 = c$

3. $x - \dfrac{1}{y} = c$ 4. $xy = c$

5. $\ln V = \dfrac{1}{P} + c$ 6. $2\ln y = x + \ln x + c$

7. $3y + \ln(x^3 + 5) = c$ 8. $\ln x + \sqrt{1 + y^2} = c$

9. $y = 2x^2 + x - x\ln x + c$

10. $r^2 = -2\sqrt{1 - \theta^2} + 8\sin^{-1}\theta + c$

11. $4\sqrt{1 - y} = e^{-x^2} + c$ 12. $\sqrt{1 + 4x^2} + \dfrac{2}{y^2} = c$

13. $e^x - e^{-y} = c$ 14. $y = e^{-x} + c$

15. $\ln(4 + y) = x + c$ 16. $\dfrac{1}{3}\tan^{-1}\dfrac{s}{3} = t + c$

17. $y(1 + \ln x)^2 + cy + 2 = 0$

18. $y^2 = (\tan^{-1} x)^2 + c$ 19. $\tan^2 x + 2\ln y = c$

20. $\cos x + \sin y = c$ 21. $x^2 + 1 + x\ln y + cx = 0$

22. $-e^{\cos\theta} + y = c$

23. $y^2 + 4\sin^{-1}x = c$

24. $2x^3 + 3y^2 = c$

25. $i = c - (\ln t)^2$

26. $(y^2-1)(x^3+1) = c$

27. $\ln(e^x+1) - \dfrac{1}{y} = c$

28. $(\sin x + 1)(y+1) = c$

29. $3\ln y + x^3 = 0$

30. $y = 3 - 2e^{-2x}$

31. $\dfrac{1}{3}y^3 + y = \dfrac{1}{2}\ln^2 x$

32. $\sin s = t$

33. $2\ln(1-y) = 1 - 2\sin x$

34. $x = 2\ln y$

35. $e^{2x} - \dfrac{2}{y} = 2(e^x - 1)$

36. $x = \ln\dfrac{\pi \sin^2 y}{2y}$

14.3   Integrating Combinations

1. $2xy + x^2 = c$

2. $y^2 + xy = c$

3. $x^3 - 2y = cx - 4$

4. $x - \dfrac{x}{y} = c$

5. $A^2 r - r = cA$

6. $x + \sin(xy) = c$

7. $(xy)^4 = 12\ln y + c$

8. $3\ln xy + 4y^3 = c$

9. $2\sqrt{x^2+y^2} = x + c$

10. $\ln(R^2 + T^2) + 2T = c$

11. $y = c - \dfrac{1}{2}\ln\sin(x^2+y^2)$

12. $y(x^2+y^3) = 1 + c(x^2+y^3)$

13. $\ln(y^2 - x^2) + 2x = c$

14. $e^{x+y} + 2x^2 = c$

15. $15xy^2 + y^3 = c$

16. $(\ln(uv))^2 + u^3 = c$

17. $2xy + x^3 = 5$

18. $\ln(t^2 + s^2) = 4t - 4$

19. $2x = 2xy^2 - 15y$

20. $y^3 + 3e^{x/y} = 11$

14.4   The Linear Differential Equations of the First Order

1. $y = e^{-x}(x + c)$

2. $y = e^{-3x}(x + c)$

3. $y = -\dfrac{1}{2}e^{-4x} + ce^{-2x}$

4. $ie^t = \sin t + c$

5. $y = -2 + ce^{2x}$

6. $y = \dfrac{1}{6}(5 + ce^{-3x})$

7. $y = x(3\ln x + c)$

8. $x^3(3y - 1) = c$

9. $y = \dfrac{8}{7}x^3 + \dfrac{c}{\sqrt{x}}$

10. $2y = 9x + cx^{1/3}$

11. $r = -\cot\theta + c\csc\theta$

12. $y = -3 + ce^{x^3/3}$

13. $y = (x + c)\csc x$

14. $y = \dfrac{1}{2}x(\ln^2 x + c)$

15. $y = 3 + ce^{-x}$

16. $y = \dfrac{1}{5}(2\sin x - \cos x) + ce^{-2x}$

17. $2s = e^{4t}(t^2 + c)$

18. $y = e^{2x}(2x + c)$

19. $y = \dfrac{1}{4} + ce^{-x^4}$

20. $y\sec x = \ln\cos x + c$

21. $3y = x^4 - 6x^2 - 3 + cx$

22. $y = t - \dfrac{\ln(t^2+1)}{2\tan^{-1}t} + \dfrac{c}{\tan^{-1}t}$

23. $xy = e^{3x}(x^3 + c)$

24. $\sqrt{1+x^2}(y - 1) = c$

25. Solve by separation of variables.

$$\frac{dy}{1-y} = 2\,dx;$$

Solve as a first order equation.

$$dy = 2\,dx - 2y\,dx$$
$$y = 1 + ce^{-2x}$$

26. $xy = x^2 + c$

27. $y = e^{-x}$

28. $q = \dfrac{1}{2}(5e^{4u} - 1)$

29. $y = \dfrac{4}{3}\sin x - \csc^2 x$

30. $y = e^{\sqrt{x}} + (3e - e^2)e^{-\sqrt{x}}$

31. $y(\csc x - \cot x) = \ln\left[\dfrac{(\sqrt{2}-1)(\csc 2x - \cot 2x)}{(\csc x - \cot x)}\right]$

32. $3y = f(x) + 10\,[f(x)]^{-2}$

14.5 Elementary Applications

1. $y^2 = 2x^2 + 1$

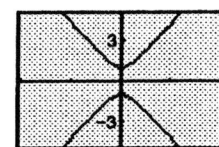

2. $y = -x \pm \sqrt{3 + x^2}$

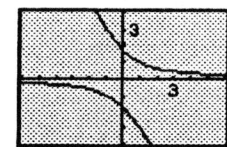

3. $y = 2e^x - x - 1$

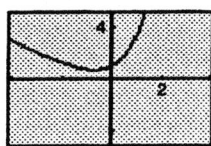

4. $y = e^{-x} + e^{-2x}$

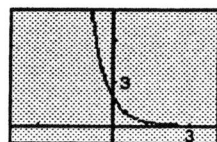

5. $y^2 = c - 2x$

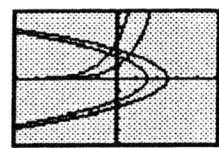

6. $3y^2 + x^2 = c$

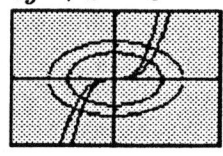

7. $y^2 = c - 2\sin x$

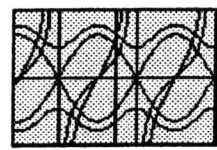

8. $y = cx$

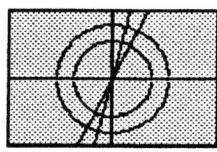

9. $N = N_0(0.5)^{0.025t}$, 35.4%

10. 1620 years

11. 3.82 days

12. $N = \dfrac{r}{k}(1 - e^{-kt})$

13. $S = a + \dfrac{c}{r^2}$

14. $v = \sqrt{2GM\left(\dfrac{r_0 - r}{r_0 r}\right)}$

15. $5250e^{0.0196t}$

16. $P = xe^{-x^2}$

17. 13 min

18. $T = 20 + 80(0.375)^{t/10}$

19. \$1040.81

20. 41.1 ft

21. $\displaystyle\lim_{i \to \infty}\left(\dfrac{E}{R} - \dfrac{E}{R}e^{-(R/L)t}\right) = \dfrac{E}{R}$

22. $i = 0.020e^{-15t}$

23. $i = \dfrac{E}{R^2 + L^2\omega^2}(R\sin\omega t - L\omega\cos\omega t + L\omega e^{-Rt/L})$

24. $i = 2.0 - 2.0 \times 10^{-4}(100 - t)^2$

25. $q = q_0 e^{-t/RC}$

26. 80 nC

27. 11 lb

28. 74.2 lb

29. $v = 32 - ce^{-t}$, 32

30. 1.5 s

31. 10 ft/s

32. $v = 17.9\left(\dfrac{1 + 0.833e^{-3.6t}}{1 - 0.833e^{-3.6t}}\right)$

33. $x = 3t^2 - t^3$; $y = -t^6 + 6t^5 - 9t^4 - 2t^3 + 6t^2$

34. $x = 4 + 2t$; $y = \dfrac{10}{5 + 2t}$

35. $p = 15(0.667)^{10^{-4}h}$

36. 280 min

37. \$2490

38. 5.91 min

39. $x = 4(1 + 2e^{-0.25t})$

40. $x^2 = cy$

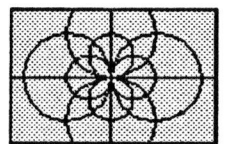

Chapter 14 Review Exercises

1. $2\ln(x^2 + 1) - \dfrac{1}{2y^2} = c$

2. $e^y = e^x + c$

3. $y^2 = 2x - 4\sin x + c$

4. $2xy = y^2 + c$

5. $2x^2 + 4xy + y^4 = c$

6. $\ln^2 x = 2\ln|y| + c$

7. $y = cx^3 - x^2$

8. $y = e^x(1 - x) + ce^{2x}$

9. $y = c(y + 2)e^{2x}$

10. $\sin y - y\cos y = -\dfrac{1}{x} + \ln|x| + c$

11. $y = e^{-2x} + ce^{-4x}$

12. $2x^2 = 4y - \ln^2 y + c$

13. $y = \dfrac{1}{2}(c - x^2)\csc x$

14. $\ln(x^2 + y^2) = 2x + c$

15. $y = \dfrac{cx^{5/2}}{(x + 2)^{1/2}}$

16. $y = e^{-x}[\ln(1 + e^x) + c]$

17. $y = cxe^{x^3/3}$

18. $x^2 y^2(y^2 + c) + 1 = 0$

19. $(x^2 + y^2)(4x + c) + 1 = 0$

20. $y = 2x + \dfrac{1}{9}e^{3x}(3x - 1) + c$

21. $y^3 = 8\sin^2 x$

22. $3y^3 - 29y + 6x = 0$

23. $y = 2x - 1 - e^{-2x}$

24. $3y = 2ye^{-x} + 2xye^{-x} + 2$

25. $x^2 + 2\ln(1-y) - 4 = 0$

26. $y = 2 - e^{-x}$ **27.** $y = \dfrac{1}{4}x^2 \sin 4x$

28. $y^2 = \cos 1 - \ln x - \cos x^2$ **29.** $r = r_0 + kt$

30. $128°F$ **31.** 3.93 m/s

32. $v = 96(1 - e^{-t/3})$ **33.** 5.31×10^8 years.

34. $p = cV^k$ **35.** 7.1 billion

36. $V = \left(\dfrac{kt + c}{3}\right)^3$ **37.** $5y^2 + x^2 = c$

38. $x^2 + y^2 = c$ **39.** $q = c_1 e^{-t/RC} + EC$

40. $i = 0.5(1 - e^{-20t})$ **41.** $V = 2.47$ L

42. $\dfrac{dv}{dt} = \dfrac{dv}{dr}\dfrac{dr}{dt} = \dfrac{dr}{dt}\dfrac{dv}{dr} = v\dfrac{dv}{dr};$

$v^2 = \dfrac{2gR^2}{r} + v_0^2 - 2gR$

43. $r = c\cos\theta$ **44.** $\dfrac{\partial N}{\partial x} = -3x^2 \sin 2y = \dfrac{\partial M}{\partial y}$

Chapter 15

HIGH–ORDER DIFFERENTIAL EQUATIONS

15.1 Higher-Order Homogeneous Equations

1. $y = c_1 e^{3x} + c_2 e^{-2x}$ **2.** $y = c_1 + c_2 e^{-x}$

3. $y = c_1 e^{-(1/3)x} + c_2 e^{-x}$ **4.** $y = c_1 e^{4x} + c_2 e^{-2x}$

5. $y = c_1 + c_2 e^{3x}$ **6.** $y = c_1 e^{-6x} + c_2 e^{-x}$

7. $y = c_1 e^{(2/3)x} + c_2 e^{6x}$ **8.** $y = c_1 e^{(1/2)x} + c_2 e^{-(7/2)x}$

9. $y = c_1 e^{x/3} + c_2 e^{-3x}$ **10.** $y = c_1 e^{(3/4)x} + c_2 e^{-(3/2)x}$

11. $y = c_1 e^{(1/3)x} + c_2 e^{-x}$

12. $y = c_1 e^{(3/2)x} + c_2 e^{2x}$

13. $y = e^x (c_1 e^{x(\sqrt{2}/2)} + c_2 e^{-x(\sqrt{2}/2)})$

14. $y = e^{-x/2} \left[c_1 e^{(\sqrt{21}/2)x} + c_2 e^{-(\sqrt{21}/2)x} \right]$

15. $y = e^{(3/8)x} \left[c_1 e^{(\sqrt{41}/8)x} + c_2 e^{-(\sqrt{41}/8)x} \right]$

16. $y = e^{(3/4)x} \left[c_1 e^{(\sqrt{17}/4)x} + c_2 e^{-(\sqrt{17}/4)x} \right]$

17. $y = e^{3x/2} (c_1 e^{x(\sqrt{13}/2)} + c_2 e^{-x(\sqrt{13}/2)})$

18. $y = e^{(1/10)x} \left[c_1 e^{(\sqrt{61}/10)x} + c_2 e^{-(\sqrt{61}/10)x} \right]$

19. $y = e^{-(1/2)x} \left[c_1 e^{(\sqrt{33}/2)x} + c_2 e^{-(\sqrt{33}/2)x} \right]$

20. $y = e^{x/16} \left[c_1 e^{(\sqrt{33}/16)x} + c_2 e^{-(\sqrt{33}/16)x} \right]$

21. $y = \dfrac{1}{5}(3e^{7x} + 7e^{-3x})$ **22.** $y = -4 + 8e^{x/4}$

23. $y = \dfrac{e^3}{e^7 - 1}(e^{4x} - e^{-3x})$

24. $y = \dfrac{2}{(e^{-5/2} - 1)}(e^{-(5/2)x} - 1)$

25. $y = c_1 + c_2 e^{-x} + c_3 e^{3x}$

26. $y = c_1 e^x + c_2 e^{2x} + c_3 e^{3x}$

27. $y = c_1 e^x + c_2 e^{-x} + c_3 e^{2x} + c_4 e^{-2x}$

28. $y = c_1 e^{-3x} + c_2 + c_3 e^x + c_4 e^{3x}$

15.2 Auxiliary Equations with Repeated or Complex Roots

1. $y = (c_1 + c_2 x)e^x$ **2.** $y = e^{3x}(c_1 + c_2 x)$

3. $y = e^{-6x}(c_1 + c_2 x)$ **4.** $y = e^{-x/4}(c_1 + c_2 x)$

5. $y = c_1 \sin 3x + c_2 \cos 3x$

6. $y = c_1 \sin x + c_2 \cos x$

7. $y = e^{-x/2} \left(c_1 \sin \dfrac{\sqrt{7}}{2}x + c_2 \cos \dfrac{\sqrt{7}}{2}x \right)$

8. $y = e^x (c_1 \sin \sqrt{3}x + c_2 \cos \sqrt{3}x)$

9. $y = c_1 e^x + c_2 e^{-x} + c_3 \sin x + c_4 \cos x$

10. $y = e^{3x/2}(c_1 + c_2 x)$ **11.** $y = c_1 \sin \dfrac{x}{2} + c_2 \cos \dfrac{x}{2}$

12. $y = c_1 \sin \dfrac{2}{3}x + c_2 \cos \dfrac{2}{3}x$

13. $y = e^{3x/4}(c_1 + c_2 x)$ **14.** $y = e^{(4/3)x}(c_1 + c_2 x)$

15. $y = c_1 \sin \dfrac{\sqrt{2}}{5}x + c_2 \cos \dfrac{\sqrt{2}}{5}x$

16. $y = e^{2x}(c_1 \sin x + c_2 \cos x)$

17. $y = e^x \left(c_1 \cos \dfrac{1}{2}\sqrt{6}x + c_2 \sin \dfrac{1}{2}\sqrt{6}x \right)$

18. $y = e^{-2x}(c_1 \sin \sqrt{2}x + c_2 \cos \sqrt{2}x)$

19. $y = e^{4x/5}(c_1 + c_2 x)$

20. $y = c_1 + e^{-x/30}(c_2 + c_3 x)$

21. $y = e^{(3/4)x}(c_1 e^{x(\sqrt{17}/4)} + c_2 e^{-x(\sqrt{17}/4)})$

22. $y = e^{5x/2}(c_1 e^{\sqrt{41}x/2} + c_2 e^{-\sqrt{41}x/2})$

23. $y = c_1 e^{(-6+\sqrt{42})(x/3)} + c_2 e^{(-6-\sqrt{42})(x/3)}$

24. $y = c_1 e^{(5/6)x} + c_2 e^{-(5/6)x}$

25. $y = e^{2x}(c_1 + c_2 x + c_3 x^2)$

26. $y = e^x(c_1 + c_2 x) + c_3 \sin x + c_4 \cos x$

27. $y = (c_1 + c_2 x)\sin x + (c_3 + c_4 x)\cos x$

28. $y = c_1 e^{(\sqrt[4]{8}/2)x} + c_2 e^{(-\sqrt[4]{8}/2)x} + c_3 \sin[(\sqrt[4]{8}/2)x]$
$\qquad + c_4 \cos[(\sqrt[4]{8}/2)x]$

29. $y = e^{-x} \sin 3x$ **30.** $y = \sqrt{3} \sin \frac{4}{3}x - \cos \frac{4}{3}x$

31. $y = e^{4x}(4 - 14x)$ **32.** $y = 2 - 2e^{-2x}$

33. $(D^2 - 9)y = 0$ **34.** $(D^2 - 6D + 9)y = 0$

35. Complex roots: $\alpha = 0, \beta = 3j, D^2y + 9y = 0$

36. $(D^2 - 4D + 5)y = 0$

15.3   Solutions of Nonhomogeneous Equations

1. $y = c_1 e^{2x} + c_2 e^{-x} - 2$

2. $y = c_1 e^{3x} + c_2 e^{-2x} + \frac{1}{9} - \frac{2}{3}x$

3. $y = c_1 e^{x} + c_2 e^{-x} - 4 - x^2$

4. $y = c_1 e^{-x} + c_2 e^{-3x} + \frac{1}{8}e^{x} + \frac{2}{3}$

5. $y = c_1 + c_2 e^{3x} - \frac{3}{4}e^{x} - \frac{1}{2}xe^{x}$

6. $y = c_1 e^{-2x} + c_2 e^{x} - 5 - 2x - \frac{5}{8}e^{2x} + \frac{1}{2}xe^{2x}$

7. $y = c_1 e^{(1/3)x} + c_2 e^{-(1/3)x} - \frac{1}{10} \sin x$

8. $y = c_1 \sin 2x + c_2 \cos 2x + 1 + \frac{1}{3} \sin x$

9. $y = e^{x}(c_1 + c_2 x) + 10 + 6x + x^2$
$\qquad - \frac{2}{25} \sin 3x + \frac{3}{50} \cos 3x$

10. $y = c_1 e^{x} + c_2 e^{-x} - \frac{1}{2}xe^{-x}$

11. $y = c_1 \sin 2x + c_2 \cos 2x + 3x \cos 2x$

12. $y = e^{x}(c_1 + c_2 x) + 3 + \frac{1}{2}x^2 e^{x}$

13. $y = c_1 e^{-5x} + c_2 e^{6x} - \frac{1}{3}$

14. $y = c_1 e^{-6x} + c_2 e^{x/2} - \frac{22}{9} - \frac{4x}{3}$

15. $y = c_1 e^{-5x} + c_2 e^{(2/3)x} + \frac{1}{4}e^{3x}$

16. $y = c_1 \sin 2x + c_2 \cos 2x - \frac{2}{5} \sin 3x$

17. $y = c_1 e^{2x} + c_2 e^{-2x} - \frac{1}{5} \sin x - \frac{2}{5} \cos x$

18. $y = c_1 e^{x/2} + c_2 e^{-3x} + \frac{1}{4}e^{x} + \frac{4}{15}e^{2x}$

19. $y = c_1 \sin x + c_2 \cos x + 4 - \frac{1}{3} \sin 2x$

20. $y = e^{x/2}\left(c_1 \sin \frac{\sqrt{3}}{2}x + c_2 \cos \frac{\sqrt{3}}{2}x\right) + 1 + x + \cos x$

21. $y = c_1 e^{-x} + c_2 e^{-4x} - \frac{7}{100}e^{x} + \frac{1}{10}xe^{x} + 1$

22. $y = c_1 e^{(2/3)x} + c_2 e^{-x} - \frac{5}{2} - x + \frac{1}{2}e^{x}$

23. $y = c_1 + c_2 e^{x} + c_3 e^{-x} + \frac{1}{10} \cos 2x$

24. $y = c_1 e^{x} + c_2 e^{-x} + c_3 \sin x + c_4 \cos x - x$

25. $y = c_1 \sin x + c_2 \cos x + \frac{1}{2}x \sin x$

26. $y = e^{x/2}(c_1 + c_2 x) + \frac{1}{2}x^2 e^{x/2}$

27. $y = c_1 + c_2 e^{-2x} + 2x^2 - 2x - \frac{1}{2}xe^{-2x}$

28. $y = c_1 + c_2 e^{-x} + c_3 e^{x} + 2xe^{-x} + \frac{1}{2}e^{2x}$

29. $y = \frac{1}{6}(11e^{3x} + 5e^{-2x} + e^{x} - 5)$

30. $y = \frac{-135}{392}e^{x/3} - \frac{9}{200}e^{3x} + \frac{1}{35}xe^{-2x} + \frac{12}{1225}e^{-2x}$

31. $y = -\frac{2}{3} \sin x + \pi \cos x + x - \frac{1}{3} \sin 2x$

32. $y = e^{x}(1 + 8x) + e^{2x}(x - 3)$

15.4   Applications of Higher-Order Equations

1. $\theta = 0.1 \cos 3.1t$

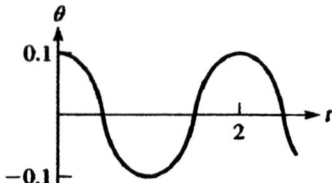

2. 0.056 in   **3.** 10

4. $x = 0.150 \cos(6.26t)$ **5.** $x = 0.250 \cos 16.0t$

6. $x = e^{-4.00t}(0.065 \sin 15.5t + 0.250 \cos 15.5t)$

7. $x = 0.250 \cos 16.0t + 0.127 \sin 2.00t - 0.016 \sin 16.0t$

8. $x = e^{-4.00t}(0.050 \sin 15.5t + 0.258 \cos 15.5t)$
$+ 0.126 \sin 2.00t - 0.008 \cos 2.00t$

9. $q = 2.23 \times 10^{-4} e^{-20.0t} \sin 2240t$

10. $q = 10^5 \cos 10^5 t$ **11.** $q = 0.01(1 - \cos 316t)$

12. $i = 3.16 \sin 316t$

13. $q = e^{-10.0t}(c_1 \sin 99.5t + c_2 \cos 99.5t)$
$-1.81 \times 10^{-3} \sin 120\pi t - 1.03 \times 10^{-4} \cos 120\pi t$

14. $i_p = 0.039 \sin 120\pi t - 0.682 \cos 120\pi t$

15. $i = 10^{-6}[2.00 \cos(1.58 \times 10^4 t)$
$+ 158 \sin(1.58 \times 10^4 t) - 2.00 e^{-200t}]$

16. $i = e^{-75.0t}(0.46 \times 10^{-3} \sin 3530t$
$+ 5.00 \times 10^{-3} \cos 3530t) - 1.60 \times 10^{-5} e^{-100t}$
(e^{-100t} term is negligible for all t.)

17. $i_p = -3.52 \cos 100t + 0.528 \sin 100t$

18. $i_p = 4.02 \times 10^{-2} \cos 10t + 1.61 \times 10^{-4} \sin 10t$

19. $y = \dfrac{w}{24EI}(6L^2 x^2 - 4Lx^3 + x^4)$

20. $y = 0.14x - 0.002x^3 + 6 \times 10^{-6} x^5$

Chapter 15 Review Exercises

1. $y = c_1 + c_2 e^{-x/2}$ **2.** $y = c_1 e^{2x} + c_2 e^{1/2x}$

3. $y = (c_1 + c_2 x)e^{-x}$ **4.** $y = e^{-x}(c_1 \sin x + c_2 \cos x)$

5. $y = e^{-x}(c_1 \sin \sqrt{5}x + c_2 \cos \sqrt{5}x)$

6. $y = e^{1/2x}(c_1 + c_2 x)$ **7.** $y = c_1 e^{0.2x} + c_2 e^{-0.4x}$

8. $y = e^{0.1x}(c_1 \sin 0.4x + c_2 \cos 0.4x)$

9. $y = c_1 e^x + c_2 e^{-3x/2} - 2$

10. $y = (c_1 + c_2 x)e^{-3x} - \dfrac{2}{9} + \dfrac{1}{3}x$

11. $y = e^{-x/2}(c_1 e^{x\sqrt{5}/2} + c_2 e^{-x\sqrt{5}/2}) + 2e^x$

12. $y = c_1 + c_2 \sin \dfrac{3}{2}x + c_3 \cos \dfrac{3}{2}x + \dfrac{1}{13}xe^x - \dfrac{21}{169}e^x$

13. $y = c_1 e^{2x/3} + c_2 e^{4x/3} + \dfrac{1}{2}x + \dfrac{25}{8}$

14. $y = c_1 \sin x + c_2 \cos x - \dfrac{4}{3}\cos 2x$

15. $y = c_1 e^x + c_2 \sin 3x + c_3 \cos 3x - \dfrac{1}{16}(\sin x + \cos x)$

16. $y = c_1 x + c_2 e^{-x} + \dfrac{1}{10}\sin 2x - \dfrac{1}{5}\cos 2x + \dfrac{1}{2}e^x$

17. $y = c_1 e^{-x} + c_2 e^{8x} + \dfrac{-2}{9}xe^{-x}$

18. $y = c_1 + c_2 e^{2x} - \dfrac{2}{3}x - \dfrac{1}{3}xe^x$

19. $y = c_1 \sin 5x + c_2 \cos 5x + 5x \cos 5x$

20. $y = c_1 \sin 2x + c_2 \cos 2x + \dfrac{1}{2}x \sin 2x - x^2 \cos 2x$

21. $y = 2e^{-x/2} \sin\left(\dfrac{1}{2}\sqrt{15}x\right)$

22. $y = \dfrac{-44}{13}e^{-2x} + \dfrac{70}{13}e^{3x/5}$

23. $y = \dfrac{1}{25}[16 \sin x + 12 \cos x - 3(4 + 5x)e^{-2x}]$

24. $y = e^x\left(\dfrac{1}{2}x^2 + x - 2\right) + x + 2$

25. $x = 0.25 e^{-2t}(\sin 4t + 2 \cos 4t)$ underdamped

26. $x = 0.50 \cos 2\sqrt{5}t$

27. $x = 0.661 e^{-1.60t} \sin 6.81t$

28. $\theta = e^{-0.10t}(0.0032 \sin 3.1t + 0.10 \cos 3.1t)$

29. $y = e^{-0.100t}(3.00 \cos 63.2t)$

30. $x_p = -\dfrac{3}{8}\sin 2t + \dfrac{1}{8}\cos 2t$

31. $q = e^{-6t}(0.3 \sin 8t + 0.4 \cos 8t) - 0.4 \cos 10t$

32. $q = 8.05 \times 10^{-7} \sin 4.47 \times 10^3 t$
$- 2.00 \times 10^{-6} \cos 4.47 \times 10^3 t$
$+ 2.00 \times 10^{-6} e^{-200t}$

33. $i = 0$

34. $q = \dfrac{CE_0}{1 - w^2 LC}\left(\sin wt - w\sqrt{LC}\,\sin \dfrac{t}{\sqrt{LC}}\right)$

35. $y = \dfrac{10}{3EI}(100x^3 - x^4 + L^3 x - 100L^2 x)$

36. $\theta = \dfrac{w_0}{w}\sin wt + \theta_0 \cos wt$ where $w = \sqrt{\dfrac{2k}{mr^2}}$

OTHER METHODS OF SOLVING DIFFERENTIAL EQUATIONS

16.1 Numerical Solutions

1.

x	y
0.0	1.00
0.2	1.20
0.4	1.44
0.6	1.72
0.8	2.04
1.0	2.40

$y = \dfrac{1}{2}x^2 + x + 1$

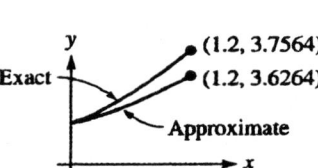

2.

x	y
0.0	2.0000
0.3	2.3000
0.6	2.6795
0.9	3.1244
1.2	3.6264

$y = \dfrac{(2x+1)^{3/2}}{3} + \dfrac{5}{3}$

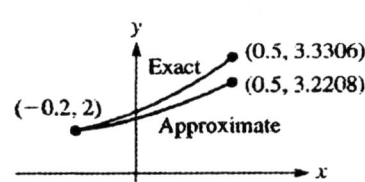

3.

x	y
−0.2	2.0000
−0.1	2.1840
0.0	2.3937
0.1	2.6330
0.2	2.9069
0.3	3.2208

$y = 2.4233e^{0.2x^2 + x}$

4.

x	y
0.0	0
0.1	0.1000
0.2	0.2205
0.3	0.3647
0.4	0.5362
0.5	0.7390

$y = xe^x$

5.

x	y
0.0	1.00
0.2	1.21
0.4	1.46
0.6	1.75
0.8	2.08
1.0	2.45

6.

x	y
0.0	2.0000
0.2	2.2095
0.4	2.4544
0.6	2.7299
0.8	3.0332
1.0	3.3618
1.2	3.7139

7.

x	y
−0.20	2.0000
−0.10	2.1903
0	2.4079
0.10	2.6573
0.20	2.9436
0.30	3.2732

8.

x	y
0.00	0.0000
0.10	0.1051
0.20	0.2319
0.30	0.3840
0.40	0.5652
0.50	0.7799

9.

x	y
0.0	0.0000
0.1	0.1003
0.2	0.2027
0.3	0.3092
0.4	0.4220

10.

x	y
0.0	1.0000
0.1	1.1115
0.2	1.2530
0.3	1.4397
0.4	1.6961

11.

x	y
0.0	0.0000
0.2	0.2027
0.4	0.4232
0.6	0.6884
0.8	1.0588
1.0	1.7722

12.

x	y
0.00	0.0000
0.05	1.0506
0.10	1.1026
0.15	1.1560
0.20	1.2110

13.

x	y
0.0	1.5708
0.1	1.5660
0.2	1.5521
0.3	1.5302
0.4	1.5011
0.5	1.4656

14.

x	y
0.5	0.0000
0.6	0.0549
0.7	0.1242
0.8	0.2089
0.9	1.3097
1.0	1.4278

15. $i = 0.0804$ A approx.
$i = 0.0898$ A exact

16. $13.3°$

16.2 A Method of Successive Approximations

1. $y_2 = \dfrac{1}{3}x^3 + x^2 + x + 1$,

$y_2(0.1) = 1.1103, y = \dfrac{1}{1-x}$,

$y(0.1) = 1.1111$

2. $y_2 = -\dfrac{x^3}{6} + x^2 - x + 1,$

$y_2\left(\dfrac{1}{2}\right) = 0.729,$

$y = 2e^{-x} + x - 1,$

$y_{\text{exact}}\left(\dfrac{1}{2}\right) = 0.713$

3. $y_3 = x^2 + \dfrac{1}{2}x^4 + \dfrac{1}{6}x^6;$

$y_3(1) = 1.67,$
$y = e^{x^2} - 1,$
$y(1) = 1.72$

4. $y_3 = 3e^x - \dfrac{x^2}{2} - 2x - 3,$

$y_3(0.2) = 0.244,$
$y = xe^x,$
$y_{\text{exact}}(0.2) = 0.244$

5. $y_3 = \dfrac{1}{2}x^2 + \dfrac{1}{20}x^5 + \dfrac{1}{160}x^8 + \dfrac{1}{4400}x^{11}$

6. $y_2 = x + \dfrac{x^4}{4}$

7. $y_2 = \dfrac{3}{4} + x + \dfrac{1}{2}x^2 + \dfrac{1}{4}\cos 2x - \dfrac{1}{2}\sin 2x$

8. $y_2 = \dfrac{1}{2}(x^2 + 2x\cos x + x^2\sin x + \sin^2 x + 2)$

9. Maclaurin: $y = 1 + x + x^2 + \dfrac{1}{3}x^3 + \dfrac{1}{12}x^4 + \cdots$

Example 1: $y_3 = 1 + x + x^2 + \dfrac{1}{3}x^3 + \dfrac{1}{24}x^4 + \cdots$

10. Maclaurin: $y = x^2 + \dfrac{x^4}{2} + \dfrac{x^6}{6} + \cdots,$

$y_3 = x^2 + \dfrac{1}{2}x^4 + \dfrac{x^6}{6},$ Exercise 3.

11. 0.58 ft/s

12. $i_2(0.5) = 0.0813$ A approximate

The approximate and exact values differ by 9.5%.

16.3   Laplace Transforms

1. $F(s) = \displaystyle\int_0^\infty e^{-st}dt = \dfrac{1}{s}$

2. $F(s) = \displaystyle\int_0^\infty e^{-st}e^{-at}dt = \dfrac{1}{s+a}$

3. $F(s) = \displaystyle\lim_{c\to\infty}\int_0^c e^{-st}\sin at\, dt$

$= \displaystyle\lim_{c\to\infty}\left[\dfrac{e^{-st}(-s\sin at - a\cos at)}{s^2 + a^2}\right]\Bigg|_0^c$

$= \dfrac{a}{s^2 + a^2}$

4. $F(s) = \displaystyle\int_0^\infty e^{-st}te^{-at}dt = \dfrac{1}{(s+a)^2}$

5. $\dfrac{1}{s-3}$ **6.** $\dfrac{4}{s(s^2+4)}$

7. $\dfrac{30}{(s+2)^4}$ **8.** $\dfrac{8}{s^2+6s+25}$

9. $\dfrac{s-2}{s^2+4}$

10. $\dfrac{s^5 + 3s^4 + 30s^3 + 126s^2 + 201s + 243}{(s^2+9)^2(s^2+6s+10)}$

11. $\dfrac{3}{s} + \dfrac{2(s^2-9)}{(s^2+9)^2}$ **12.** $\dfrac{6}{s^4} - \dfrac{3}{(s+1)^2}$

13. $s^2L(f) + sL(f)$ **14.** $L(f)(s^2 - 3s) - 2s + 7$

15. $L(f)(2s^2 - s + 1) - 2s + 1$

16. $L(f)(s^2 - 3s + 2) + s - 5$

17. t^2 **18.** $\dfrac{3}{2}\sin 2t$ **19.** $\dfrac{1}{2}e^{-3t}$

20. $\dfrac{3}{8}(2t - \sin 2t)$ **21.** $\dfrac{1}{2}t^2 e^{-t}$

22. $t\cos t$ **23.** $\dfrac{1}{54}(9t\sin 3t + 2\sin 3t - 6t\cos 3t)$

24. $\dfrac{1}{3}e^{-2t}(3\cos 3t + \sin 3t)$

25. $-\dfrac{1}{3}e^{-t} - \dfrac{8}{3}e^{2t} + 7e^{3t}$

26. $-2\cos t + \sin t + 2e^t$

27. $e^t\left(2\cos 2t + \dfrac{5}{2}\sin 2t\right)$

28. $-2\cos t + 2\sin t + \dfrac{t^2}{2} + t + 5$

16.4 Solving Differential Equations by Laplace Transforms

1. $y = e^{-t}$ **2.** $y = 2e^{2t}$ **3.** $y = -e^{3t/2}$

4. $y = \frac{1}{2}(1 - e^{-2t})$ **5.** $y = (1 + t)e^{-3t}$

6. $y = \frac{1}{2}t^2 e^{-2t}$ **7.** $y = \frac{1}{2}\sin 2t$

8. $y = \frac{1}{2}\left(e^{-(2/3)t} + e^{(2/3)t}\right)$ **9.** $y = 1 - e^{-2t}$

10. $y = -2te^{-t}$ **11.** $y = e^{2t}\cos t$

12. $y = \frac{1}{2}e^{-(1/2)t}(2 + t)$ **13.** $y = 1 + \sin t$

14. $y = \frac{1}{4}(2t - \sin 2t)$ **15.** $y = e^{-t}\left(\frac{1}{2}t^2 + 3t + 1\right)$

16. $y = \frac{3}{16}(\sin 2t - 2t\cos 2t)$ **17.** $y = 3e^{-2t} + 2e^{3t}$

18. $y = e^{2t} + te^t$

19. $y = -\sin 2t + \frac{3}{2}e^t - \frac{3}{2}e^{-t}$

20. $y = -\frac{3}{130}\cos 3t - \frac{11}{130}\sin 3t - \frac{1}{13}e^{-2t} + \frac{1}{10}e^t$

21. $v = 6(1 - e^{-t/2})$ **22.** $\theta = 0.089\sin 4.5t$

23. $q = 1.60 \times 10^{-4}(1 - e^{-5000t})$

24. $i = 0.1(1 - e^{-40t})$ **25.** $i = 5t\sin 50t$

26. $q = 2500t^2 e^{-1000t}$ **27.** $y = \sin 3t - 3t\cos 3t$

28. $y = \frac{1}{2}e^{-3t}(\cos t + 3\sin t)$

29. $i = 5.0e^{-50t} - 5.0e^{-100t}$

30. $i = \frac{3}{50}\sin 100t$

31. $i = 4.42e^{-66.7}\sin 226t$

32. $y = \frac{w}{24EI}(L^3 x - 2Lx^3 + x^4)$

Chapter 16 Review Exercises

1.

x	y
0.0	1.0000
0.1	0.9000
0.2	0.8200
0.3	0.7568
0.4	0.7085
0.5	0.6743

2.

x	y
0.0	0.0000
0.2	0.2000
0.4	0.3429
0.6	0.4576
0.8	0.5548
1.0	0.6397

3.

x	y
0.0	1.0000
0.4	1.4366
0.8	2.0115
1.2	2.7128
1.6	3.5330
2.0	4.4672

4.

x	y
0.0	1.0000
0.2	1.1735
0.4	1.3743
0.6	1.6130
0.8	1.8963
1.0	2.2246

5.

x	y
0.0	0.5000
0.1	0.5546
0.2	0.6266
0.4	0.8359
0.6	1.1843
0.7	1.4864

6.

x	y
0.0	0.0000
0.2	0.2231
0.4	0.5703
0.6	1.1269
0.8	2.0145
1.0	3.2859

7.

x	y
0.00	1.0000
0.10	0.9077
0.20	0.8329
0.30	0.7734
0.40	0.7282
0.50	0.6965

8.

x	y
0.00	0.0000
0.10	0.0955
0.20	0.1761
0.30	0.2466
0.40	0.3097
0.50	0.3669
0.60	0.4194
0.70	0.4680
0.80	0.5134
0.90	0.5560
1.00	0.5961

9.

x	y
0.0	1.0000
0.1	0.9094
0.2	0.8358
0.3	0.7772
0.4	0.7327
0.5	0.7018

10.

x	y
0.0	0.0000
0.2	0.1696
0.4	0.3002
0.6	0.4082
0.8	0.5011
1.0	0.5831

11.

x	y
0.0	0.5000
0.1	0.5637
0.2	0.6476
0.3	0.7567
0.4	0.8996

12.

x	y
0.0	0.0000
0.2	0.2490
0.4	0.6429
0.6	1.2812
0.8	2.2779

13. $y_3 = 1 + x + \dfrac{1}{2}x^2 + \dfrac{1}{2}x^3 + \dfrac{1}{12}x^4 + \dfrac{1}{60}x^5$

14. $y_3 = \cos x + \dfrac{x^2}{2} - \dfrac{x^3}{6}$

15. $y_2 = -\dfrac{7}{36} + x - \dfrac{1}{9}x^3 + \dfrac{1}{4}x^4 + \dfrac{1}{18}x^6$

16. $y_2 = \dfrac{16x^3}{3} + 4x^2 + \dfrac{3}{2}x - 7 + 9\cos x + 2\sin x$

$\qquad\qquad + 8x\cos x + \dfrac{\sin x \cos x}{2}$

17. $y = e^{t/4}$ **18.** $y = 5e^{t/2} - 4$

19. $y = \dfrac{1}{2}(e^{3t} - e^t)$ **20.** $y = e^{-2t}(t + 2)$

21. $-4\sin t$ **22.** $y = e^{-2t}(\cos t + 3\sin t)$

23. $y = \dfrac{1}{10}(3e^t - \sin 3t - 3\cos 3t)$

24. $y = e^x\left(\dfrac{x^2}{2} + 2x - 2\right) + x + 2$

25. $y_2 = \dfrac{7}{2} + x - (3 + x)e^{-x} + \dfrac{1}{2}e^{-2x};$

$\qquad y(0.5) = 2.0611$

26. $y_2(0.5) = 1.084$

27.

x	y
0.0	1.0000
0.1	1.2000
0.2	1.4086
0.3	1.6239
0.4	1.8442
0.5	2.0678

28.

x	y
0.0	1.0000
0.1	1.2164
0.2	1.4275
0.3	1.7812
0.4	2.1605
0.5	2.6359

29. $i = 12(1 - e^{-t/2});$

$\qquad i(0.3) = 1.67$ A

30. $i = -\dfrac{4}{51}\cos 20t + \dfrac{1}{51}\sin 20t + \dfrac{4}{51}e^{-5t}$

31. $q = 10^{-4}e^{-8t}(4.0\cos 200t + 0.16\sin 200t)$

32. $q = 0.01e^{-6t}[\cos 100t + 0.06\sin 100t]$

33. $y = 0.25t\sin 8t$ **34.** $y = \cos 3.16t$

35.

t	i
0.00	0.0000
0.05	0.3000
0.10	0.5988
0.15	0.8963
0.20	1.1925
0.25	1.4875
0.30	1.7813

36. $i_3 = 6t - \dfrac{3}{2}t^2 - \dfrac{t^3}{4}$

$\qquad i_3 = 1.66$ A as compared with 1.67 A from Exercise 29 and 1.78 A from Exercise 35.

37. $y = 0.75\cos 8t$

38. $y = e^{-t}\left(\cos 3t + \dfrac{1}{3}\sin 3t\right)$

39. $F(s) = \dfrac{b - a}{(s + a)(s + b)} = \dfrac{1}{s + a} - \dfrac{1}{s + b};$

$\qquad L^{-1}(F(s)) = e^{-at} - e^{-bt}$

40. $F(s) = \dfrac{1}{s} - \dfrac{s}{s^2 + a^2}$

$\qquad L^{-1}(F(s)) = L^{-1}\left(\dfrac{1}{s}\right) - L^{-1}\left(\dfrac{s}{s^2 + a^2}\right)$

$\qquad L^{-1}(F(s)) = 1 - \cos at$

SUPPLEMENTARY TOPICS

Exercises A-1 Rotation of Axes

1. $2x'y' + 25 = 0$, hyperbola

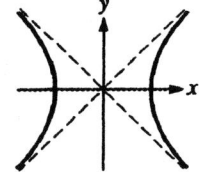

2. $x'^2 + y'^2 = 16$, circle

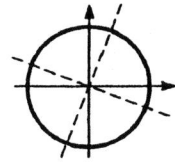

3. $4x'^2 + 9y'^2 = 36$, ellipse

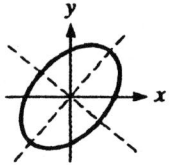

4. $11x'^2 - 14y'^2 = 8$, hyperbola

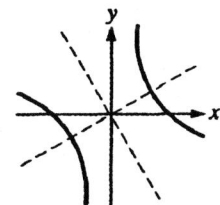

5. $x'^2 + \sqrt{2}y' = 0$, parabola

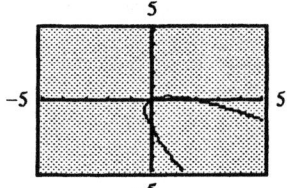

6. $x'^2 + 4y'^2 = 16$, ellipse

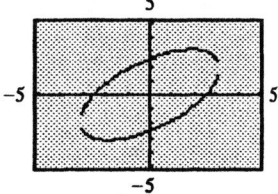

7. $4x'^2 - y'^2 = 4$, hyperbola

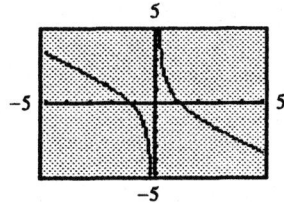

8. $y'^2 = 16x'$, parabola

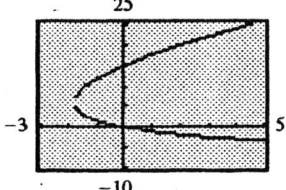

9. $x'^2 + 2y'^2 = 2$, ellipse

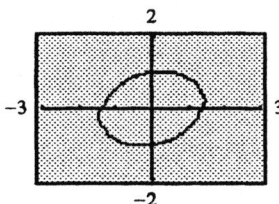

10. $2x'^2 - 3y'^2 = 6$, hyperbola

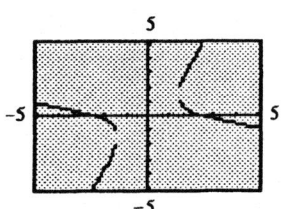

11. $y''^2 = 4x''$, parabola

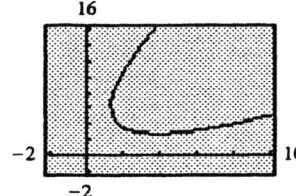

12. $x''^2 + 4y''^2 - 4 = 0$, ellipse

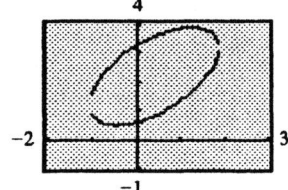

Exercises A-2 Regression

1. $y = 1.0x - 2.6$

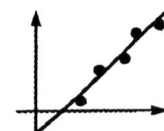

2. $y = -1.77x + 191$

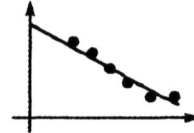

3. $y = 3.5\sqrt{x} + 1.3$

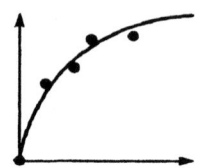

4. $y = 0.99(10^x) + 5.05$

5. $V = -0.590i + 11.3$

6. $T = 0.32t + 20.4$

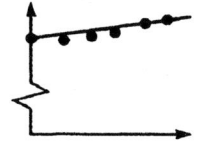

7. $p = -0.200x + 649$

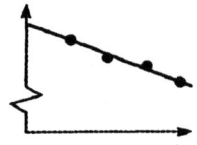

8. $L = -860t + 8330$

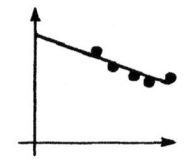

9. $P = \dfrac{1343}{S}$

10. $f = \dfrac{488}{\sqrt{L}} + 6$

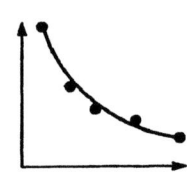

11. $y = 6.20e^{-t} - 0.05$

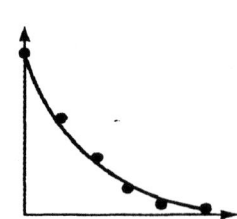

12. $y = -29.7\cos\left[\dfrac{\pi}{6}(t - 0.5)\right] + 44.7$

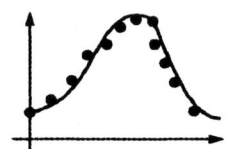

THE GRAPHING CALCULATOR

(Most answers have been rounded off to four significant digits.)

1. 56.02　　2. 1061.8　　3. 4162.1　　4. −7.1405　　5. 18.65　　6. 24.71　　7. 0.3954

8. 693.3　　9. 14.14　　10. 0.9722　　11. 0.5251　　12. 7.769　　13. 13.35　　14. 0.001645

15. 944.6　　16. 41.92　　17. 0.7349　　18. 0.9128　　19. −0.7594　　20. −0.4863　　21. −1.337

22. 0.5954　　23. 1.015　　24. −1.133　　25. 41.35°　　26. 2.552　　27. −1.182　　28. 4.227°

29. 0.5862　　30. −0.04518　　31. 6.695　　32. 4.256　　33. 3.508　　34. 0.8100　　35. 0.005685

36. 5.323　　37. 2.053　　38. 1.595　　39. 5.765　　40. 383.1　　41. 4.501×10^{10}　　42. 6.313×10^{20}

43. 497.2　　44. 1.706　　45. 6.648　　46. 0.8411　　47. 401.2　　48. −1.251　　49. 8.841

50. 558.2　　51. 2.523　　52. −2.088　　53. 10.08　　54. 3.658　　55. 22.36　　56. 3122

57. 20.3°　　58. 1.044　　59. 4729　　60. 94.82°　　61. 3.301×10^4　　62. -3.083×10^{-3}　　63. 1.056

64. 2.781　　65. 55.5°　　66. −61.16°　　67. 3.277　　68. 0.8210　　69. 8.125　　70. 123.5

71. 1.000　　72. 1.000　　73. 1.000　　74. −0.5962　　75. 12.90　　76. 5.031　　77. 8.001

78. 7.001　　79. 8.053　　80. 574.2　　81. 0.04259　　82. 8.686　　83. 0.4219　　84. −0.05282

85. 0.7822　　86. 2.170　　87. 2.0736465　　88. 0.51504　　89. 124.3　　90. 0.06083　　91. 252

92. 0.9999989

93.
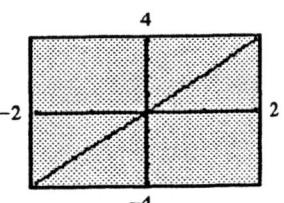

94.
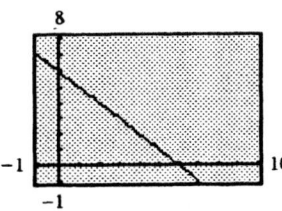

95.
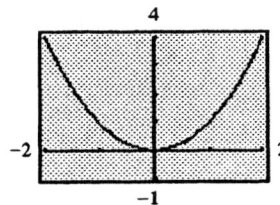

96.
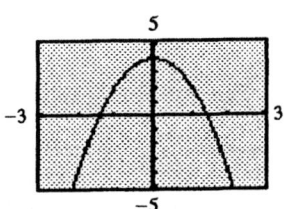

97.
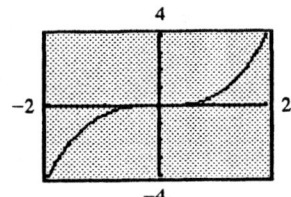

98.
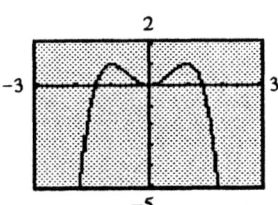

99.
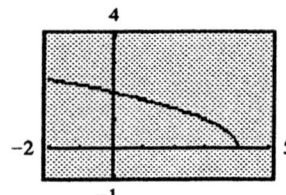

100.
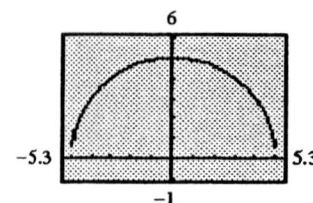

101.
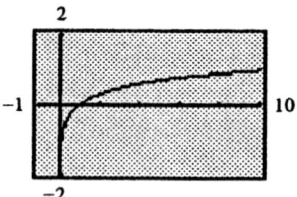

102.
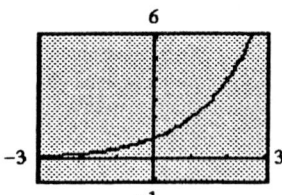

103.
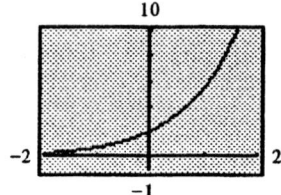

104.
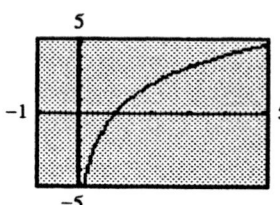

105.
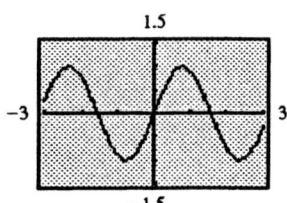

106.
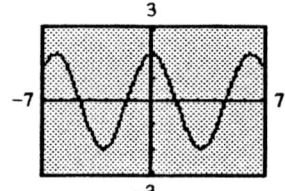

107.
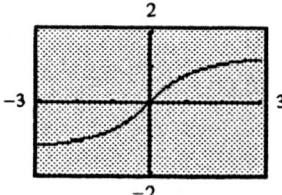

108.
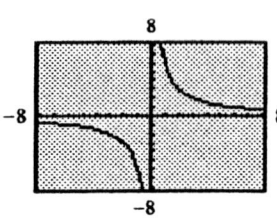